LONE STAR
SPORTS LEGENDS

LONE STAR SPORTS LEGENDS

On This Day In HISTORY

RYAN SPRAYBERRY

THE History PRESS

Published by The History Press
Charleston, SC
www.historypress.net

Cover: All images courtesy of the Texas Sports Hall of Fame.

First published 2017

Manufactured in the United States

ISBN 9781467137751

Library of Congress Control Number: 2017938331

Notice: The information in this book is true and complete to the best of our knowledge. It is offered without guarantee on the part of the author or The History Press. The author and The History Press disclaim all liability in connection with the use of this book.

A special thanks to my wife, whom I would be lost without,
and to my family for their constant support through life's ups and downs.

CONTENTS

JANUARY

January 1, 1937: Cotton Weaves into Texas Culture

Trains were roaring from the Lone Star State to the Golden State. Thousands of fans—more than ten thousand, in fact—crammed into one hundred railway cars. Among them was James Allred, the governor of Texas; Matty Bell, the first-year head coach of Southern Methodist University; and, of course, thousands of SMU fans. The Mustang faithful were itching to watch SMU, the undefeated and untied number one team in the nation, take on Stanford in the Rose Bowl on January 1, 1936.

While SMU would end up falling to Stanford, 7–0, one passenger on the trip asked a simple question: "Why travel thousands of miles for a bowl game, when Dallas is a hotbed of football fans and a much closer destination?" That man was J. Curtis Sanford, an early Texas oil executive. His question was a common one. After the Rose Bowl became college football's first postseason game in 1902, it was joined by the Orange Bowl in 1933, the Sugar Bowl in 1935 and the Sun Bowl in 1936 as college football fans looked to bring postseason games to their region.

Within a month, Sanford had applied to copyright the name "Cotton Bowl" and made plans to rent the forty-six-thousand-seat Fair Park Stadium for the event. After the failure of the Dixie Classic, another postseason game held in Dallas, Sanford found that he was unable to garner many investors. Undeterred, he covered the expenses of the first Cotton Bowl himself.

So, on January 1, 1937, the country was introduced to the Cotton Bowl. The game featured No. 16 Texas Christian University, with head coach

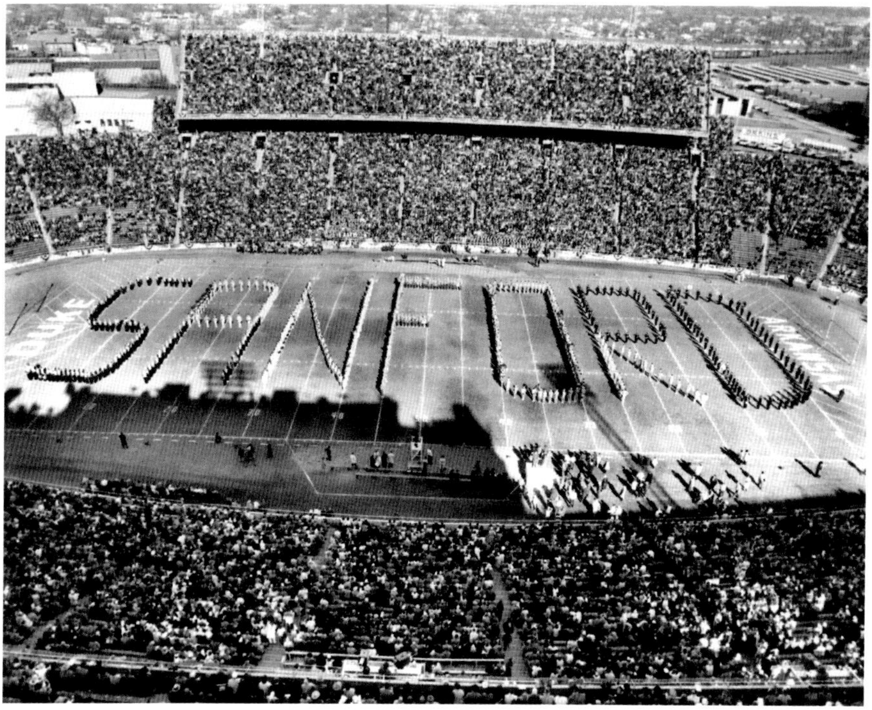

In honor of Cotton Bowl founder J. Curtis Sanford, a halftime band spells out his name at the 1961 Cotton Bowl. *Courtesy of the Texas Sports Hall of Fame.*

Dutch Meyer, "Slingin'" Sammy Baugh and Ki Aldrich, against No. 20 Marquette. After going down 6–3 early in the first quarter, TCU held a 16–6 edge at halftime. By the end of the third quarter, Coach Meyer had used all of his bench players, including a little-known sophomore quarterback, Davey O'Brien. Neither team scored after the half, as the TCU Frogs held on to win. Baugh would end his collegiate career in the Cotton Bowl, becoming the first in a long line of great quarterbacks to play in the game. After leaving TCU, he spent sixteen years in the NFL, where he won six passing titles and became a charter member of the Pro Football Hall of Fame.

Despite featuring a pair of top-twenty teams, including a near-hometown team, the first Cotton Bowl was a failure. With just seventeen thousand fans in attendance, Sanford took a $6,000 hit on his new venture. Detractors began calling the Cotton Bowl "Sanford's Folly," but he was driven to see the game succeed. Within two years, he had doubled attendance—forty thousand fans filled the stands to see St. Mary's knock off undefeated Texas Tech, 20–13. The game was gaining momentum.

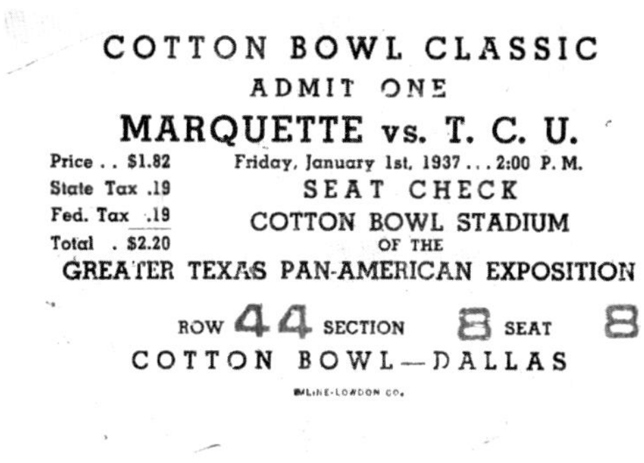

Original ticket from the first Cotton Bowl played between Texas Christian University and Marquette. *Courtesy of the Texas Sports Hall of Fame.*

While Sanford had envisioned the game as a promotion for the Southwest Conference (SWC), the conference began urging its champions to decline any invitation to the Cotton Bowl. Unhappy that Sanford exercised exclusive authority, the conference wanted the game removed from private control. Accordingly, the 1938 national champions, TCU, and 1939's national champs, Texas A&M, snubbed Sanford, accepting instead invitations to the Sugar Bowl. Seeing the game's long-term viability dependent on locking down the SWC champion, Sanford struck a deal. On January 1, 1941, No. 6 Texas A&M beat No. 12 Fordham, 13–12, in the first SWC-sponsored Cotton Bowl.

From modest beginnings, the Cotton Bowl Classic has been woven into the fabric of Texas culture. Even today, it is arguably the most iconic Texas sporting contest, continuing a legacy as one of the premier postseason college football games.

January 2, 1922: Aggies Stand to Serve

The 1921 college football season was a legendary one. The Praying Colonels of Centre College in Kentucky had routed TCU in the Fort Worth Classic by a score of 63–7 to end the 1920 season, but no one expected them to post a 6–0 victory over college football's premiere team, Harvard, in 1921. Led by Charley Moran (who coached Texas A&M from 1909 to 1914, compiling a 38-8-4 record), Centre looked to be a formidable team, and it backed up this reputation, outscoring opponents by a staggering 282–6. Not surprisingly, it would claim the Southern Intercollegiate Athletic Association title with a perfect regular season record of 9-0 (many consider the SIAA the primary precursor to today's Southeastern Conference [SEC]). With just

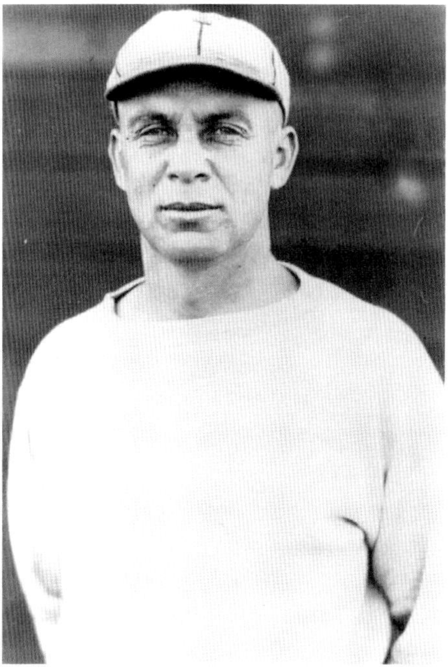

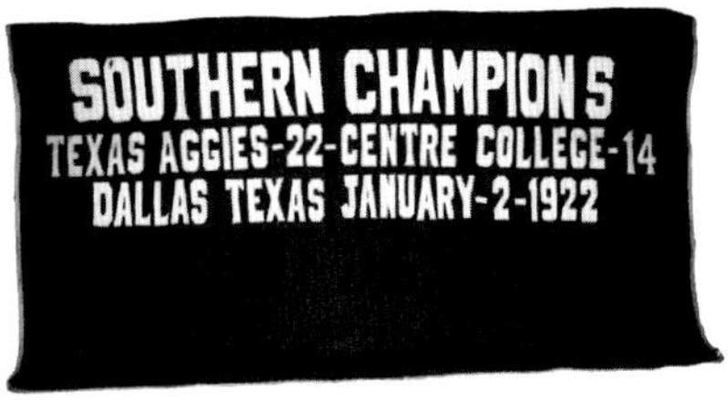

Above: Blanket presented to the Texas A&M Aggies for defeating powerful Centre College in the 1922 Dixie Classic. *Courtesy of the Texas Sports Hall of Fame.*

Left: Dana X. Bible poses in his coaching cap. Bible is responsible for some the earliest football success at both the University of Texas and Texas A&M University. *Courtesy of the Texas Sports Hall of Fame.*

three college postseason matchups in 1922, Centre was invited to two of them, accepting both. The first, played on December 28, was the San Diego Christmas Classic. Traveling cross-country to face the Arizona Wildcats, Centre won by a typical margin. The final score was 38–0.

On its way back to Kentucky from California, Centre stopped in Dallas to play the Southwest Conference champions, Texas A&M, in the Dixie Classic. The Aggies, coached by the legendary Dana X. Bible, looked to give the Centre team a hard fight despite its underwhelming 5-1-2 record. On the opening drive, Texas A&M lost its team captain to a leg injury. After a punt, the Aggies tackled Centre for a safety, putting Texas A&M up, 2–0. It was the first time all season that Centre had fallen behind in a game. To end the half, A&M stopped Centre three times from two yards out for a turnover on downs and the halftime lead.

The Aggies continued to suffer injuries, and Coach Bible took notice. Concerned about his lack of depth, Bible approached E. King Gill in the stands. Gill had left the football team to focus on the 1922 basketball season, but when Bible asked him to come to the aid of the football team, he immediately obliged, switching clothes with the injured Heine Weir under the stadium. Gill reported to the A&M sideline for the second half, ready to serve his team at a moment's notice.

After going down 7–2, A&M forced two turnovers, scoring each time to take a 16–7 lead. With such a large deficit, Centre was forced to pass to try and save its perfect season. On the ensuing drive, Texas A&M's Ted Winn stepped in front of a pass, intercepting it and returning it forty-five yards for the final Aggie score. Centre scored one more time, but A&M triumphed, 22–14.

Although Gill never entered the game for the Aggies, he reportedly later said, "I wish I could say that I went in and ran for the winning touchdown, but I did not. I simply stood by in case my team needed me." In honor of Gill, the Aggies still stand today. Texas A&M's student body remains standing throughout football games, as a sign of solidarity and commitment to serve fellow students. One of collegiate athletics' most notable traditions, Texas A&M's "12th Man" began with E. King Gill at the 1922 Dixie Bowl.

January 3, 1971: The Cowboys' First Chance to Be Super

The first NFC championship game pitted the Dallas Cowboys against the San Francisco 49ers. Played at San Francisco's Kezar Stadium, the game took place on a bright, sunny afternoon. The contest was knotted 3–3 at halftime, but the Cowboys opened it up in the second half.

Up 10–3, the Cowboys' Mel Renfro intercepted a 49er pass. Looking to ice the game, Dallas rode Walt Garrison on the ensuing sixty-two-yard drive. The injured Garrison had a twelve-yard carry, a twenty-four-yard run on a screen pass and, at last, a five-yard touchdown reception. Up 17–3, the Cowboys defense took over, and Dallas won, 17–10.

Garrison had the gutsiest performance of the day, playing with a broken collarbone and an ankle injury. Garrison is still remembered as a fan favorite and a true "cowboy." When not playing football, he spent time roping and participating in rodeo competitions. His Dallas Cowboys signing bonus even included a horse trailer.

The victory over San Francisco propelled Dallas to its first Super Bowl appearance, but the 'Boys would fall to the Baltimore Colts, 16–13, in Super Bowl V. The Cowboys fought hard; it is the only time a Super Bowl MVP award was given to a member of the losing team. Dallas linebacker Chuck Howley was given the award after intercepting two passes, but he refused to accept it, saying it was meaningless, since the Cowboys had lost the game.

January 4, 2006: Lone Star BCS

With head coach Mack Brown, quarterback Vince Young, freshman running back Jamaal Charles, tight end David Thomas and sophomore safety Michael Griffin, the Texas Longhorns won the 2005 Bowl Championship Series (BCS) national title. UT is the only Texas school to claim a title in the BCS era. Vince Young put on a one-man show, setting multiple Rose Bowl records.

Up 16–10 at half, the Longhorns found themselves down 38–33 with 1:50 left in the game. Completions to Quan Cosby, Limas Sweed and Brian Carter, and a facemask penalty, moved the ball to the University of Southern California eight-yard line. On fourth down, Young scanned the field and, finding no one open, trotted into the end zone to put the Longhorns up 39–38 with nineteen seconds left. After a two-point conversion on a Young rush, the 'Horns had the final score of 41–38. Young's final statistics included completing thirty of forty passing attempts for 267 yards, with nineteen carries for another 200 yards and three touchdowns.

January 5, 1931: Two-Sport Star Walter "Buddy" Davis Is Born

Born in Beaumont, Walter Davis contracted polio at the age of nine. Despite not being able to walk for three years, Davis would grow to be six feet, eight inches tall and earn an athletic scholarship to Texas A&M. While an Aggie, Davis made a name for himself as a two-sport athlete, excelling in field events and on the basketball court.

In 1952, after being chosen in the second round of the NBA draft by the Philadelphia Warriors, Davis won a gold medal at the Helsinki Olympics in the high jump. He returned to the United States, playing for the Warriors from 1953 to 1958 and helping the team win a NBA championship in 1956. After moving to the St. Louis Hawks in 1958, Davis won a second NBA title with that team.

January 6, 1929: George "Tex" Rickard Passes Away

Born in Kansas City, Missouri, George Rickard moved with his family to Sherman, Texas, when he was four. His early life took him from cattle rancher to marshal, from gambler to casino owner. While working in Nevada, Rickard tried his hand at boxing promotion and showed an immediate ability to thrive. Offering an unheard-of purse—$30,000—Rickard still managed to make a profit when gate receipts went over $60,000. For his second fight, Rickard matched fellow Texan Jack Johnson against James Jeffries. This time, Rickard offered a purse of over $100,000 and, again, came out on top.

After a six-year hiatus from boxing, Rickard returned to promotion and arranged a fight in 1916 at Madison Square Garden. The bout between Jess Willard and Frank Moran earned $156,000 in gate receipts, a record for an indoor fight at the time. Rickard remained in boxing promotion for the rest of his life. His most successful draw was a series of fights featuring Jack Dempsey from 1921 to 1927. Each fight earned over $1 million in gate receipts. The highlight of this series was a rematch between Dempsey and Gene Tunney, held at Chicago's historic Soldier Field. The fight earned an astounding $2.6 million in receipts.

Rickard made a lasting impression on the city of New York after he acquired the rights to Madison Square Garden. He established the Madison Square Garden Corporation, dedicated to creating profitable sporting events. Rickard opened Madison Square Garden III in 1925, which stood until 1968. In 1926, the National Hockey League granted Rickard a franchise, nicknamed "Tex's Rangers." The name stuck, and today, the team plays as the New York Rangers. Rickard passed away at the age of fifty-nine from complications following an appendectomy. He was working in Miami Beach at the time, an area he believed held great promise for future growth.

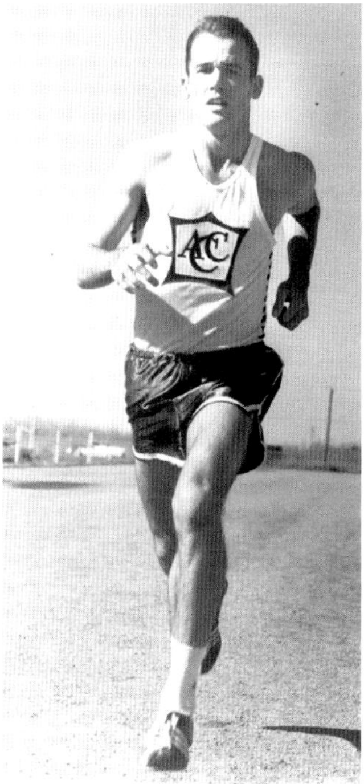

Bobby Morrow trains in his Abilene Christian College gear. *Courtesy of the Texas Sports Hall of Fame.*

January 7, 1957: Bobby Morrow on the Cover of *Sports Illustrated*

The "Fastest Man in the World" and *Sports Illustrated*'s Sportsman of the Year, Bobby Morrow became one of the greatest Olympic athletes in history when he won gold medals in the 100-meter dash, the 200-meter dash and the 4x100 relay at the 1956 Melbourne Olympics. Born in Harlingen, Texas, Morrow's track career began at Abilene Christian University, where he was coached by the legendary Oliver Jackson. Coach Jackson produced athletes that set or broke fifteen world records while winning four Olympic gold medals.

January 8, 1921: First Sanctioned High School Championship Game

Cleburne and Houston Heights battled to a 0–0 draw in a game played at Clark Field in Austin. The Interscholastic Athletics Association was created by the University of Texas Extension Service in 1910. In 1913, the group merged with the Debating League of Texas to create the University Interscholastic League (UIL), which would be responsible for governing athletic and academic contests in Texas high schools. With just one division, the 1921 game represented a matchup between the champions of North Texas and South Texas.

January 9, 1975: Grant Teaff Wins AFCA "Coach of the Year"

Teaff was named the recipient of the American Football Coaches Association "Coach of the Year" award after leading Baylor to an 8-3 record in 1974. The Bears won the Southwest Conference title that year, their first conference title in five decades. Even more impressive, Teaff accomplished the feat with a team that went 2-9 in 1973. The '74 season was highlighted by a 34–24 victory over No. 12 Texas. Down 24–7 at halftime, the Bears rallied to victory, their first win over UT in seventeen years. The game was almost immediately immortalized as the "Miracle on the Brazos."

January 10, 1956: Nelson and Hogan Play Venturi and Ward

Golf is a game of historic moments. People discuss for years how a single stroke defines a major tournament. A moment of brilliance or mental

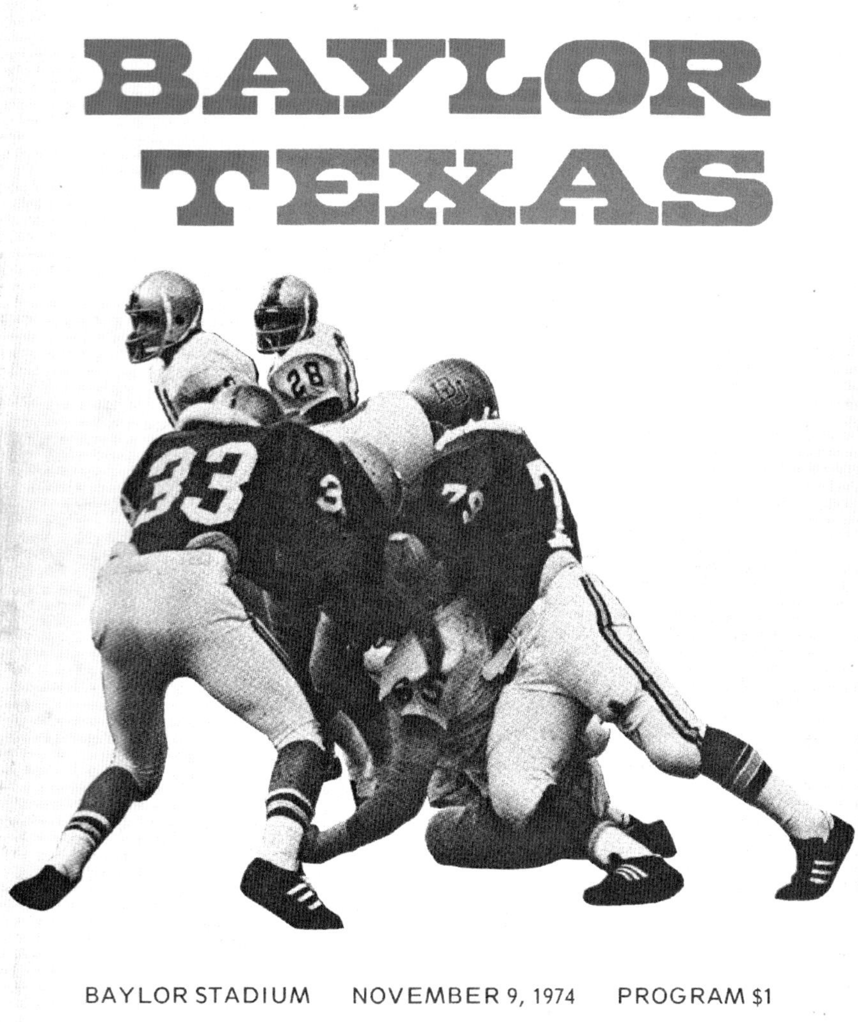

Baylor-Texas program from the Bears' "Miracle on the Brazos" win in 1974. *Courtesy of the Texas Sports Hall of Fame.*

breakdown leads to victory or defeat. Interestingly enough, perhaps the most legendary single round of golf was witnessed by virtually no one.

Golfers, celebrities and businessmen were in San Francisco for the Bing Crosby Clambake (today known as the Pebble Beach Pro-Am). Among the group were millionaires Eddie Lowery and George Coleman. Lowery claimed that no two players could beat his amateurs, Harvie Ward and Ken

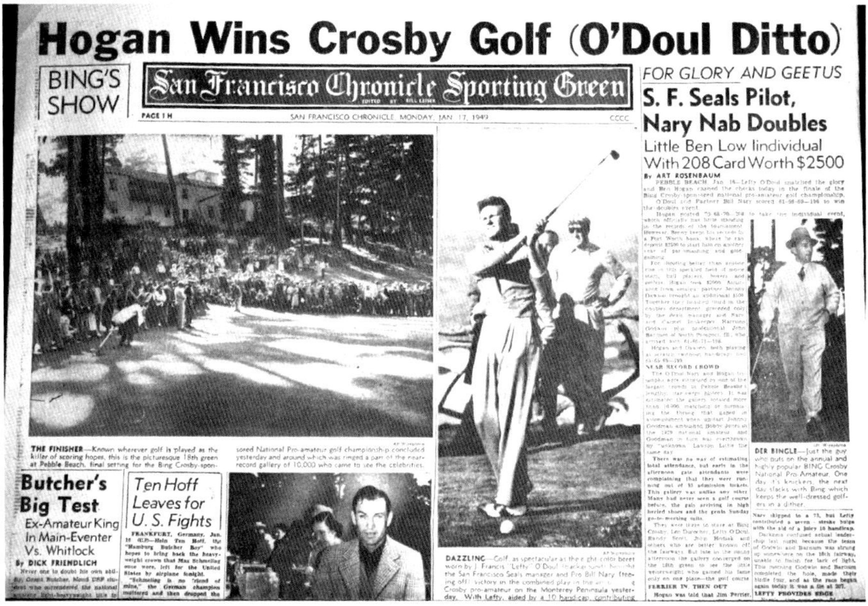

Hogan Wins Crosby Golf (O'Doul Ditto)

BING'S SHOW

San Francisco Chronicle Sporting Green

SAN FRANCISCO CHRONICLE, MONDAY, JAN. 17, 1949

FOR GLORY AND GEETUS

S. F. Seals Pilot, Nary Nab Doubles

Little Ben Low lindividual With 208 Card Worth $2500

By ART ROSENBAUM

THE FINISHER—Known wherever golf is played as the killer of scoring hopes, this is the picturesque 18th green at Pebble Beach, final setting for the Bing Crosby-sponsored National Pro-amateur golf championship concluded yesterday and around which was ringed a part of the near-record gallery of 10,000 who came to see the celebrities.

Butcher's Big Test

Ex-Amateur King In Main-Eventer Vs. Whitlock

By DICK FRIENDLICH

Ten Hoff Leaves for U. S. Fights

FRANKFURT, Germany, Jan. 16 (U.P.)—Hein Ten Hoff, the "Hamburg Butcher Boy" who hopes to bring back the heavyweight crown that Max Schmeling once wore, left for the United States by airplane tonight.

"Schmeling is no friend of mine," the German champion muttered and then dropped the

Headline of the *San Francisco Chronicle Sporting Green*, announcing Hogan the winner of the Bing Crosby Clambake in 1949. Today, the Clambake has morphed into the Pebble Beach Pro-Am. *Courtesy of the Texas Sports Hall of Fame.*

Venturi. Coleman wagered he could put together a team that could defeat the pair. After the bet is made, Coleman announces his team: Ben Hogan and Byron Nelson, the two greatest living professional golfers.

What followed was an epic best ball match that Nelson would later refer to as the best round he ever played. At the end of the match, Hogan remarked, "That's as hard as I can ever remember playing." Nelson and Hogan won, helping to establish professional golf as the way of the future rather than the amateur route made standard by Bobby Jones. The event is compellingly recounted in Mark Frost's *The Match.*

January 11, 1951: Texas Sports Hall of Fame's First Induction

Originally created by the sports editor of the *Beaumont Enterprise*, Thad Johnson, the Texas Sports Hall of Fame is the oldest such state institution in the country. After Johnson worked with the Texas Sportswriters Association, Hubbard, Texas native Tris Speaker was announced as the hall's first

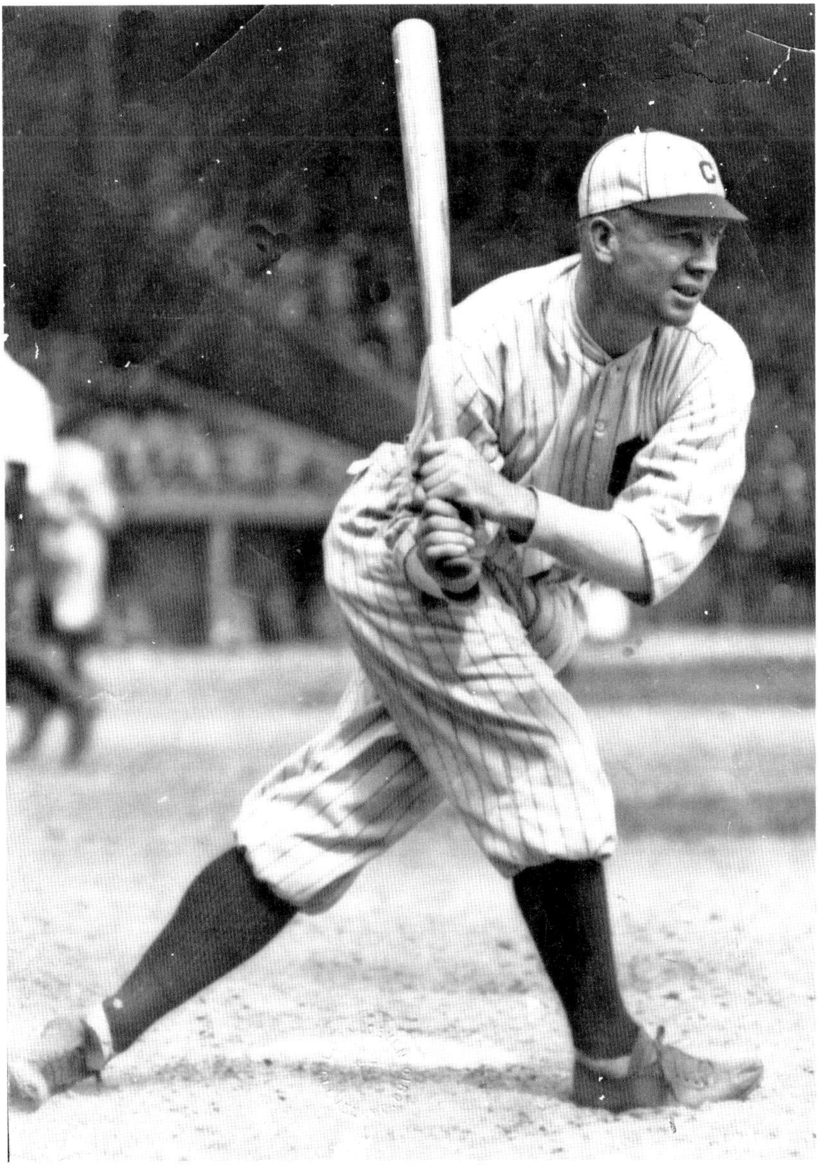

Tris Speaker in swinging motion while playing for Cleveland. *Courtesy of the Texas Sports Hall of Fame.*

inductee. Today, the Texas Sports Hall of Fame includes well over three hundred inductees and uses the state's great sports history to inspire and educate people of all ages.

JANUARY 12, 1975: "MEAN" JOE GREENE LEADS PITTSBURGH TO A TITLE

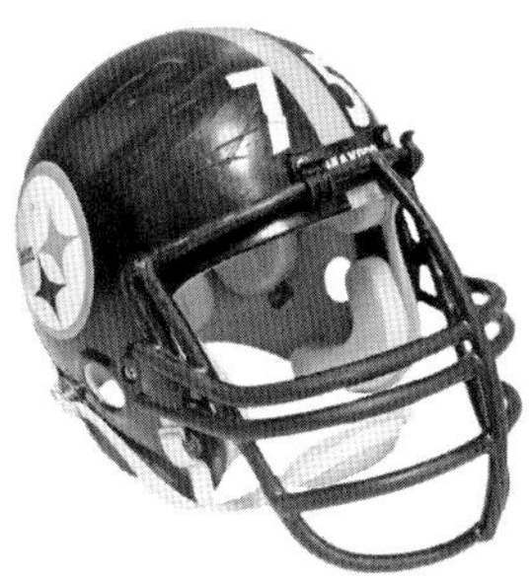

"Mean" Joe Greene's Pittsburgh Steelers helmet. *Courtesy of the Texas Sports Hall of Fame.*

Super Bowl IX, played at Tulane Stadium in New Orleans, featured two of the NFL's best defensive units as the Pittsburgh Steelers faced the Minnesota Vikings. As the first half finished with Pittsburgh leading, 2–0, it was evident that this would be a tight defensive battle. While offenses got going in the second half, the Steelers would hold on to win, 16–6. The Pittsburgh defense held Minnesota to 119 yards of offense, 17 yards rushing and just nine first downs. Elgin, Texas native Joe Greene recorded a great individual game, with an interception and a fumble recovery. Before turning pro, Greene made a name for himself as one of college football's most fearsome and dominant defenders at North Texas State (today, the University of North Texas).

JANUARY 13, 1974: FIRST SUPER BOWL IN TEXAS

Super Bowl VIII would be the first time the NFL's premier game was played in a city other than Los Angeles, Miami or New Orleans—the game was coming to Houston's Rice Stadium. It was also the first Super Bowl held at a site that was not the home of an NFL franchise. Miami won the game, 24–7, over the Minnesota Vikings.

JANUARY 14, 1973: CHARLEY TAYLOR LEADS THE REDSKINS IN SUPER BOWL VII

The main offensive weapon for the Redskins, Taylor led Washington against the Miami Dolphins in Super Bowl VII. It was clear that Miami keyed its coverage to limit Taylor—he was held to just two receptions for twenty yards and one rush for eight yards, as Miami won, 14–7. From Grand Prairie, Texas, Charley Taylor began his Washington Redskins career as a running back, winning the United Press International NFL Rookie of the

Year award. However, the six-foot, three-inch athlete made the switch to wide receiver and wrote his name in the record books. Taylor retired after fourteen seasons, at which point he was the NFL record-holder for career receptions, with 649.

January 15, 1972: Super Bowl I

Lamar Hunt's Kansas City Chiefs appeared in Super Bowl I against Vince Lombardi's legendary Green Bay Packers. While the Chiefs kept it close in the first half, down just 14–10, the Packers opened up in the second half, winning by a final score of 35–10. It was fitting that Hunt's team made the first Super Bowl, as he was a key player in the AFL-NFL merger. He coined the term "Super Bowl," later saying he was likely inspired by his kids playing with a Wham-O Super Ball toy. The Chiefs started out as the Dallas Texans, but after recognizing a losing battle with the NFL's Dallas Cowboys, Hunt moved the team to Kansas City.

January 16, 1972: Dallas Cowboys Win Their First Super Bowl

After Dallas finished the regular season 11-3, it dispatched the Minnesota Vikings and San Francisco 49ers in the playoffs for a shot at the NFL's ultimate achievement. By this point, the Cowboys had earned a reputation for not being able to win big games, due largely to their losses in the NFL championship games in 1966 and 1967, as well as a loss in Super Bowl V. The team's front office and roster were flooded with talent, including Tex Schramm, Clint Murchison, Tom Landry, Gil Brandt, Bob Lilly, Roger Staubach, Bob Hayes, Forrest Gregg, Mel Renfro and Rayfield Wright. Dallas would assert itself early and often in the big game, winning 24–3 for its first Super Bowl title.

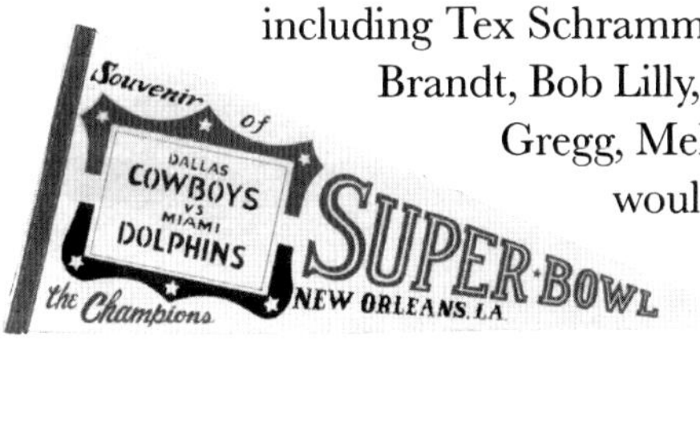

Souvenir pennant from the Cowboys' Super Bowl game against the Miami Dolphins in New Orleans. *Courtesy of the Texas Sports Hall of Fame.*

January 17, 2013: Dr. Donna Lopiano Honored by the NCAA

One of the leading advocates of equality and fairness in sports, Lopiano made her mark in athletics administration when she became the first athletic director of women's sports at the University of Texas in 1975. She held that post until 1992, building UT into one of the finest women's programs in the entire country. From 1975 to 1992, she grew the UT women's budget from $57,000 to over $4 million while producing eighteen national championships in team sports and another fifty-one individual national champions. In 2013, the NCAA honored Lopiano with the Ford Award for being a leader and advocate of intercollegiate athletics over her career.

January 18, 1976: Swann Song

It was the first time two prior Super Bowl champions met in the big game. The Dallas Cowboys and Pittsburgh Steelers, two of the NFL's dominant teams, met to decide the world championship. Unfortunately for Dallas, Steeler wide receiver Lynn Swann proved too much. Swann reeled in four receptions for 161 yards and a touchdown as Pittsburgh knocked off the 'Boys, 21–17.

January 19, 1972: Presidential Congratulations

Tyler Junior College head coach Floyd Wagstaff received a letter from President Richard Nixon congratulating him on his 660th career victory, a national junior college record. Wagstaff led Tyler to the NJCAA national titles in 1949 and 1951.

January 20, 1968: Cougars Win College Basketball's Game of the Century

Orchestrated by the University of Houston's Guy V. Lewis, UCLA came to Houston to play the Cougars in the first basketball game at the Astrodome. UCLA was ranked No. 1 by the Associated Press, and UH was ranked No.

THE WHITE HOUSE

WASHINGTON

January 19, 1972

Dear Coach Wagstaff:

It is a pleasure to join your many friends in extending my warmest congratulations to you for your 660th victory as basketball coach at Tyler Junior College. This triumph, which establishes a new record in junior college coaching, is eloquent testimony to your superb teaching skills. More importantly, hundreds of students at Tyler Junior College have had the privilege of playing under your inspired leadership and, in so doing, have gained the satisfaction of excelling to the limits of their potential. This is in the finest traditions of athletic competition, and you are to be commended for your outstanding contributions to the growth of these young men.

With my best wishes,

Sincerely,

Mr. Floyd Wagstaff
Basketball Coach
Tyler Junior College
Tyler, Texas

Letter from Richard Nixon congratulating Floyd Wagstaff on his 660th career victory, which reads in part, "This is in the finest traditions of athletic competition, and you are to be commended for your outstanding contributions to the growth of these young men." *Courtesy of the Texas Sports Hall of Fame.*

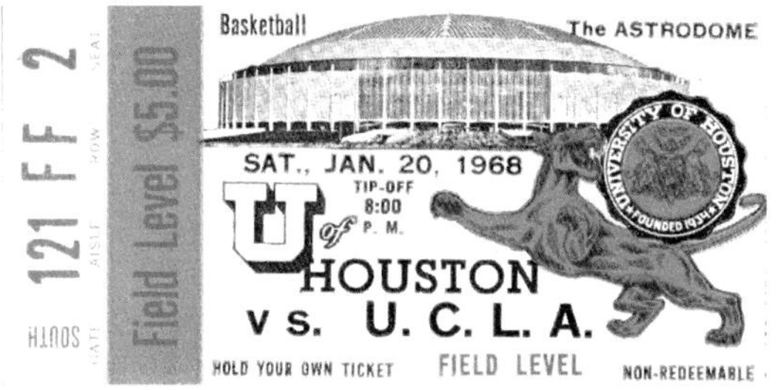

Game ticket from the "game of the century" between UCLA and Houston. *Courtesy of the Texas Sports Hall of Fame.*

2. The contest was the first NCAA regular season basketball game broadcast nationally in prime time.

However, this wasn't the first meeting between the two programs. In fact, UH had fallen to UCLA, 73–58, in the previous year's NCAA tournament. Led by Lew Alcindor (today known as Kareem Abdul-Jabbar) and John Wooden, UCLA had not lost a single game in over two seasons. Houston, for its part, had not lost a game since falling to UCLA the year before. Despite this incredible matchup, many were skeptical about the game and its national broadcast.

A great game took place, and the nation proved that it was ready to consume regular season collegiate basketball. Over fifty thousand fans poured into the Astrodome to watch the game, as Houston knocked off UCLA, 71–69. Each school received $125,000 for playing, nearly four times as much as they earned for their 1968 tournament appearance. Many credit this game for laying the foundation for today's March Madness, one of the most successful and exciting collegiate athletic events every year.

Both UH and UCLA would go through the rest of the 1968 season undefeated until they met again in the NCAA tournament semifinals. This time, the rankings were reversed—UH held the No. 1 spot, and UCLA was No. 2. Whether it was the absence of Astrodome magic and home court advantage or just that UCLA made better adjustments after the first meeting, Game 2 would not go the Cougars' way. The Bruins beat UH, 101–69, advancing to the NCAA title game.

January 21, 1957: Defensive Standout Jacob Green Is Born

Born in Pasadena, Texas, Jacob Green would go on to become one of the most disruptive defensive football players ever produced by the Lone Star State. After a standout career at Kashmere High School in Houston,

Green joined the Texas A&M Aggies. During his time in College Station, Green set a school record for sacks in a season with twenty during his All-American year in 1979. Drafted tenth overall by the Seattle Seahawks, Green set a team record for career sacks over his twelve seasons. At the time of his retirement, he was third on the NFL's career sacks list, behind Reggie White and Lawrence Taylor.

January 22, 1973: The Sunshine Showdown

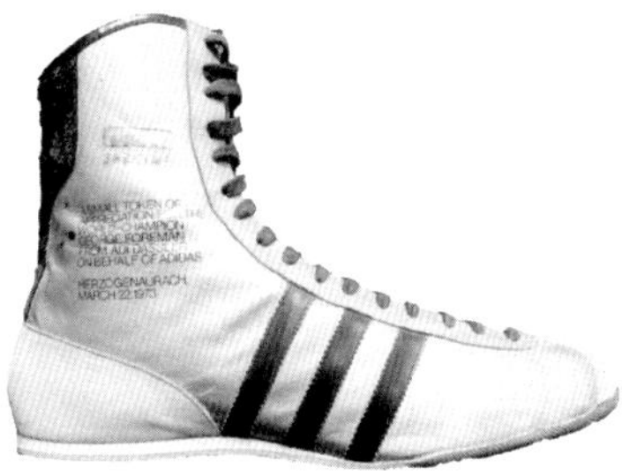

Special shoe designed by Adidas to help with George Foreman's powerful punch. While many shoes would slip when Foreman threw as hard as he could, this new shoe limited that problem. *Courtesy of the Texas Sports Hall of Fame.*

"Down goes Frazier! Down goes Frazier! Down goes Frazier!" In one of the most famous calls in boxing history, Howard Cosell emphatically described George Foreman's dominance over Joe Frazier. Held at Jamaica's National Stadium, "The Sunshine Showdown" saw Foreman score a technical knockout just 1:35 into the second round. Originally from Marshall, Texas, Foreman became the undisputed heavyweight champion of the world.

January 23, 1980: Gervin Scores Big

The San Antonio Spurs defeated the Indiana Pacers, 144–130, and George Gervin scored 55 points. It wasn't the first time Gervin put up such gaudy numbers; he scored 63 against the New Orleans Jazz to end the 1978 season and win his first NBA scoring title. Gervin would win the scoring title again in 1979, 1980 and 1982. At the time of his retirement, he held many of the Spurs' shooting and scoring records, most of which have since been taken over by Tim Duncan.

JANUARY 24, 1986: FLO HYMAN COLLAPSES ON SIDELINE

University of Houston legend Flo Hyman collapsed on the sideline during a professional volleyball game in Japan. Within moments, she had passed away. Hyman was the first female scholarship athlete at the University of Houston, where she played for three years (1974–76). She took the Cougars to three consecutive volleyball finals of the Association for Intercollegiate Athletics for Women (AIAW) and, in 1984, led Team USA to a silver medal in the Olympics—still tied for the country's best finish in US Olympic women's volleyball history. After an autopsy, it was ruled that Hyman's death was the result of Marfan syndrome. Her untimely passing has helped save lives today by raising awareness and leading to earlier diagnosis, such as the case with Baylor's Isaiah Austin.

JANUARY 25, 1975: "THE MEN HAVE MORE STRENGTH, BUT I'VE GOT PRETTIER LEGS"

The first female to earn a varsity letter from SMU and the first to earn a varsity letter in the Southwest Conference, Christine Loock spent her entire diving career competing almost exclusively against men. In a meet on January 25, 1975, she defeated all of her male teammates and males from other schools to claim first place. Later that year, she placed third at the SWC meet in the 3-meter event. Once asked how she felt about competing against the men, she quickly replied, "The men have more strength, but I've got prettier legs."

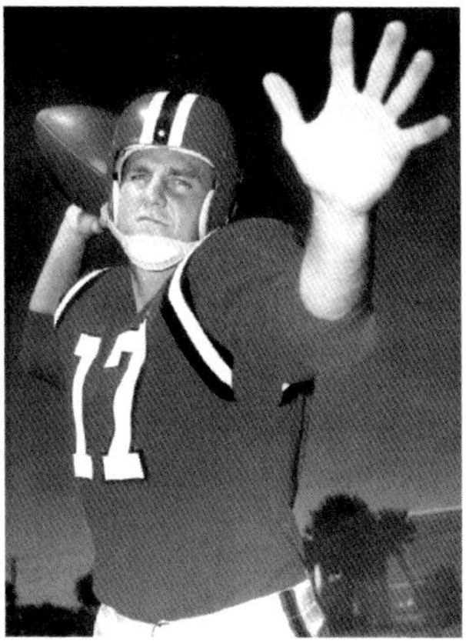

Don Meredith poses in his red SMU uniform. *Courtesy of the Texas Sports Hall of Fame.*

JANUARY 26, 1969: THE BIRTH OF TEXAS STADIUM

Dallas Cowboy legends Clint Murchison, Tex Schramm, Tom Landry and Don Meredith broke ground on Texas Stadium, the new home of the Cowboys. The team would make the move from the Cotton Bowl to Irving, Texas. Texas Stadium would be home to the Cowboys from 1971 to 2008. It was demolished in 2010.

January 27, 1955: Cotton Bowl Icon Dicky Moegle Is Drafted

A standout halfback for Rice, Dicky Moegle is probably best remembered for the 1954 Cotton Bowl Classic. Playing against Alabama, Rice was leading, 7–6, when Moegle broke through the Alabama line on what appeared to be a clear path to the end zone. Moegle was stopped when Alabama's Tommy Lewis ran off the sideline and tackled him. After a quick conference, the referees awarded Moegle a 95-yard touchdown on the play. Moegle finished the game with eleven carries for 265 yards and three touchdowns, and Rice won, 28–6.

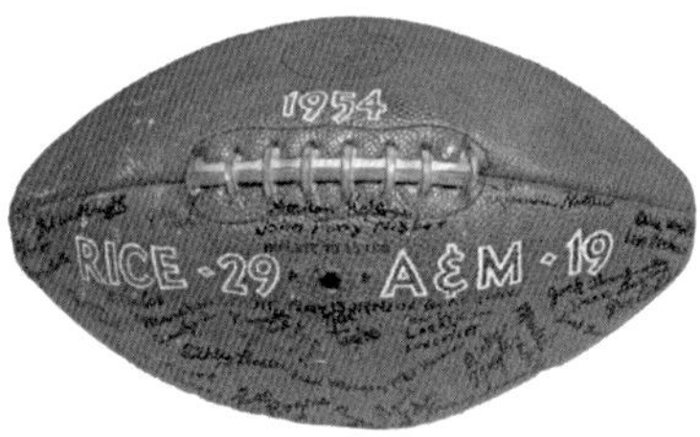

Following their trip to the 1954 Cotton Bowl, the Owls had high expectations for the 1954 SWC season. However, Rice would finish the year 4-2 in conference play. One of its victories came over Texas A&M under its first-year head coach Paul Bryant. The game ball from Rice's 1954 victory over A&M is pictured. Moegle would earn consensus All-American status after 1954—just one of two SWC players to earn the honor that year. *Courtesy of the Texas Sports Hall of Fame.*

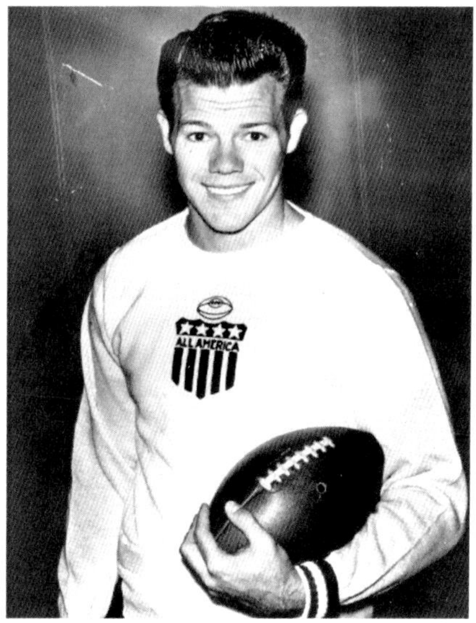

Rice halfback Dicky Moegle poses in his All-American sweater. *Courtesy of the Texas Sports Hall of Fame.*

January 28, 1996: Super Bowl XXX

The Dallas Cowboys defeated the Pittsburgh Steelers, 27–17, to win Super Bowl XXX. It was the Cowboys' fifth Super Bowl title. Larry Brown became the first cornerback to win the Super Bowl MVP—he intercepted two Pittsburgh passes in the second half, both of which the Cowboys' offense turned into touchdowns. While Dallas coach Barry Switzer and owner Jerry Jones were aglow after the game, things would turn sour with the NFL.

Jones had spent $62 million on player salaries for the season, blowing the $37.2 million salary cap out of the water. To cover these fees, he signed multimillion-dollar deals with powerhouse brands such as Nike, American Express and Pepsi. The deals threatened the NFL Trust, a group that had begun negotiating licensing agreements for NFL teams collectively in 1993. This led the league to sue Jones for $300 million. Never one to back down, Jones countersued for $750 million and eventually forced the NFL to settle. The settlement allowed teams to pursue their own endorsements, arguably the main reason Jones was able to build the Cowboys into one of the most valuable sports franchises in the world.

January 29, 1989: Matthews's First Pro Bowl

Bruce Matthews played in the 1989 Pro Bowl, which featured Pro Bowl selections from the 1988 season. Over his career, Matthews would make a record fourteen Pro Bowls and play in 296 games—more than any positional player in NFL history at the time of his retirement.

January 30, 1915: The First Southwest Conference Game

Rice and Baylor faced off in the first official competition of the new Southwest Conference. The SWC officially began on December 8, 1914, making the 1915 basketball season the first in conference history. Rice's team defeated Baylor, 45–10, but the University of Texas would claim the SWC title with a perfect 5-0 record (Rice finished 5-1). UT was coached by L. Theo Bellmont, the father of the SWC, and captained by Clyde Littlefield, one of the greatest figures in Longhorn athletic history.

January 31, 1957: Don Maynard, 109th Pick in the Draft

Born in Crosbyton, Texas, Don Maynard played collegiate football for Texas Western (today, the University of Texas–El Paso) after competing for Rice for just one season. Not a standout at any one position, Maynard registered only 28 catches for the Miners, but he did average over 27.0 yards per catch with ten touchdowns. As a running back, he accumulated over 800.0 yards, averaging 5.4 yards per carry. Maynard also returned punts and kickoffs and recorded ten interceptions on defense. Drafted by the New York Giants in the ninth round of the NFL draft, Maynard went on to record 633 career NFL receptions for 11,834.0 yards and eighty-eight touchdowns, good enough to enter the Pro Football Hall of Fame.

FEBRUARY

February 1, 1922: The Normal Boys

Mascots engender passionate feelings among sports fans, but they might be even more compelling to college sports fans. A school's mascot is meant to convey a message about the school's community and educational standard, not just its athletic teams. At the University of North Texas, teams went by the nicknames "Normalities" and the "Normal Boys" before a council made up of students and faculty announced a list of finalists for an official mascot. Wanting a symbol that was not used by any other major Texas college, the council recommended the Dragons, Eagles, Hawks and Lions. After a vote by the student body in January 1922, the new mascot was announced on February 1. The Eagles garnered almost seventeen times more votes than the runner-up, the Dragons. In 1950, the mascot came to life when Denton resident Tommy Laney gave the university what he believed to be a live golden eagle. It was later discovered to be a Southeast Asian sea eagle, but the students voted to name it Scrappy, and it became a fixture at UNT athletic events.

February 2, 1949: "You'll Never Play Again"

Driving home with his wife, Texas native Ben Hogan broke through a fog bank to the terror of oncoming headlights. Hogan dove in front of his

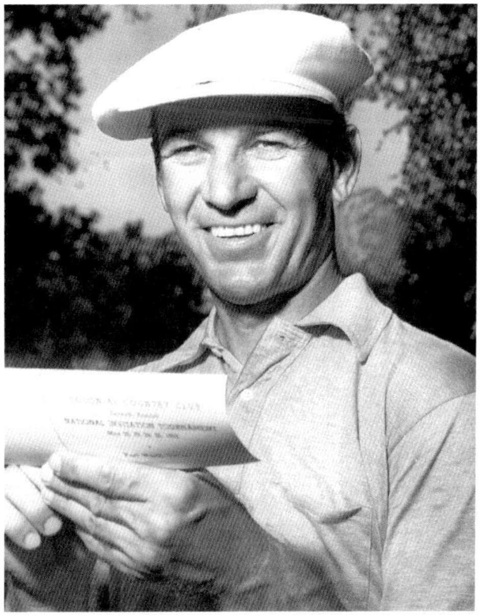

Ben Hogan opens his invitation to the Seventh Annual Colonial tournament in Fort Worth. Hogan would win the tournament. *Courtesy of the Texas Sports Hall of Fame.*

wife to protect her from the ensuing collision. While the act was committed entirely for her safety, it ended up saving Hogan's life. A Greyhound bus slammed into their car, driving the steering column deep into Ben's seat. Just thirty-six, Hogan suffered a broken pelvis, broken collarbone, a fractured ankle and life-threatening blood clots. As the doctors worked to stabilize him, they questioned whether Hogan would ever walk again. Many told him he would never return to competitive golf. However, just fifty-nine days after the accident, Hogan left the hospital. By November of the same year, he began to work on his golf game. He joined the PGA Tour to start the 1950 season and immediately competed for a title. Hogan would struggle the rest of his career with severe pain, and his condition had to be constantly monitored. Always stubborn and a strong competitor, Ben Hogan returned from the accident to win an astounding six more major PGA tournaments on his way to becoming one of the greatest golfers who ever lived.

February 3, 2005: Emmitt Smith Announces Retirement

Although he played for the Arizona Cardinals from 2003 to 2004, there is no doubt that Emmitt Smith is synonymous with the blue and silver of the Dallas Cowboys. Originally from Florida, Smith became arguably the greatest running back in NFL history while a member of the Cowboys. From 1990 to 2002, he played in 201 games for Dallas, racking up 17,162 yards and 153 touchdowns. His career rushing marks of 18,355 yards and 164 touchdowns remain NFL records.

FEBRUARY 4, 2007: LOVIE SMITH HELPS MAKE HISTORY

Born in Gladewater and raised in Big Sandy, Lovie Smith remains one of the most influential coaches in Texas history. While Smith has made countless lasting impressions around the country, one of his greatest marks came with the Chicago Bears in 2007. After defeating the New Orleans Saints, 39–14, in the NFC championship game, Smith became the first African American head coach to take his team to the Super Bowl. Just hours later, Tony Dungy led the Indianapolis Colts to the AFC title. Both Super Bowl teams would be led by African American head coaches. While Dungy's Colts won the contest, 29–17, Smith helped make NFL history.

FEBRUARY 5, 1964: MURCHISON SHOWS A LITTLE FAITH

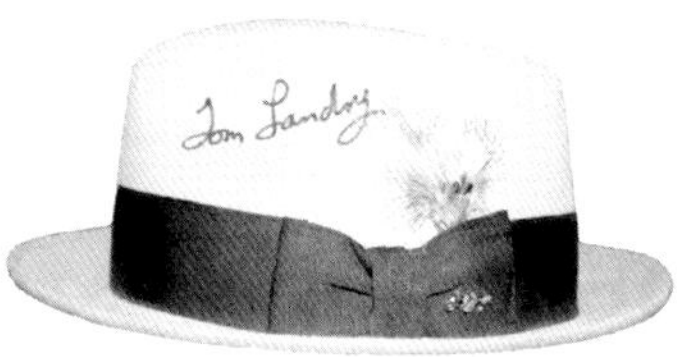

One of Tom Landry's signature fedoras, signed by the legendary head coach. *Courtesy of the Texas Sports Hall of Fame.*

In an era of instant criticism, and in a profession driven by wins and losses, coaches can often find themselves on the proverbial hot seat after just two or three seasons. Imagine a coach posting an abysmal record of 13-38-3 in his first four seasons. Now imagine that coach works in the NFL and his contract has just ended. In today's world, he most certainly would be let go (assuming he even made it to season four). Dallas Cowboys owner Clint Murchison faced the decision to re-sign or fire head coach Tom Landry after his contract ended in 1963. Landry had just posted a 4-10 record. On February 5, Murchison announced that he had made the decision to sign Landry to a ten-year extension—the longest head-coaching contract in professional sports history at the time. Landry responded by winning at least ten games seven times over the next ten years while taking the Cowboys to the playoffs eight times and winning the franchise's first Super Bowl title in 1971.

February 6, 2011: "Jerry World" Hosts Super Bowl XLV

Opened in 2009, AT&T Stadium (also known as "Jerry World," after Cowboys owner Jerry Jones) played host to its first major championship game when the Green Bay Packers met the Pittsburgh Steelers in Super Bowl XLV. In its relatively short existence, the Arlington stadium has become an icon in the sports world. From its record-setting video board to hosting the first major college football national championship decided by a playoff, AT&T is a destination for all sports fans.

February 7, 2016: Texans Lead Denver to Super Bowl Glory

On January 20, 2015, the Denver Broncos hired Gary Kubiak to become the franchise's fifteenth head coach. The Houston native had a long Texas history, first as a high school star at St. Pius X in Houston before quarterbacking the Texas A&M Aggies in the 1980s, where he was an All-SWC selection in 1982. Kubiak gained his first head coaching job in the NFL with the Houston Texans, leading the team from 2006 to 2013. Despite his Texas background, Kubiak's signing with the Broncos was a homecoming of sorts, as he spent his entire NFL playing career with the Broncos (1983–1991).

Shortly after signing Kubiak, the Broncos added Wade Phillips to their staff. Born into a coaching family, Wade is the son of longtime Houston Oilers head coach Bum Phillips. Wade began his NFL coaching career as an assistant for his dad in 1976, using the next three decades to hone his defensive schemes before joining Denver in 2015. He proved to be a great hire by the Broncos, as the team led the NFL in defense in 2015. While plenty of credit was due to Phillips, he did have one of the NFL's greatest individual defensive players at his disposal, Von Miller.

Born in Dallas, Miller was recruited by Texas A&M after a standout career at DeSoto High School. An immediate impact player, Miller was named to the freshman All–Big 12 team. In his final collegiate season, in 2010, he won the Butkus Award and was named a consensus first team All-American. The second overall pick in the NFL draft, Miller made a difference on the professional level, being named the 2011 AP NFL Defensive Rookie of the Year.

After an outstanding 2015 regular season, these three Texans were ready to play a key role in Super Bowl 50. Phillips unleashed his defense, and the

Broncos harassed the Carolina Panthers all night. The Broncos led the entire game, despite the offense not scoring a touchdown until just three minutes remained. Miller forced a fumble in the end zone that was recovered for Denver's first score, then forced another fumble that led to the offensive touchdown to seal the game. While the total team effort led to the Broncos winning, 24–10, Miller's individual statistics of five solo tackles, two and a half sacks and two forced fumbles led to him being named Super Bowl MVP.

February 8, 2004: T.J. Ford's Number Is Retired

While the state of Texas has been fortunate to see many great collegiate basketball teams and even more inspiring individual players, T.J. Ford remains one of the best. After leading Willowridge High School to a 75-1 record and a pair of state championships, Ford joined the University of Texas. Despite being diagnosed with spinal stenosis, Ford continued to excel. During the 2001–02 college basketball season, he was named the consensus Big 12 Freshman of the Year after leading UT to a Sweet Sixteen appearance in the NCAA tournament. For his sophomore campaign, Ford led UT to its first Final Four appearance since 1947 while winning the Naismith Award and the John R. Wooden Award as the best individual player in college basketball. Drafted eighth overall by the Minnesota Timberwolves, Ford's rookie season was cut short when he suffered a contusion of the spinal cord. Not sure if he would ever play again, Ford slowly worked back onto the court, but his career was plagued by injuries. On February 8, Ford became just the fourth University of Texas athlete to have his jersey retired, joining Earl Campbell, Ricky Williams and Roger Clemens. The first UT basketball player to have his jersey retired, Ford has since been joined by Slater Martin and Kevin Durant.

February 9, 2002: Priest Holmes's First Pro Bowl

A standout for Marshall High School in San Antonio, Priest Holmes had an up-and-down collegiate career at the University of Texas. Whether dealing with injuries or the depth chart, Holmes was never able to sustain a full season of high individual achievement. There were flashes, though. In the

1994 Sun Bowl, Holmes was named the MVP after rushing for 161 yards and four touchdowns. In the first Big 12 championship game, Holmes led Texas against No. 3 Nebraska. He rushed for 120 yards and three scores as UT shocked the Cornhuskers, 37–27. Not too surprisingly, Holmes went undrafted, landing with the Baltimore Ravens in 1997. In his rookie season, he led Baltimore with over 1,000 yards rushing, but by 2000, he was overtaken on the depth chart by Jamal Lewis. Leaving the Ravens, Holmes joined the Kansas City Chiefs in 2001. He led the NFL in rushing with 1,555 yards that year, becoming the first undrafted player to lead the league in rushing, a feat not replicated until the Houston Texans' Arian Foster accomplished it in 2010. The performance earned him a spot in his first Pro Bowl on February 9, where he was the game's leading rusher with seven carries for 77 yards and a score. Holmes would finish his NFL career with 8,172 yards rushing and eighty-six touchdowns.

February 10, 1968: Oilers to the 'Dome

When the "Eighth Wonder of the World" opened in 1965, the Houston Oilers would not be playing there. Instead of heading to the Astrodome, the Oilers continued to call Rice Stadium home. Oilers owner K.S. "Bud" Adams Jr. stated that the city wanted an "unrealistic lease agreement," so he signed with Rice to stay put for another five years. On February 10, Adams and the Oilers announced that an agreement had been reached; the Oilers would be moving to the Harris County Domed Stadium (as the Astrodome was known when it opened) for the 1968 season. Of course, the contract with Rice wasn't up yet, forcing the Oilers to settle the contract before the move was complete.

February 11, 2003: Winningest Coach in High School Hoops

Led by head coach Robert Hughes, Fort Worth Dunbar defeated Fort Worth Poly, 71–62, making Hughes the winningest head coach in high school basketball history. Over his career, Hughes won five state basketball titles and 1,333 games.

February 12, 2010: Vancouver Olympics Opening Ceremonies

While a state the size of Texas covers many different geographies, cultures and demographics, there is one stereotype about the state that's mostly true—it's hot. While unpredictable Texas weather can mean a pleasant afternoon plunges into freezing temperatures overnight, most Texans are familiar with the oppressive summer heat. Certainly, no one thinks of Texas as a stronghold for winter sports. That may be true, but the Lone Star State has done its fair share to produce high-quality winter Olympians. At the 2010 games, athletes such as Justin Olsen (San Antonio), Jordan Malone (Denton) and Chad Hedrick (Spring) won Olympic medals for the United States. Olsen helped the national team to gold in the four-man bobsleigh, and Malone and Hedrick earned a combined three medals in speedskating.

February 13, 1920: "We Are the Ship, All Else the Sea"

Born in tiny Calvert, Texas, Andrew "Rube" Foster was destined for big things. While African Americans had been virtually banned from professional baseball, highly skilled players would join to form barnstorming teams that played across the country and around the world. Foster made a name for himself as a pitcher with the Cuban X-Giants, winning an astounding forty-four games in a row in 1902. Nicknamed the "Black Christy Mathewson," he was considered by some spectators to be the best pitcher in baseball when he was at his peak.

While there was no doubt of Foster's talent as a player, his lasting impact would come as an owner. Partnering with John Schorling, the son-in-law of Chicago White Sox owner Charles Comiskey, Foster founded the Chicago American Giants in 1911 and turned them into one of baseball's premier teams. In fact, the American Giants routinely outdrew both the White Sox and the Cubs with a style of play that was aggressive and exciting. Foster and other African American team owners found that they were often short-changed on gate receipts. The clubs were also tightly controlled in terms of when and where they could play.

That changed on February 13, 1920, as a group of African American owners led by Foster founded the Negro National League (NNL) during a meeting at the Kansas City YMCA. Foster surprised the other owners when he showed up to the meeting with an official charter for the NNL already in hand—a move made even more surprising by the fact that, if anything, the NNL would dampen Foster's personal success. Owning one of the most popular teams, Foster enjoyed substantial financial success and had no reason to seek an official organization. However, he saw how other teams were being treated and, instead of ignoring the problem, led the charge to create the NNL.

With teams such as Chicago, Cincinnati, Dayton, Detroit, Indianapolis, Kansas City and St. Louis, the NNL decided to chart its own course, adopting as its official slogan, "We Are the Ship, All Else the Sea." The NNL became the first African American baseball league to last more than onc season. It produced some of baseball's greatest players, including James "Cool Papa" Bell, Bill Foster and Satchel Paige. While the Great Depression would eventually force the NNL to shut down, the league paved the way for the Negro American League, which would produce Jackie Robinson who broke MLB's color barrier in 1947.

February 14, 2010: NBA All-Star Game Record Attendance

While the Dallas Mavericks hosted the 2010 NBA All-Star Game, AT&T Stadium, not American Airlines Center, was the site of the contest. It was the first time the league's showcase game was hosted at a football stadium since 1996, when San Antonio's Alamodome hosted the event. The East beat the West, 141–139, but the most notable aspect of the game was that it set a new attendance record: 108,713 people were on hand to watch.

February 15, 2004: Shaquille O'Neal, All-Star MVP

One of the greatest post players in NBA history, Shaquille O'Neal (better known as Shaq) first made a splash at San Antonio's Robert G. Cole High School, where he led his team to a 68-1 record and a state title over a two-year period. After a strong collegiate career at Louisiana State University, Shaq went to the NBA, where he racked up dozens of awards and recognitions. On February 15, O'Neal led the West to a 136–132 victory while scoring twenty-four points and grabbing eleven rebounds. The performance earned Shaq his second NBA All-Star Game MVP award.

February 16, 1994: Lowry Sets the SWC Scoring Record

Baylor University's Mary Lowry set the Southwest Conference single-game women's basketball scoring record with fifty-four points against the University of Texas. The previous single-game record had been held by Texas Tech's Sheryl Swoopes (fifty-three points).

February 17, 1941: Kimbrough Signs with the Yankees

The decade of the 1930s was arguably the "Golden Age" of Texas college football. Three times that decade, a Texas school claimed the national title: SMU earned a nod in 1935, and the Associated Press named TCU the champions in 1938 and Texas A&M in 1939. Players such as Sammy Baugh, Davey O'Brien, Harrison Stafford, Johnny Vaught, Joe Routt, Ki Aldrich and Joe Boyd became household names across the country. One of those great 1930s players was "Jarrin'" John Kimbrough, Texas A&M's star fullback. After the 1940 season, Kimbrough finished second in Heisman voting to Michigan's Tom Harmon. Kimbrough was known not only for his football skills, but also for his winning personality. This combination led the owner of the New York Yankees, Douglas Hertz, to sign Kimbrough to an astronomical one-year contract at $37,500. The Yankees were part of the fledgling American Football League, which lasted just two years. However, the contract was only partially about football. Hertz also wrote into the contract that, during Kimbrough's off time, he would serve as a polo player in Jersey, lecture on a nationwide tour, act in westerns, serve as a radio personality and complete odd jobs. Like that of many others, Kimbrough's career was interrupted when the Japanese attacked Pearl Harbor. He served in the Pacific theater as a pilot in the army. Although he tried to return to football after the war, he began experiencing a series of heart attacks at the age of thirty, requiring him to retire.

February 18, 1986: The Spurs' First Quadruple-Double

Alvin Robertson achieved just the second quadruple-double in NBA history, recording twenty points, eleven rebounds, ten assists and ten steals for the

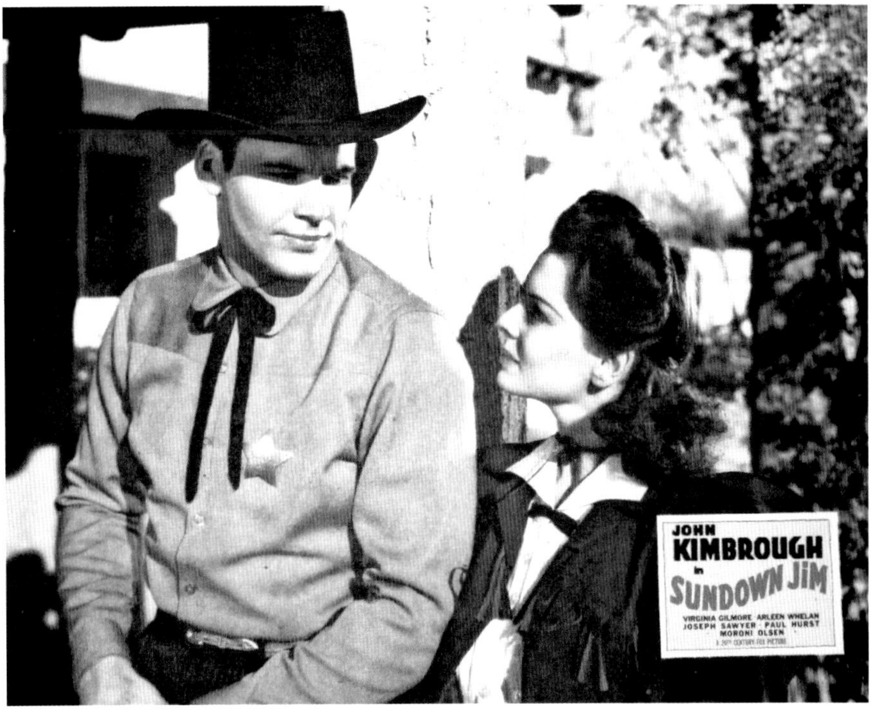

Poster promoting John Kimbrough in the movie *Sundown Jim*. Kimbrough's first professional contract required of him everything from playing football to working as a handyman and acting. *Courtesy of the Texas Sports Hall of Fame.*

San Antonio Spurs in a game against Phoenix. Almost exactly eight years later, David Robinson recorded the league's fifth quadruple-double and the second in Spurs history, scoring thirty-four points, grabbing ten rebounds, dishing out ten assists and blocking ten shots. Of the five quadruple-doubles in NBA history, four have been recorded by Texas teams. Along with Robertson and Robinson, Hakeem Olajuwon recorded two quadruple-doubles for the Houston Rockets in 1990.

February 19, 1994: Sheryl Swoopes's Jersey Is Retired

After leading Texas Tech to the NCAA women's basketball title in 1993, the school honored Sheryl Swoopes by retiring her jersey on February 19, 1994. Coached by Marsha Sharp, the Red Raiders finished the regular season

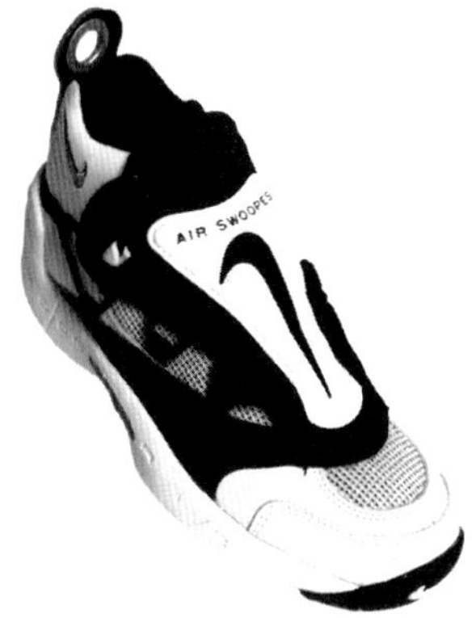

31-3 (13-1 in the SWC), earning a number two seed in the NCAA tournament. After fairly comfortable wins over Washington, Southern California, Colorado and Vanderbilt, Tech faced Ohio State in the final. Swoopes absolutely dominated, setting multiple NCAA records for a championship game (men's or women's), including most points scored (forty-seven). The Red Raiders would pull out a close one, winning 84–82, bringing Texas Tech its first team national championship.

The "Air Swoopes," Sheryl Swoopes was the first women's player to have her own signature shoe. Released in 1996, the new Nike shoe also broke with tradition, as many female players had to count on finding men's basketball shoes that fit. With the introduction of the Swoopes shoe, Nike was showing a commitment to creating equipment specifically for female athletes. *Courtesy of the Texas Sports Hall of Fame.*

February 20, 1974: Gordie Howe Comes Out of Retirement

After an operation on his wrist, Gordie Howe came out of retirement to join his sons Mark and Marty on the Houston Aeros. The Aeros, members of the upstart World Hockey Association, were looking to create an attractive team for fans. By signing with the team, Howe became a part of the first father-son combination to play together in professional hockey. The signing wasn't just a gimmick, though; Howe was named the WHA's MVP in 1974 after totaling one hundred points. In addition, Gordie Howe helped lead the Aeros to back-to-back WHA titles in 1974 and 1975.

February 21, 1896: On a Sandbar in the Rio Grande

One of the earliest popular sports, boxing continues to capture the imagination. While Las Vegas has been the home of most major prizefights in recent years, many of the greatest boxing matches of all time have occurred in distant locations, including the Rumble in the Jungle (Zaire), the Brawl in Montreal and the Thrilla in Manila. Once upon a time, a tiny sandbar in the middle of the Rio Grande counted itself as one of boxing's most unique locations.

In the mid-1890s, boxing promoters began working to secure a heavyweight title match between Bob Fitzsimmons and James Corbett. However, the fight was delayed after multiple states, including Texas, Arkansas, Wisconsin, Illinois and Missouri, made it clear that the event would not happen within their borders. (Once it was even suggested that the fight be staged on a hot-air balloon, literally placing the fighters above the law.) After seeing Corbett surrender his title to newcomer Peter Maher, Fitzsimmons became enraged and immediately challenged Maher. With the prospect of a Fitzsimmons-Maher match, promoters again began looking for a site.

At this point, Judge Roy Bean, known as the "Law West of the Pecos," became involved. Bean arranged for a fight in El Paso with a purse of $10,000—a huge sum at the time. Fitzsimmons traveled to El Paso to begin training, and Maher held camp at nearby Las Cruces. As the fighters prepared, so did law enforcement. Large contingents of U.S. marshals and the Texas Rangers moved in, prepared to uphold the ban on prizefighting. On February 20, Judge Bean instructed everyone to meet at the train station by 9:45 p.m. That night, spectators, members of the press and law enforcement agents boarded train cars headed east.

The next day, February 21, the train pulled to a stop in tiny Langtry, Texas, where passengers debarked and Bean pointed them toward the Rio Grande. Bean had set up a boxing ring on a sandbar in the middle of the river, out of reach of legal jurisdiction. The imaginative Bean had created the perfect location for the long-anticipated bout, but he hadn't counted on the vantage points the cliff above the river provided for spectators. With seats at ringside costing $25, most spectators opted to sit on the cliffs. The ding of a hammer against a tin pail signaled the start of the fight. After a blistering early attack by Maher, Fitzsimmons regrouped and countered, knocking Maher out just ninety-five seconds into the fight.

One spectator had traveled all the way from New York to see the fight, but he missed the short-lived match as he turned around to light his cigar. By the time he turned back to the ring, Fitzsimmons had won. The fight was intended to be the first filmed match in history, and an Edison kinetoscope had been brought to capture the action. However, the brevity of the fight prevented it from being captured; a Fitzsimmons-Corbett fight a year later became the first filmed fight. Fitzsimmons's victory earned him his second class title (he had won the middleweight title in 1881). In 1903, he won the light heavyweight title, making him the first triple titleholder in boxing history.

February 22, 1899: Madison "Matty" Bell Is Born

Born in Fort Worth, Madison A. Bell joined a long line of the city's natives in attending Centre College to play for head coach Charley Moran. Bell would eventually become the captain of the school's football team, showing an early penchant for leadership that would guide him to great success as a head coach after graduation. Bell landed multiple head coaching jobs, including stops at Texas Christian (1923–28) and Texas A&M (1929–33) before landing at Southern Methodist. He immediately made an impact, leading SMU to a national championship in 1935, his first season as head coach. The 12-0 Mustangs became the first team west of the Mississippi (besides Pacific Coast teams) to be invited to the Rose Bowl, helping to put the Southwest Conference on the map. Bell served as SMU's head coach from 1935 to 1941 and again from 1945 to 1949, only taking a break to serve in World War II. Bell led the Mustangs to one national title and four SWC titles and brought the likes of Doak Walker and Kyle Rote to SMU. After stepping down as head coach, Bell served as SMU's athletic director until 1964. He passed away in 1983.

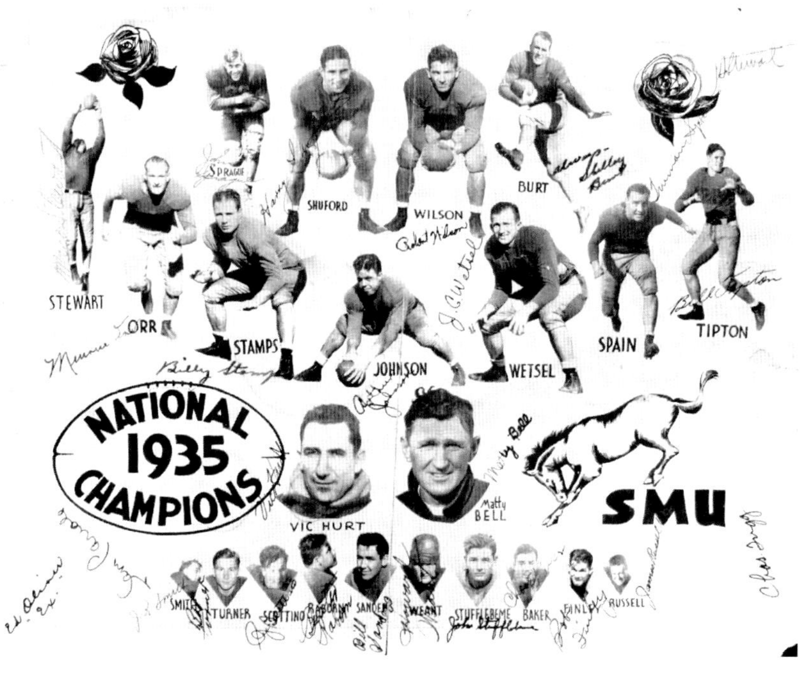

Southern Methodist's 1935 national championship team, which played Stanford in the Rose Bowl. Each coach and player has signed the image. *Courtesy of the Texas Sports Hall of Fame.*

February 23, 1982: Malone's Scoring Streak

Moses Malone recorded his thirteenth straight game of thirty or more points. His streak began on January 26 and ended nearly one month later, on February 23. The thirteen-game streak remains one of the many Rockets' records held by Malone, one of the franchise's greatest players.

February 24, 1968: Sports for More

There is no doubt that sports play a vital role in modern society. Nowhere is that more true than in Texas. Sports are a foundational aspect of culture in the Lone Star State—a source of entertainment, pride and community. However, we all recognize that there is more to life than sports. Whether overly prioritizing victories and losses or placing athletic achievement over academic performance, there are many examples of people placing too much emphasis on sports.

On February 24, 1968, Texas Christian's basketball team defeated Texas A&M, 85–78, to start a three-game winning streak that culminated in a 72–65 victory over Baylor to capture the SWC title. TCU was led by All-SWC player James Cash. A phenomenal athlete, Cash made waves when he was signed by TCU head coach Buster Brannon as the first African American basketball player in the conference. Coming out of Fort Worth Terrell, Cash had ninety-two scholarship offers. (That number would be reduced to ninety-one when the University of Texas retracted its offer for unknown reasons. Texas's Harold Bradley mentioned that UT athletes needed "a balanced perspective regarding athletics and education.") Cash chose to stay in his hometown. A six-foot, six-inch center, Cash was a phenomenal athlete, constantly among the team's leaders in scoring and rebounding. In the 1968 Baylor game, Cash scored twenty-five points to help TCU clinch the SWC title. For all of his on-court success, Cash had his sights set on making an impact off it.

When he first came to TCU, Cash told his advisor that he wanted to major in math. According to the *Dallas Morning News*'s Kevin Sherrington, the advisor responded by saying, "You know you people aren't very good in this discipline." Despite the deplorable remark, Cash later credited the same advisor for being a driving force behind his academic success at TCU. Cash used his athletic scholarship to support his academic goals,

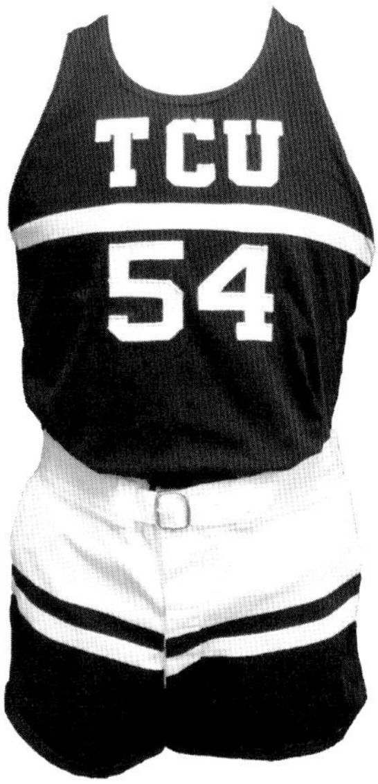

earning academic All-American status before graduating from TCU in 1969 with a degree in math. He went on to Purdue, where he earned his master's degree and a PhD. A lifelong leader, Cash became the first tenured African American at Harvard Business School. In addition to teaching, he served on multiple boards, including Microsoft, General Electric and Walmart. Never one to forget his love of sports, Cash is a minority owner of the NBA's Boston Celtics. James Cash remains a premier example of how athletics can be properly utilized and balanced in everyday life.

James Cash's TCU basketball uniform. *Courtesy of the Texas Sports Hall of Fame.*

FEBRUARY 25, 1950: MCMILLIN INKS WALKER TO A LONG-TERM CONTRACT

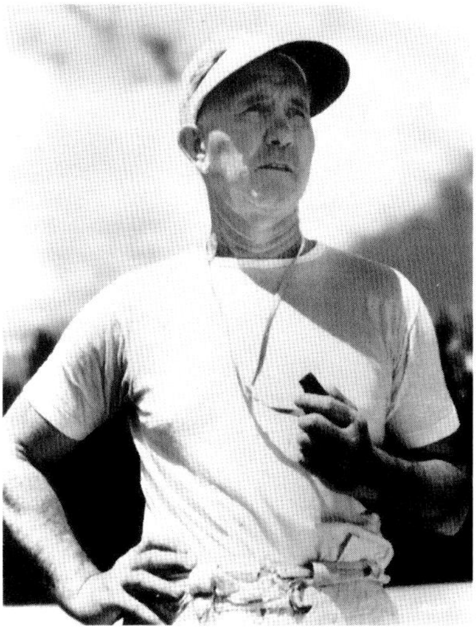

A legend for scoring the Centre touchdown that upset Harvard, 6–0, Bo McMillin is seen here as the head coach of the Detroit Lions. *Courtesy of the Texas Sports Hall of Fame.*

In 1948, Bo McMillin, a Texas native and a hero of Centre College, left his post at the University of Indiana. McMillin had taken over Indiana's football program in 1934 and, by 1945, had led the lowly Hoosiers to an undefeated season and their first outright conference title. Despite what appeared to be lifetime job security, McMillin left to become the head coach of the NFL's Detroit Lions. Ultimately, McMillin's time in Detroit would be short-lived, as he butted heads with players and once even went so far as to change the Lions' colors from blue to maroon. However, for all of McMillin's failures on the field, he did build the core of the Lions' future roster. On February

25, 1950, he inked fellow Texan Doak Walker to a long-term deal before bringing in another Texan, Bobby Layne, just weeks later. McMillin was fired in 1950 and replaced by yet another Texan, Buddy Parker. Parker, Walker and Layne formed the core of a Detroit Lions team that would dominate the 1950s, including securing NFL championships in 1952, 1953 and 1957.

February 26, 1989: A Legend Is Let Go

Shortly after Bum Bright sold the Dallas Cowboys to Jerry Jones, head coach Tom Landry was dismissed. Bright once claimed that he had been ready to fire Landry as early as 1987 but had been persuaded to keep the head coach by Tex Schramm. Jones, ready for fresh blood, hired his University of Arkansas teammate Jimmy Johnson to lead the 'Boys. Not long after Landry's dismissal, Schramm was removed from his position as general manager. Schramm and Landry had been together for 29 years—since the Cowboys' debut in 1960—and had helped lead the team to two Super Bowl championships, seven conference championships and eighteen division titles. Although many observers were displeased with how the situation was handled, Johnson would help Dallas to back-to-back Super Bowl titles in 1992 and 1993.

February 27, 2010: Bobsleigh Gold

For the first time since 1948, the U.S. men's bobsleigh team won a gold medal, at the Vancouver Olympics. Led by driver Steve Holcomb, the four-man team won gold, defeating second-place Germany by 0.38 seconds. One of the members of Holcomb's team, nicknamed "Night Train," was Justin Olsen. Olsen is a native of San Antonio, where he graduated from Sandra Day O'Connor High School. A football player in high school and college, today Olsen is a sergeant in the New York National Guard and a member of the Army's World Class Athlete Program.

February 28, 1941: Jenkins KOs Ambers

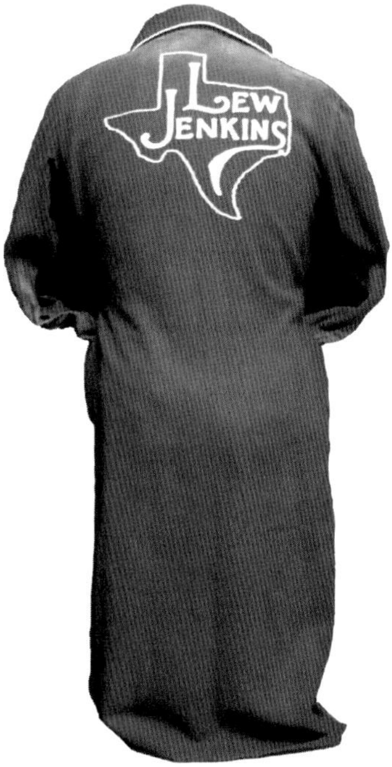

Lew Jenkins's warmup robes. The purple robe has white embroidery outlining Texas and showcasing Jenkins's name. *Courtesy of the Texas Sports Hall of Fame.*

Born in Milburn, Texas, Lew Jenkins was one of the wildest characters in boxing history. Known as the "Sweetwater Swatter," Jenkins became boxing's lightweight world champion after defeating Lou Ambers at Madison Square Garden on May 10, 1940. After claiming the title, Jenkins went on a spree, spending money on alcohol, women and cars. On February 28, 1941, Jenkins was to meet Ambers in a rematch, but after indulging a little too much on Broadway, he stumbled into his dressing room just a half hour before the fight was to begin. Despite his condition, Jenkins still knocked out Ambers in the seventh round to maintain his title. Jenkins would lose his title in December 1941 after being outpointed by Sammy Angott. At the time of the Angott fight, Jenkins was nursing a neck injury suffered during a motorcycle crash—one of many road accidents Jenkins was involved in during his boxing career. At the outbreak of World War II, Jenkins joined the United States Coast Guard. He was later decorated with a Silver Star for gallantry in action.

MARCH

March 1, 1940: First PVIL Basketball Title

The first Prairie View Interscholastic League basketball state tournament begins. Houston Yates defeated Houston Wheatley, 33–19, in the title game, held on March 2, to win the championship.

March 2, 1984: Phi Slama Jama

When you ask most people about Texas sports, the first thing that comes to mind is football. However, the Lone Star State has a long history of excellent teams in many other sports. That is especially true for basketball. Texas college teams have produced greats like Slater Martin, Jackie Robinson, T.J. Ford, Kevin Durant and Sonny Parker. The best two-year period in Texas college basketball history was the product of one team in particular: the Houston Cougars.

On March 2, 1984, the Cougars began that season's NCAA tournament. Led by head coach Guy V. Lewis and players Clyde Drexler and Hakeem Olajuwon, Houston earned a No. 1 seed in the Midwest region. After defeating Maryland, Memphis State, Villanova and Louisville, the Coogs reached the title game against North Carolina State and head coach Jim Valvano. After a heartbreaking last-second loss to NC State, the Cougars regrouped the next year. Again, Houston made the title game, this time facing Georgetown. Unfortunately, the Cougars again came up short, losing 84–75. But the back-to-back appearances in the NCAA championship game undoubtedly ranks as the best two-year stretch in Texas college basketball history.

March 3, 1990: Larry Johnson Leads UNLV

Larry Johnson, born in Tyler, Texas, played high school basketball at Dallas Skyline. After originally committing to Southern Methodist, Johnson began his collegiate career at Odessa College. Playing for Odessa in the 1987 and 1988 seasons, he earned the Junior College Player of the Year award both years. After junior college, Johnson chose to forgo the NBA draft and join the University of Nevada–Las Vegas. On March 3, 1990, led by Johnson, UNLV finished the regular season with a 103–85 victory over Cal State–Fullerton. Johnson played the most games of any Rebel that season, averaging team highs in points (20.7) and rebounds (11.6). A No. 1 seed, the Rebels ran through the NCAA tournament, defeating Duke, 103–73, in the title game, setting records for points scored in a title game and margin of victory. Johnson opted to return to UNLV for his senior season, winning the prestigious John R. Wooden Award and being named the Naismith College Player of the Year in 1991. Drafted first overall, Johnson would be named the NBA's Rookie of the Year before being named a two-time NBA All-Star over a ten-year career.

March 4, 1995: Refusal to Fight

On March 4, 1995, the World Boxing Association voted to strip George Foreman of his heavyweight title for refusing to participate in a bout against Tony Tucker. While the WBA mandated that Foreman fight Tucker, Foreman instead chose to make his first title defense against Axel Schulz. It was Foreman's second time holding the heavyweight title, having recaptured it on November 5, 1994, at the age of forty-five—the oldest heavyweight champion in history. Instead, the WBA set up a contest between Tucker and Bruce Seldon to determine the vacant heavyweight crown. Seldon defeated Tucker by TKO.

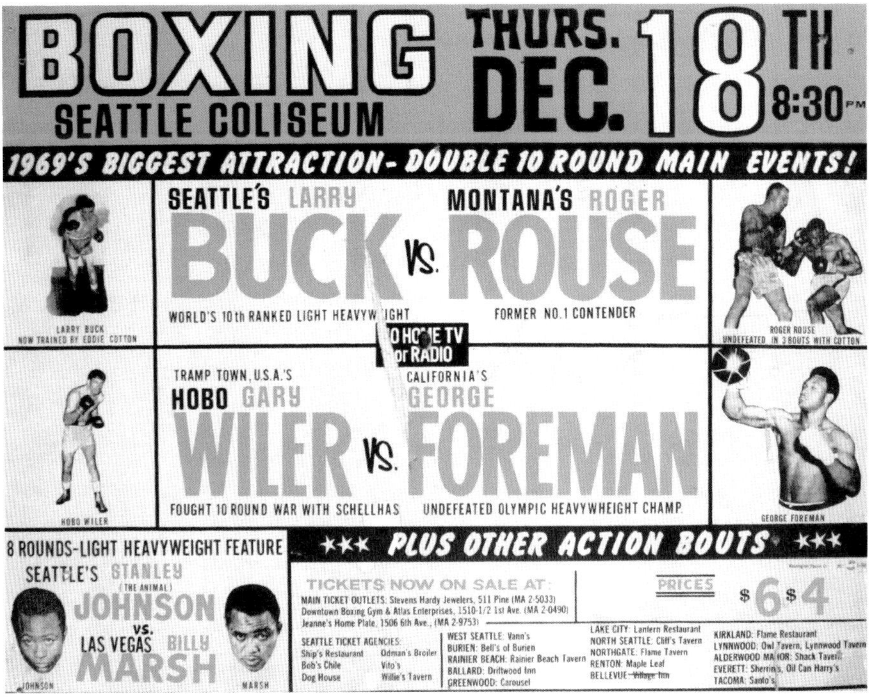

Fight promotion from early in George Foreman's career. He fought Gary Wiler in the Seattle Coliseum. *Courtesy of the Texas Sports Hall of Fame.*

March 5, 2016: Presidential First Pitch

President George H.W. Bush threw out the first pitch before a contest between Texas A&M and Yale in College Station. The pitch was filled with meaning, as Bush had played baseball for Yale, where he was captain and led the team to the finals of the 1947 and 1948 College World Series (Yale finished as runners-up both years). Meanwhile, after a life of service in Texas, Bush chose Texas A&M to house his presidential library, and he remains active on the campus, especially at sporting events.

March 6, 1982: Two Over Forty

Mike Mitchell and George Gervin led the San Antonio Spurs to a win over the Milwaukee Bucks in triple overtime. The two players combined for ninety-five points, as Gervin scored fifty and Mitchell added forty-five—the most points by a pair of teammates in a single game at the time.

March 7, 1996: The Final Men's SWC Basketball Tournament

March 7, 1996, marked the first day of the final men's Southwest Conference Basketball Tournament. Texas Tech would defeat Texas A&M, 58–57, in the first round and Rice, 68–53, in the second round, to set up a match against Texas in the title game. The year before, Tech and Texas had battled in a classic, as UT defeated the Red Raiders, 107–104, in overtime to claim the SWC tournament title. In the final tournament, Tech exacted revenge, winning 75–73 in another close contest.

March 8, 1945: Medal of Honor

A two-sport athlete at Baylor University, Jack Lummus played baseball and football for the Bears from 1937 to 1941. Not just a participant, Lummus excelled at both sports, earning All-SWC honors as a centerfielder and as an end. When the Japanese attacked Pearl Harbor, Lummus responded by enlisting in the Marines in January 1942. Not surprisingly, Lummus excelled as a soldier. During the Battle of Iwo Jima, he single-handedly destroyed three enemy positions, allowing his unit to reach its objective. Unfortunately, Lummus was mortally wounded when he stepped on a land mine, losing both of his legs. For his actions that day, March 8, 1945, Lummus was awarded the Congressional Medal of Honor, the nation's highest military decoration.

Lummus was the second Bear to win the Medal of Honor in World War II. A Baylor basketball and football player by the name of John Riley Kane earned the award as the commander of a B-24. Nicknamed "Killer" Kane by German intelligence, Kane earned his Medal of Honor for leading a daring raid against oil refineries in Romania. Baylor University is believed to be the only school with two athletes who received the Medal of Honor.

March 9, 1964: Aggies Go Dancing

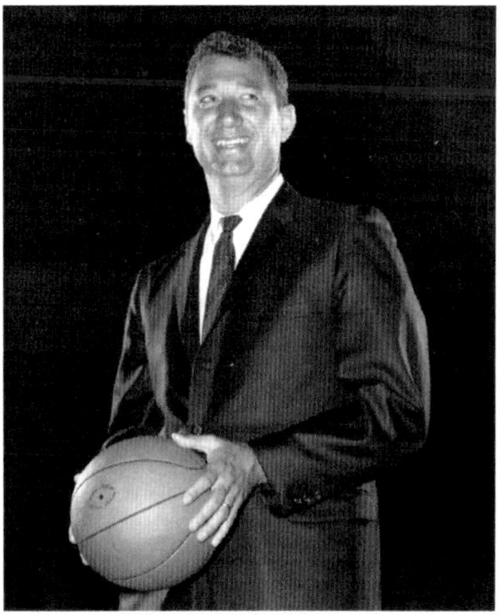

A young Shelby Metcalf just at the start of his career as Texas A&M's head coach. *Courtesy of the Texas Sports Hall of Fame.*

Texas A&M men's basketball played its first season in 1912, but it did not make an NCAA tournament until 1951. On March 9, 1964, the Aggies played in their second NCAA tournament game. Under first-year head coach Shelby Metcalf, the Aggies won the SWC with a record of 13-1. Led by team captain Bennie Lenox, the 1964 SWC title team was just the Aggies' second outright conference title since 1948. For its efforts, Texas A&M would have to play a tough Texas Western team led by Don Haskins. The Miners defeated the Aggies in round one, 68–62, but Coach Metcalf had shown that he could lead Texas A&M to greatness. He would be the face of Texas A&M basketball for more than a quarter century, guiding the Aggies to six regular-season SWC titles, two SWC tournament titles, five NCAA tournaments and two Sweet Sixteens. Metcalf finished his career as the winningest coach in SWC history; only SMU's Doc Hayes had more career SWC titles. After Metcalf was let go by Texas A&M, the team went into a downward spiral, posting just one winning season in the next fifteen years.

March 10, 1976: "The Opera Ain't Over 'til the Fat Lady Sings"

The first recorded use of the adage "The opera ain't over 'til the fat lady sings" appeared in the *Dallas Morning News*. An incredibly popular saying today, the quote was first used by Texas Tech's sports information director Ralph Carpenter when Texas A&M rallied to tie the Red Raiders, 72–72, in the SWC basketball tournament. The quote was nationally attributed to broadcaster Dan Cook when he used the phrase during a San Antonio Spurs–Washington Bullets playoff game in 1978, but Fred Shapiro identified and credited Carpenter in the 2006 publication *The Yale Book of Quotations*.

March 11, 2000: Dallas Mavericks Honor Rolando Blackman

After being selected ninth overall by the Dallas Mavericks in 1981, Rolando Blackman would go on to score a career 19,823 points, grab 3,278 rebounds and dish out 2,981 assists. A four-time NBA All-Star, Blackman was the NBA's all-time leading Hispanic scorer until Pau Gasol passed him in 2015. Blackman played almost his entire career with the Mavs and was the franchise leader in scoring until passed by Dirk Nowitzki in 2008. To honor his outstanding career, the team retired Blackman's jersey number (22) on March 11, 2000. He was just the second Mav to receive such an honor (after Brian Davis's number 15).

March 12, 2011: Idalou Double Dips

The Idalou Wildcats defeated the Tatum Eagles by one point, 55–54, to win the 2A Boys' Basketball title at the Erwin Center in Austin, Texas. While the state title by itself was impressive, the win was made even more remarkable because the Wildcats had won the state football title earlier that academic year, making Idalou only the fifth school to win the Texas state titles in football and boys basketball in the same year (Dumas, 1960–61; Southlake Carroll, 1992–93; Duncanville, 1998–99; Everman, 2002–3; and Cayuga, 2009–10).

March 13, 1960: First Cowboys Draft

A special expansion draft was held to allow the Dallas Rangers (soon to be the Dallas Cowboys) to fill out its roster for the upcoming NFL season. At the time, the NFL roster limit was thirty-six players, and each franchise was allowed to protect twenty-five of its players from being selected by the Cowboys. The remaining players entered a pool from which the Cowboys could draft them. Many of the new Dallas players were homesick Texans, such as L.G. Dupre, a Baylor star who had been playing for the Baltimore Colts; Jerry Tubbs, from Breckenridge, who had been with the 49ers; former SMU running back Don McIlhenny of the Green Bay Packers; and Gene Babb of Austin College, who originally signed with the American Football

League's Houston Oilers. Prior to the draft, the Cowboys had signed Don Meredith and Don Perkins to personal service contracts, which the NFL decided to honor.

March 14, 2006: Brees Becomes a Saint

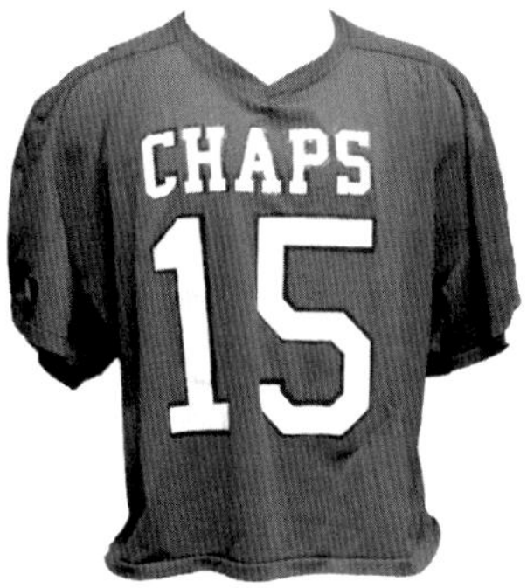

Drew Brees's high school football jersey, worn while playing for Austin Westlake. *Courtesy of the Texas Sports Hall of Fame.*

Drew Brees was used to being overlooked. After a high school career in which he led his team to a 28-0-1 record against some of Texas's strongest competition while compiling astronomical stats, he didn't receive an offer from either of his dream schools, the University of Texas or Texas A&M University. Instead, he traveled to Purdue in Indiana, the only school that offered him a scholarship besides Kentucky. While at Purdue, Brees set multiple Big Ten passing records and finished as a Heisman Trophy finalist in both his junior and senior years. Drafted by the San Diego Chargers in 2001, he went on to lead the franchise to its first AFC West title in ten years. However, the Chargers opted to add Philip Rivers in 2004; by 2006, the team made it clear that Brees would not be its long-term quarterback. So, on March 14, 2006, Brees signed with the New Orleans Saints. His Saints career has included eight Pro-Bowl selections, three First Team All-Pro selections, two NFL Offensive Player of the Year awards and, of course, a victory in Super Bowl XLIV. Brees has cemented his place as one of the greatest quarterbacks to play the game, revolutionizing ideas about what an "ideal" quarterback should look like. He continues to thrive well into his thirties.

March 15, 1967: Drafted 214th

The 1967 NFL/AFL draft was ripe with talent. The first common draft between America's two major professional football leagues, it promised to be interesting, if for no other reason than to see the strategies employed by the two different groups. The first round proved fruitful, with four future Pro Football Hall of Fame inductees. The second round brought two more. However, the following fifteen rounds would bring a total of just two more future hall of famers. One was Rayfield Wright, drafted by the Dallas Cowboys in round seven. The last future hall of famer selected was defensive back Ken Houston, out of Prairie View A&M. Houston was selected 214th overall, in the ninth round of the draft. It ended up being a steal for the Houston Oilers. Houston was a starter by the third game of his rookie year. In 1971, he set the record for touchdown returns in a single season, scoring five (four on interception returns and one on a fumble return). The record was not surpassed until Devin Hester scored six in 2006. Houston would make twelve consecutive Pro Bowls from 1968 to 1979 and, even today, regularly appears in rankings of the greatest football players of all time.

March 16, 1918: Texas's First Indoor Rodeo

From March 11 to 16, 1918, the Lone Star State saw its first indoor rodeo, held in Fort Worth. The year before, an "indoor cowboy riding contest" was held, but 1918 saw the addition of official rodeo events, which helped dramatically increase attendance. These events included men's and women's bucking bronco riding, as well as men's and juniors' steer riding. Although Texas has claimed this as the first indoor rodeo to happen anywhere, Kansas contends that it held the first indoor rodeo, in January 1918.

March 17, 1994: NCAA Tournament Kicks Off

Fans across the country begin each NCAA tournament with hopes that their team will claim basketball's highest honor. Nowhere was that more true than in Arkansas in 1994. Led by El Paso native Nolan Richardson, the Arkansas Razorbacks had established a reputation for their "40 Minutes of Hell" style of play, which focused on pressuring the other team into mistakes and constantly running the floor. On opening night, the Razorbacks won their first game, 94–79, over North Carolina A&T. In similar fashion, they defeated Georgetown, Tulsa, Michigan and Arizona before reaching the finals against a true basketball blue blood: the Duke Blue Devils. In one of the greatest final games in men's college basketball history, Arkansas prevailed, 76–72, adding to Richardson's collection of national titles. In 1980, he led Western Texas College to the National Junior College championship before leading Tulsa to the 1981 National Invitation Tournament title.

March 18, 1971: Beaty Leads Utah to Game 7

Born in Hillister, Texas, it was clear early on that Zelmo Beaty would be a basketball star. However, as an African American, many colleges in Texas were closed to him. No matter, Beaty took his talents to Prairie View A&M, as did many other outstanding athletes. He led the Panthers to the 1962 National Association of Intercollegiate Athletics national championship. Drafted third overall by the St. Louis Hawks, Beaty would play with the team from 1962 to 1969 before joining the American Basketball Association's Utah Stars. While many of Beaty's teammates were hesitant to relocate to conservative Salt Lake City, Beaty and his wife became ambassadors for the city. In 1971, Beaty would lead the Stars to the ABA Finals against the Kentucky Colonels and, on March 18, would help the Stars to win Game 7 by a score of 131–121. Beaty would win the Playoff MVP Award; Utah Stars fans carried him off the court on their shoulders.

March 19, 1966: Texas Western Makes History

Thanks to the hit movie *Glory Road*, this story has become a much more familiar one. Under the coaching of Don Haskins, Texas Western entered the 1966 NCAA tournament looking to shape history. Led by a starting five consisting entirely of African American players (the first such team in NCAA championship history), the Miners looked to prove not only that they were as competent as their white counterparts but also that they could beat them. Of course, they would do just that. The team defeated Oklahoma City, Cincinnati, powerhouse Kansas and Utah on its way to the finals, where they faced one of the greats— Kentucky. Led by Adolph Rupp, the Wildcats had won two national titles in the 1950s and were looking to add their first in the 1960s. However, in one of sport's biggest upsets, Texas

Western won, 72–65, as the Miners downed Kentucky's all-white team. On a less important note, the 1966 Texas Western team remains the only Texas squad to win the Division I men's basketball tournament.

March 20, 1967: Mookie Blaylock's Birthday

Born in Garland, Texas, Mookie Blaylock is small by NBA standards—listed at six feet tall and only 180 pounds—but with quick hands and a tenacious personality, he became one of professional basketball's best defenders. After playing at Garland High School, Blaylock joined Midland College before playing for the University of Oklahoma, where he helped the Sooners to the 1988 NCAA men's basketball championship against the Kansas Jayhawks. Although the Sooners were favored by eight points, the game was played in Kansas City and, after a 50–50 tie at half, the Jayhawks upset Oklahoma, 83–79. Blaylock had fourteen points, five rebounds and four assists in the game. In 1989, he was drafted twelfth overall by the New Jersey Nets, but he really made a name for himself playing with the Atlanta Hawks from 1992 to 1999, including leading the NBA in steals two years in a row (1996–97 and 1997–98), a feat accomplished by only four other NBA players (Allen Iverson, Magic Johnson, Chris Paul and Alvin Robertson).

March 21, 1978: Texas Wins the NIT

The University of Texas had a history of success when it came to hiring head coaches from Oklahoma. Maybe that's why it dipped into the Sooner State to hire Abe Lemmons in 1976. Lemmons was known for his quick wit, and more than a few of his quotes remain in circulation today. But there was no doubt he was an accomplished basketball coach. After his success at Oklahoma City and Texas–Pan American, the Longhorns were hopeful he could provide similar results in Austin. After a 13-13 finish in his first year (1977), some fans began to doubt. However, in year two, Lemmons took the team to a 26-5 record and a SWC title. The season culminated on March 21, 1978, when UT knocked off North Carolina State, 101–93, to win the National Invitation Tournament. Lemmons, named the 1978

National Coach of the Year, only made it to the 1981–82 season before he was let go. Regardless, Lemmons's quotes remain an entertaining aspect of Texas basketball history.

March 22, 1915: First SWC Baseball Contest

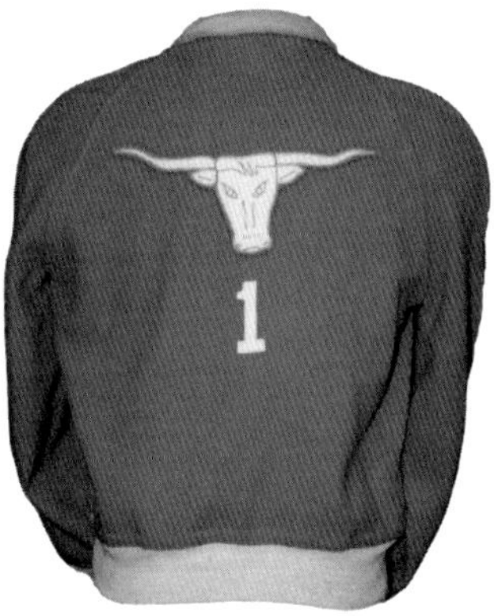

Uncle Billy Disch's University of Texas coaching jacket. Sporting the colors burnt orange and white, the jacket features a longhorn and the number "1." *Courtesy of the Texas Sports Hall of Fame.*

Arguably the greatest college baseball program in the entire country, the University of Texas has seen success on the diamond from its earliest days. The team began play in 1894, but its first Southwest Conference game wouldn't come until March 22, 1915. With the Longhorns led by head coach Billy Disch, the first SWC baseball game was played in Austin, against Southwestern. The game was almost called due to darkness, but UT would prevail in the eleventh inning by a score of 5–4. Texas would go on to claim the first SWC baseball title with a conference record of 12-2 (25-5 overall)—a common theme, as the team would win fifteen of the first seventeen conference championships. For his part, Disch led the Longhorns to 465 victories before passing the reins to one of his former players, Bibb Falk.

March 23, 1948: The Texan Jackie Robinson

There may be no name more familiar to sports fans than Jackie Robinson. In 1947, Jack Roosevelt "Jackie" Robinson broke Major League Baseball's color barrier; he remains one of the most important figures in sporting history. The following year, another Jackie Robinson led the first Texas school to a NCAA basketball final. Robert Jackson "Jackie" Robinson was born in Fort Worth, where he grew up before attending Baylor University to play basketball for coach R.E. "Bill" Henderson. Henderson's starting point guard, Robinson showed flashes of brilliance as the Bears' floor general, earning All-American status as a junior and senior. Despite Baylor's short stature, the team advanced all the way to the 1948 NCAA tournament final, where it faced none other than Adolph Rupp and the Kentucky Wildcats. Quite the opposite of Baylor, Kentucky had a towering lineup. The Wildcats finished off the Bears, 58–42. The Bears' showing is still the best finish in school history. Robinson passed on a chance of a professional basketball career to follow a life in theology.

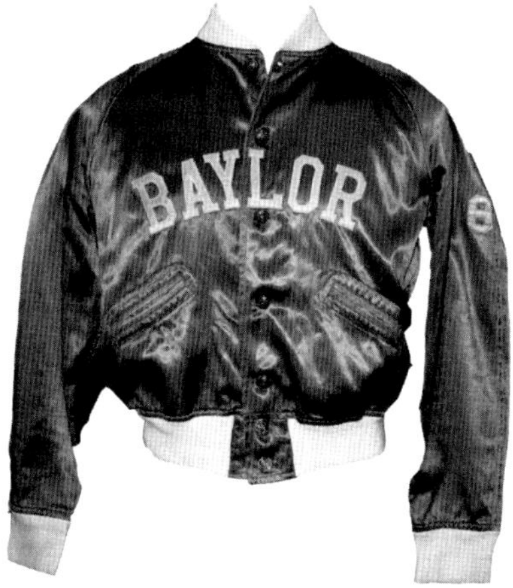

Jackie Robinson's Baylor basketball warmup jacket. *Courtesy of the Texas Sports Hall of Fame.*

March 24, 2000: Johnson Sets 300-Meter Record

In Pretoria, South Africa, Michael Johnson set the world record in the 300 meters. Johnson smashed the previous record of this rarely run event, beating it by more than a half second. Johnson recorded a time of 30.85 seconds, compared to the previous record of 31.48, set in 1990. The only other sprinter to break the 31:00-second mark in the 300 is Usain Bolt, who recorded a time of 30.97 in 2010.

March 25, 1971: Texas's First Final Four

The NCAA Final Four came to the Lone Star State for the first time, as the Astrodome hosted UCLA, Kansas, Western Kentucky and Villanova. Villanova and UCLA would advance to the championship game, played on March 27. UCLA prevailed, 68–62.

March 26, 1961: Swimming to an American Record

Just a sophomore at Highland Park High School, Ric Nesbit set an American record in the 100-yard breaststroke at the state meet. He would lead the school to three state titles in swimming while earning All-American statuses in four events. Although Nesbit originally enrolled at Texas A&M, he would transfer to the University of Texas at Arlington to join forces with Doug Russell, Charlie Smith and Ernie Siefert to create one of the greatest programs in the country. During his college career, Nesbit was a ten-time All-American and seven-time NCAA champion, and he set three NCAA records.

March 27, 1921: Malcolm Kutner Is Born

Malcolm Kutner, born in Dallas, Texas, was acknowledged early as a talented athlete, starring at Woodrow Wilson High School before accepting a scholarship to the University of Texas, where he lettered in football, basketball and track. UT coach Dana X. Bible recognized Kutner's talents and utilized him at multiple positions, including end, tackle and halfback. Over his final two seasons in Austin, Kutner helped Texas to a 16-3-1 record. He earned All-American status as a senior. Kutner and Chal Daniel were the Burnt Orange and White's first All-Americans, both recognized in 1941. After graduating, Kutner joined the U.S. Navy to serve during World War II, after which he turned pro, joining the Chicago Cardinals. He won Rookie of the Year honors in 1946. The following season, Kutner won the NFL's Most Valuable Player award as he led the league in receiving with 944 yards and seven touchdowns. For good measure, Kutner also scored on a pick six during that season.

March 28, 1975: Dave Roberts Sets World Record

While competing in the Florida Relays, Rice's Dave Roberts cleared an astounding 18 feet, 6.25 inches to set a new record in the pole vault. He would hold the record only until May 1976, when fellow American Earl Bell bested the mark—only for Roberts to reclaim it in June. With the

1976 Montreal Olympics set for July, Roberts looked to be a favorite in the competition. However, he and two other competitors would tie the Olympic record, leading to another round of jumps. Unfortunately, the other two men did not miss at any height, and Roberts missed once, relegating him to the bronze medal. His world-record jump would stand as the mark to beat until 1980.

March 29, 1968: Nancy Richey Takes Down Billie Jean King

The setting was iconic—Madison Square Garden. Over ten thousand spectators arrived to watch a match that *Sports Illustrated* described as the "Wimbledon and Forest Hills finals combined." Although the tournament certainly had no such prestige, the match was filled with symbolism.

On one side of the net was Billie Jean King, just twenty-four years old and playing her last amateur tournament. On the other side stood Nancy Richey, twenty-five, from San Angelo, Texas. King and Richey had been trading the top ranking in the United States. Richey held the spot in 1964; the two tied for No. 1 in 1965; and King held it from 1966 to 1967. Making the matchup even more intriguing was the fact that King and Richey hadn't played in nearly three and a half years. The last contest between the two had been in September 1964, when Richey won in straight sets, 6–4, 6–4, to claim her seventh victory over King in seven tries. While the opponents utilized very different styles, there was no doubt they were the top two players in America at the time.

Even though Richey held the edge over King in head-to-head matches, there was no doubt who was expected to win: Billie Jean King. The match certainly started that way, as King won the first set, 6–4, before putting Richey down 5–0 in the second. Richey battled back to 5–3, but certainly almost everyone believed the match to be over. Then King missed what should have been an easy match point, sending the ball just past the baseline. Richey pounced on the momentum swing. Over the final fifty-one points, King won just twelve of them. Richey won nine straight games after those three to win the match, 4–6, 7–5, 6–0. King had never lost twelve straight games in her career, and Richey put together one of the greatest comebacks the tennis world has ever seen. Of course, King would go on to a fantastic pro career and serve as a champion for equality in society and sports. But for that afternoon in New York, it was Richey who shone brightest.

March 30, 1986: Conradt Leads Texas to Glory

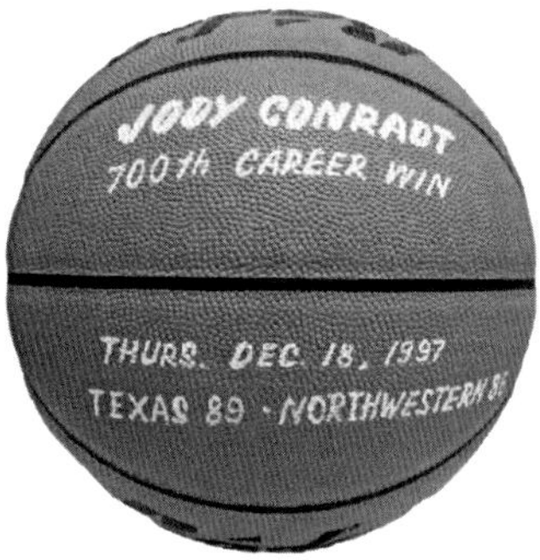

Game ball from Jody Conradt's 700th career win, as she led Texas to a victory over Northwestern. *Courtesy of the Texas Sports Hall of Fame.*

It's the final day of the 1986 NCAA women's basketball tournament, and only two teams are left vying for the title of national champion. Each had received a No. 1 seed, and each was more than talented enough to claim the title. The University of Texas, led by head coach Jody Conradt, hadn't lost a game all year. The University of Southern California was led by two of the greatest women's basketball players of all time, Cheryl Miller and Cynthia Cooper. USC had won two of the first three NCAA women's basketball national titles, going back-to-back in 1983 and 1984. With 1986 being Miller's senior year, the Trojans were looking to add a third title to their collection. Instead, the Longhorns held Miller to one of her worst performances ever. Texas's depth was the difference. Playing all eleven players, the Longhorns constantly had fresh legs and limited Miller to two of eleven shooting on the day. Meanwhile, Clarissa Davis came off the bench for Texas to score twenty-five and earn Most Outstanding Player honors (UT had an astounding 58-4 advantage in bench points). The Longhorns won, 97–81, claiming the first perfect season in NCAA women's basketball history, going 34-0.

March 31, 1980: Roger Staubach Retires

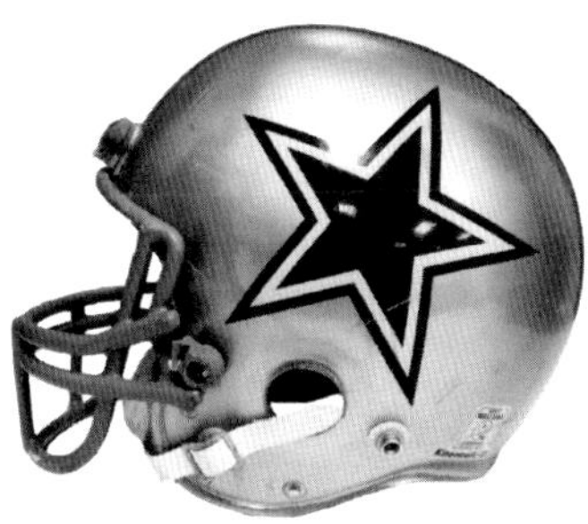

Roger Staubach's Dallas Cowboys helmet. While this helmet features the Cowboys' star logo, the team original used a logo that was solid. The star with the white-and-blue border was adopted in 1964. *Courtesy of the Texas Sports Hall of Fame.*

Few names resonate so deeply with Dallas Cowboys fans as that of Roger Staubach. Being called the "face of the franchise" is an honor; it is even more impressive when that franchise has been represented by stars such as Bob Lilly, Troy Aikman, Emmitt Smith and many more. Not drafted until the tenth round due to his naval obligations, Staubach proved worth the wait, leading the Cowboys to their first Super Bowl title in his second year. Over the course of his career, Staubach was named to six Pro Bowls and led the Cowboys to five Super Bowls, winning two.

APRIL

April 1, 2006: Dynamo Dominate

The first day of April marked the opening of the 2006 Major League Soccer season. The Houston Dynamo would go on to win the MLS Cup, becoming the first Texas team to capture the title. They would successfully defend their title in 2007, making the Dynamo just the second MLS team to win back-to-back titles.

April 2, 1967: Oilers in Kerrville

NFL training camps have become a subject of popular focus in the modern era. Fans flock to attend open practices, and shows like HBO's *Hard Knocks* reveal more about day-to-day life as a professional football player than does any game during the season. Some training sites have become as popular as the teams that inhabit them, such as the Cowboys' site in Thousand Oaks, California, or today when they travel to Oxnard for training. However, on April 2, 1967, the Houston Oilers announced they'd be making their own trip west—just not as far west. The Oilers would be going to Kerrville, Texas, to set up training camp at Schreiner University. It was only the third time in franchise history that the Oilers trained outside of Houston.

April 3, 2012: Bears Finish First Again

The final seconds ticked down, and a game that had already been decided officially ended. Baylor defeated Notre Dame, 80–61, to capture the school's second women's basketball title. The game was the crowning moment in Brittney Griner's college career. At six feet, eight inches, Griner was a well-known commodity before she even joined the college basketball ranks. After her senior year at Nimitz High School, Houston's mayor, Bill White, declared May 7, 2009, as Brittney Griner Day. No pressure, right? The top recruit in the country, Griner chose to join coach Kim Mulkey at Baylor. Mulkey had won a previous title with the Bears when they defeated Michigan State, 84–62, in the 2005 title game. Not surprisingly, such a high-profile coach-player duo brought lots of expectations. With the victory over Notre Dame, Griner and Mulkey solidified one of the greatest four-year runs in women's college basketball history.

April 4, 1937: The Green Jacket Comes to Texas

The most iconic tournament in professional golf, the Masters, was first played in 1934. Just four years later, it would see the first Texan win the coveted green jacket. On April 4, 1937, Byron Nelson charged ahead of fellow Texan Ralph Guldahl, picking up an astonishing six strokes over two holes on the back nine before finishing the final day with a score of 70 and a four-day total of 283, two strokes better than Guldahl's 285. The late surge led famous sports journalist O.B. Keeler to title his lead article the next day, "LORD BYRON WINS MASTERS," comparing Nelson's comeback to poet Lord Byron's piece about Napoleon's defeat at Waterloo. Nelson was only twenty-five years old at the time, but the article would give him a nickname for the rest of his career—Lord Byron. For his victory, Nelson earned a check for $1,500, a paltry sum compared to $1,800,000 won by another Texan, Jordan Spieth, almost eighty years later.

April 5, 2011: Aggies Win Their First Basketball Title

Led by head coach Gary Blair and the tournament's Most Outstanding Player, Danielle Adams, the Texas A&M Aggies captured their first national

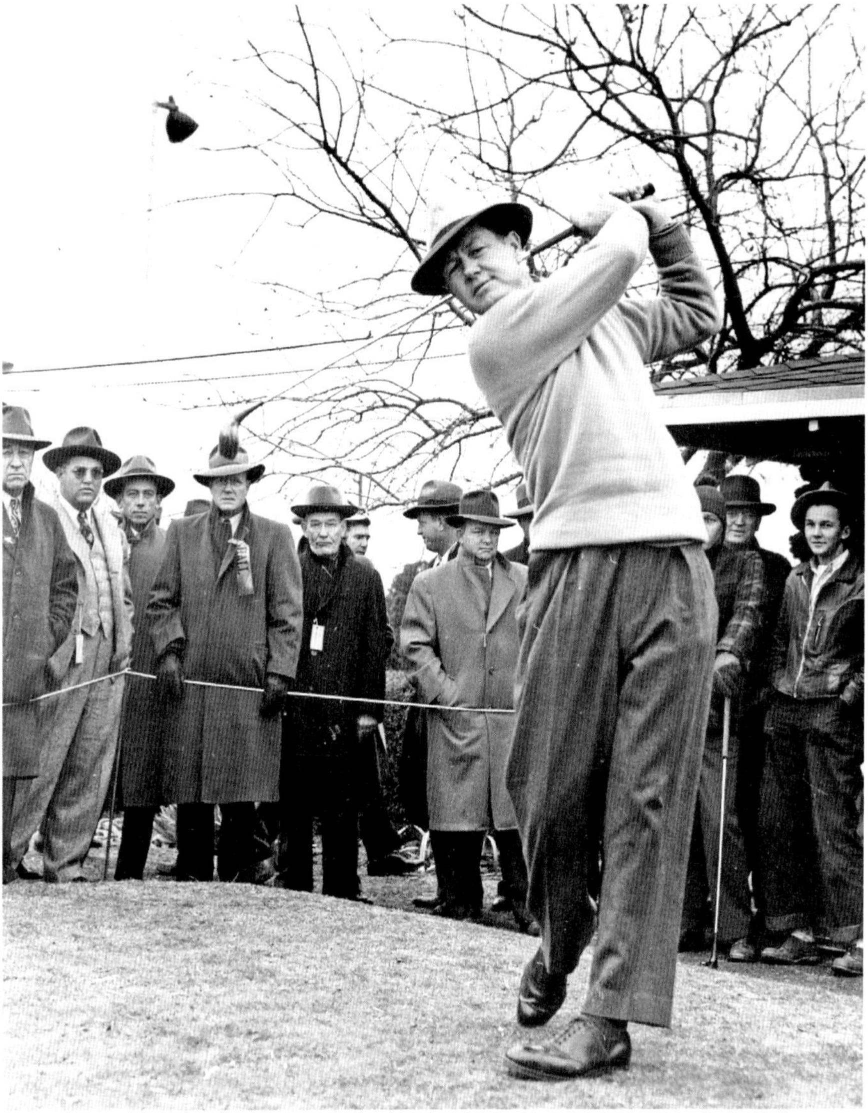

Byron Nelson follows his drive through the air while the gallery watches from behind. *Courtesy of the Texas Sports Hall of Fame.*

championship in basketball. The Aggies advanced to the Final Four after defeating Kim Mulkey and the Baylor Bears in the Regional Finals by a score of 58–46. Once there, the Ags didn't look back. They won a classic game against Stanford, 63–62, before taking down Notre Dame in the title game, 76–70.

APRIL 6, 1929: LONE STAR DYNASTY

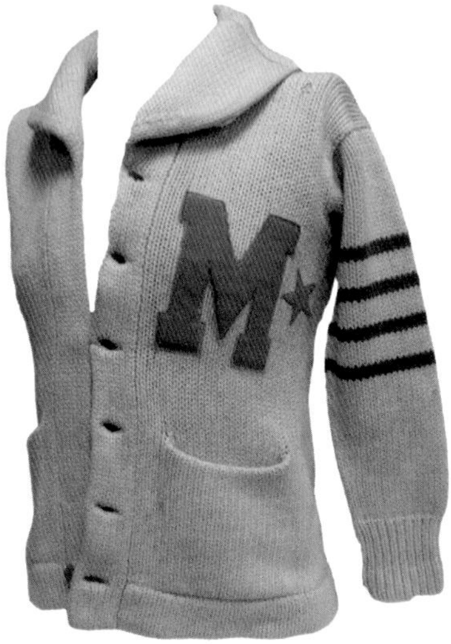

Jimmy Kitts's SMU letter jacket. *Courtesy of the Texas Sports Hall of Fame.*

The National High School Basketball Tournament in Chicago, Illinois, won by the Athens High School Hornets, began on this day in 1929. The Hornets had been led by former Baylor standout Wesley Bradshaw but, after what was viewed as limited success, Bradshaw was replaced with Southern Methodist star Jimmy Kitts. As head coach of the Hornets, Kitts proved to be a dominant force. In his first year at the helm, 1927, Kitts led the Hornets to the state title. From 1927 to 1934, the Athens Hornets never lost when they made it to a championship finals game, and their accomplishments included seven district titles, five state titles and two national championships. In 1932, Kitts moved on to Rice, where he would lead the Owls to two SWC titles in eight years, including their first conference title.

APRIL 7, 1940: DEMARET ADDS A JACKET TO "THE WARDROBE"

Jimmy the "Wardrobe" Demaret was known around the professional golf circuit for his flashy style of dress. But it was another Texan, Lloyd Mangrum, who stole the audience's attention on day one of the 1940 Masters Tournament. Mangrum opened the tournament with a blistering 64, a Masters record at the time. However, by the second round, Demaret had moved into first. He would stay there throughout the final two rounds, as Mangrum held second and Byron Nelson moved into third. The top three spots at the Masters were all held by Texans. Augusta National would prove a popular course for Demaret, who would win the Masters again in 1947 and 1950, adding a total of three green jackets to his already famous wardrobe.

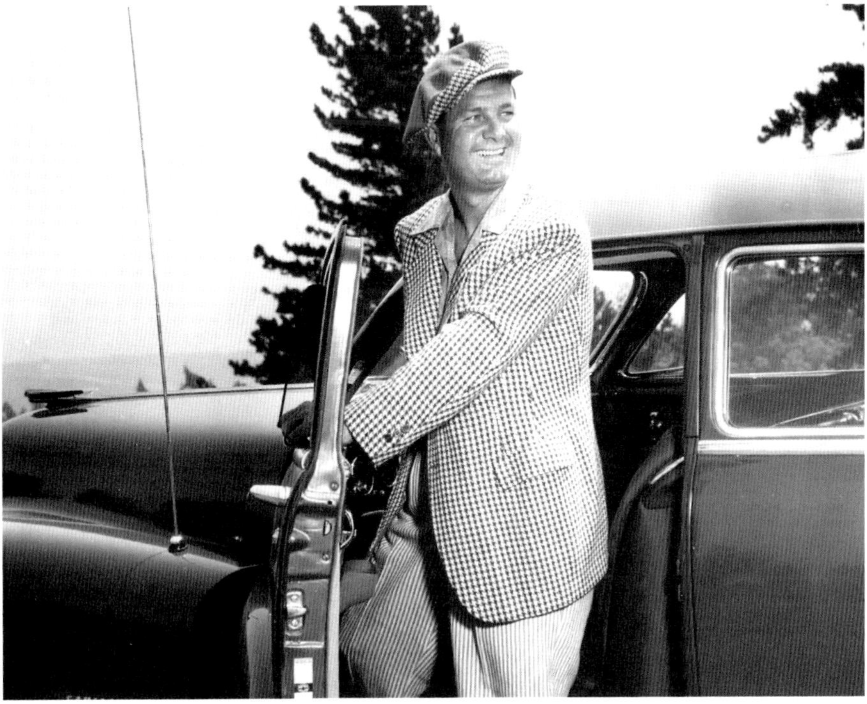

Jimmy the "Wardrobe" Demaret was known for his audacious outfits while on the PGA Tour. *Courtesy of the Texas Sports Hall of Fame.*

April 8, 1956: Burke Roars Back

On Saturday, April 7, 1956, Jack Burke Jr. sat eight strokes off the lead at the 1956 Masters. Tied for fourth place with fellow Texan Lloyd Mangrum after the third round, Burke was looking at a steep uphill climb if he wanted to compete for the coveted green jacket. Amateur Ken Venturi—who had played against Byron Nelson and Ben Hogan in the now-famous match in January of that year—had held the lead at the Masters from round one to round three. However, Venturi shot a shocking 42 on his final nine holes, leading to an 80 in his final round (+8). Burke shot a final-round 71, finishing one shot ahead of Venturi to win the tournament. Burke's final score of 289 (+1) is tied for the highest score ever to win a Masters.

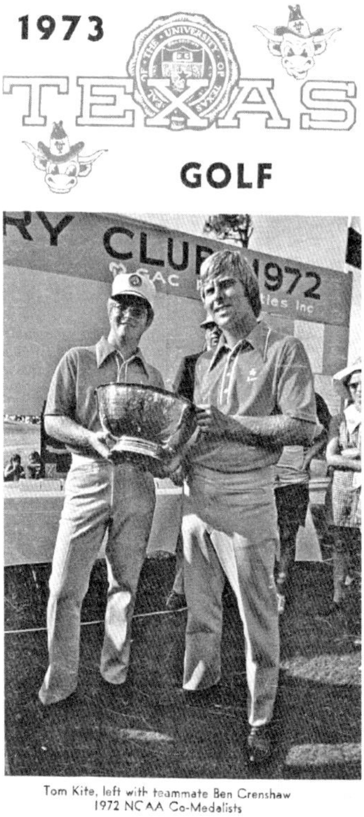

April 9, 1995: Crenshaw Honors Penick

On the final day of the 1995 Masters, Ben Crenshaw was surely riding a wave of conflicting emotions. Tied for first entering the final round, Crenshaw must have been ecstatic to be in the hunt for his second Masters (he had won in 1984). However, just days before, Crenshaw's mentor and University of Texas golf legend Harvey Penick had passed away. Penick had been one of the greatest golf instructors of all time, and Crenshaw would certainly have had him on his mind. As he navigated the final round, Crenshaw played masterfully, carding a final-round 68—his second-best score of the weekend—to win the tournament by one stroke. Perhaps Penick was there after all.

Teammates Tom Kite (*left*) and Ben Crenshaw (*right*) lift their 1972 NCAA trophy as co-medalists. *Courtesy of the Texas Sports Hall of Fame.*

April 10, 1962: Opening Day for the Colt .45s

The storied Chicago Cubs traveled to Houston on April 10 to face Major League Baseball's newest club, the Houston Colt .45s. While Houston had long had a minor-league team, the Buffaloes, many in the city were ready for the Lone Star State to be represented in the big leagues. Four men in particular led that charge: Craig Cullinan, George Kirksey, R.E. Smith and, of course, Judge Roy Hofheinz. The dream came to reality in October 1960 when the National League approved a new franchise in Houston to begin play in 1962. The city began plans to build an opulent indoor, air-conditioned stadium to combat the city's oppressive weather, but for the the first few seasons, the team played at Colt Stadium. This is where opening day 1962 would be played, as the Colt .45s downed the Cubs, 11–2, before sweeping the Chicago team to win the franchise's first series. After that, victories were few and far between, as the Colt .45s finished 1962 third to last in the NL, just one spot ahead of the Cubbies. In 1964, the team would change its name to the Astros before moving into the Astrodome, in 1965. The rest, as they say, is history.

April 11, 1995: Labontes Break Ground at Texas Motor Speedway

When a new racetrack was planned for Fort Worth, it made sense to invite two of the greatest NASCAR drivers of all time to break ground. The fact that they were brothers from Texas made it even more appropriate. Bobby and Terry Labonte, from Corpus Christi, have had careers as prolific drivers. In the NASCAR Sprint Cup Series (the association's highest division), Terry competed in 890 races over thirty-seven years claiming twenty-two wins and 361 top-ten finishes. Bobby was similarly competitive, driving in 728 races over twenty-five years, with twenty-one wins and 203 top-ten finishes. The brothers joined another NASCAR legend, Jeff Gordon, in April 1995 to help break ground on Texas Motor Speedway. The new circuit, completed in 1996, would see its first Texan win in 1999, as Terry claimed the checkered flag.

April 12, 2015: Spieth's First Major

The history of Texas sports is as impressive as it is long. Of course, football receives most of the attention, and there have been many great basketball and baseball teams over the years. Often, other sports get a little lost in the shuffle. For instance, Texas could make a strong argument for being one of the greatest golfing states in America. It has a pantheon of storied athletes: Ben Hogan, one of the five greatest golfers of all time; Byron Nelson, easily a top-ten all-time golfer, despite retiring at an early age; Babe Zaharias, the greatest female golfer of all time and in the top ten, regardless of gender; and Lee Trevino, one of the greatest fifteen golfers ever. While there have been plenty of other golfers from the Lone Star State, the only one who looks to challenge this group of all-time greats is Jordan Spieth. From Dallas, Spieth played a brief collegiate career at the University of Texas before turning professional at the age of nineteen. By his third year as a pro, it was clear why Spieth was being hyped as potentially the next great Texas golfer. On April 12, 2015, Spieth claimed his first major title, leading the Masters Tournament from beginning to end and becoming the second-youngest person to win the prestigious tournament. Just a few months later, he would claim his second major, winning the 2015 U.S. Open. Needless to say, some of Texas's best athletes may have competition for the title "greatest ever."

April 13, 1983: Green Speed

Known as one of the greatest defensive backs in football history, Darrell Green showed off his world-class speed on April 13, 1983, as he ran the 100-meter dash in 10.08 seconds—a personal best. While Green was a multiple All-American in track and field for Texas A&I, he was even more impressive on the gridiron. A graduate of Jesse H. Jones High School in Houston, Green attended Texas A&I before being selected twenty-eighth overall in the 1983 NFL draft by the Washington Redskins. The selection paid dividends immediately, as Green played in all sixteen games as a rookie before finishing a twenty-year career with the Redskins, making the Pro Bowl seven times, being named an All-Pro four times and winning two Super Bowls (XXII and XXVI).

April 14: National Pecan Day

A state of symbols, Texas is known for everything from the bluebonnet to the mockingbird. However, two of Texas's most popular symbols have to be the pecan and football. So, what could be better than combining the two? National Pecan Day is April 14, and from 1964 to 1970, the pecan and Texas football were on full display at the Pecan Bowl. Although not a major bowl, the game served as a college postseason playoff game for seven years. Played four times in Abilene and three times in Arlington, the Pecan Bowl was never kind to Texas teams—the only Lone Star winner was UT–Arlington in 1967.

April 15, 1968: Twenty-Four Innings, Six Hours, One Run

In April 1968, the Houston Astros and New York Mets played one of the longest, lowest-scoring contests in Major League Baseball history. With a total of 158 at-bats, the Astros and Mets combined for a total of twenty-two hits—three players made nine appearances each at the plate without recording a hit. Mercifully, the Astros loaded the bases in the bottom of the twenty-fourth inning. With one out, Bob Aspromonte hit a single that skidded off the AstroTurf and through the Mets' infield to let Norm Miller score from third base, ending the game, 1–0. While no one knows for sure how many fans remained at thc end of the game, somewhere between one thousand and three thousand people made it all the way to 1:37 a.m. to see the Astros triumph.

April 16, 1972: Hooton Makes the Majors

After three shining seasons on the Forty Acres of the University of Texas, Burt Hooton was drafted second overall by the Chicago Cubs. Just one week after that, Hooton made his first start for the Cubs, jumping straight from college to the majors. On April 16, 1972, in just his fourth start, Hooton looked like he might become one of the greatest pitchers of all time. In a game that played in wet conditions and with temperatures that fluctuated between just above freezing and the mid-forties, Hooton threw a no-hitter against the Philadelphia Phillies. That night, fellow Texan turned Cub turned Chicago sports announcer, Ernie Banks, described the scene this way: "at Wrigley Field, everybody was rootin' and tootin' for Burt Hooton." One of the main reasons for Hooton's success was his control of a nasty off-speed pitch known as the knuckle curve. Some claim Hooton invented the pitch, but that is debatable. What isn't in doubt is that Hooton became the first major leaguer to utilize the knuckle curve, and he dominated with it. However, over time, hitters adjusted to the pitch, and Hooton's effectiveness declined. Still, with 151 career wins and pitching appearances in three World Series, Hooton remains a Lone Star legend.

April 17, 1965: Matson Sets Shot Record

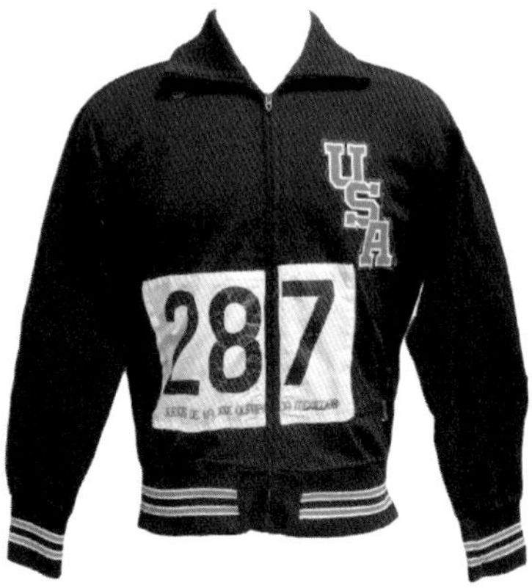

Randy Matson's Olympic warmup jacket, worn at the 1968 Mexico City Games. *Courtesy of the Texas Sports Hall of Fame.*

At the Fortieth Annual Kansas Relays, Texas A&M track-and-field legend Randy Matson set an intercollegiate shot put record by throwing sixty-five feet, ten and three-fourths inches, beating the old mark by a quarter of an inch. Matson was still an underclassman at the time, and setting records would become commonplace. Later in 1965, over a two-month period, Matson would break the world record three times, adding nearly two feet to the previous mark. After graduating from A&M, Matson was drafted by the NFL and the NBA, but he turned down those offers to focus on his track and field career. Matson would win silver in shot put at the 1964 Tokyo Olympics and then earn gold in the 1968 Mexico City Olympics. When he retired in 1972, Matson was the only athlete to have thrown the shot over seventy feet.

April 18, 1982: Malone's Streak Ends

Moses Malone remains one of the greatest Houston Rockets to ever play. The holder of many franchise records, Malone saw one come to an end on April 18. After 319 games of scoring ten or more points, Malone's streak ended. It had begun nearly a decade earlier, in November 1972. The streak remains a Houston Rockets record.

April 19, 1908: "Smokey" Joe Turns Pro

Born in Seguin, Texas, to parents of African American and Comanche descent, "Smokey" Joe Williams was barred from Major League Baseball due to the color of his skin. While it took decades, Williams has finally been recognized for being one of the greatest pitchers in baseball history. Unfortunately, records from the Negro leagues have often faded into history, but some give April 19, 1908, as Williams's first professional start. Playing for the San Antonio Black Bronchos, Williams was an immediate success before spending nearly two decades at the pinnacle of Negro league baseball. Discussing Williams's tremendous fastball, Chicago Giants owner Frank Leland once wrote, "If you have ever witnessed the speed of a pebble in a storm you have not even then seen the equal of the speed possessed by this wonderful Texan Giant." Ty Cobb once called Williams a "sure 30-game winner" if he had been allowed to play in the majors. The records we do know show exactly how dominant Williams was. One season, he was credited with forty-one wins and only three losses. In one of his most famous games—a 1930 contest between Williams's Homestead Grays and the Kansas City Monarchs—Williams struck out an astounding twenty-seven batters over twelve innings as the Grays won, 1–0. Williams was thirty-four at the time. While modern history often remembers Satchel Paige as the greatest Negro league pitcher, a 1952 poll by the *Pittsburgh Courier*, the contemporary authority on African American sports, selected Williams as the greatest pitcher in Negro league history, just ahead of Paige. What is clear is that Williams remains one of the greatest players to ever hurl a fastball.

April 20, 1927: Barnstorming Japan

On this date, the Fresno Athletic Club and the Philadelphia Royal Giants met at Meiji Shrine Stadium in Tokyo. The two teams were on a four-month barnstorming tour of Hawaii, Japan and Korea. The Royal Giants were composed of some of the biggest stars in the Negro National League, including Texans Andy Cooper (Waco) and Biz Mackey (Eagle Pass). Although his conclusions are contested, Japanese historian Kazuo Sayama has argued that this 1927 tour was the inspiration for professional baseball in Japan—a distinction usually given to a team made of MLB All-Stars in 1934. For instance, Sayama points to how the Royal Giants attempted to play a gentlemanly game, giving the highest consideration to their less-experienced Japanese counterparts. On the other hand, the 1934 All-American team showboated, running up the score on the Japanese teams they faced. One specific example of the respect shown by the Royal Giants occurred when Mackey was hit by an errant pitch. The pitcher, wishing to apologize to Mackey, bowed toward him. Mackey returned the bow before taking first base. The Royal Giants finished the tour with a record of 35-2-1.

April 21, 1868: "Texas State Championship"

Few events have had such a lasting impact on the United States as the Civil War. Even today, the war remains a divisive topic that can be a flashpoint for controversy. Yet, one of the interesting, unintended consequences of the war was the birth of a national pastime. While Americans had long enjoyed sports, including some early forms of baseball, games were largely dictated by regional rules and styles. However, as Americans from throughout the country came together in military garrisons and prison camps, the game became more uniform. It also grew in popularity throughout the country. In a nod to both Texas and U.S. history, the Houston Stonewalls played the Galveston Robert E. Lees on April 21, 1868, at the site of the Battle of San Jacinto in what newspapers described as the "Texas State Championship." The Stonewalls won.

April 22, 1934: Fiesta Tournament

Cecil Smith led his Austin team into the San Antonio Fiesta Polo Tournament. One of the greatest polo players to ever live, Smith was born in Llano, Texas, and learned the game as a horse trader. He was a ten-goal player—the highest status available—from 1938 to 1962, the longest that an American has held that status. Smith became famous enough to play polo with the likes of Will Rogers and Walt Disney. He won the U.S. Open Polo Championship five times. Smith retired to Boerne, Texas, where he passed away in 1999.

April 23, 1950: Slater and the Lakers Claim the NBA Championship

One of the earliest hard-court legends to come out of the Lone Star State, Slater Martin first made a name for himself playing for the Texas Longhorns

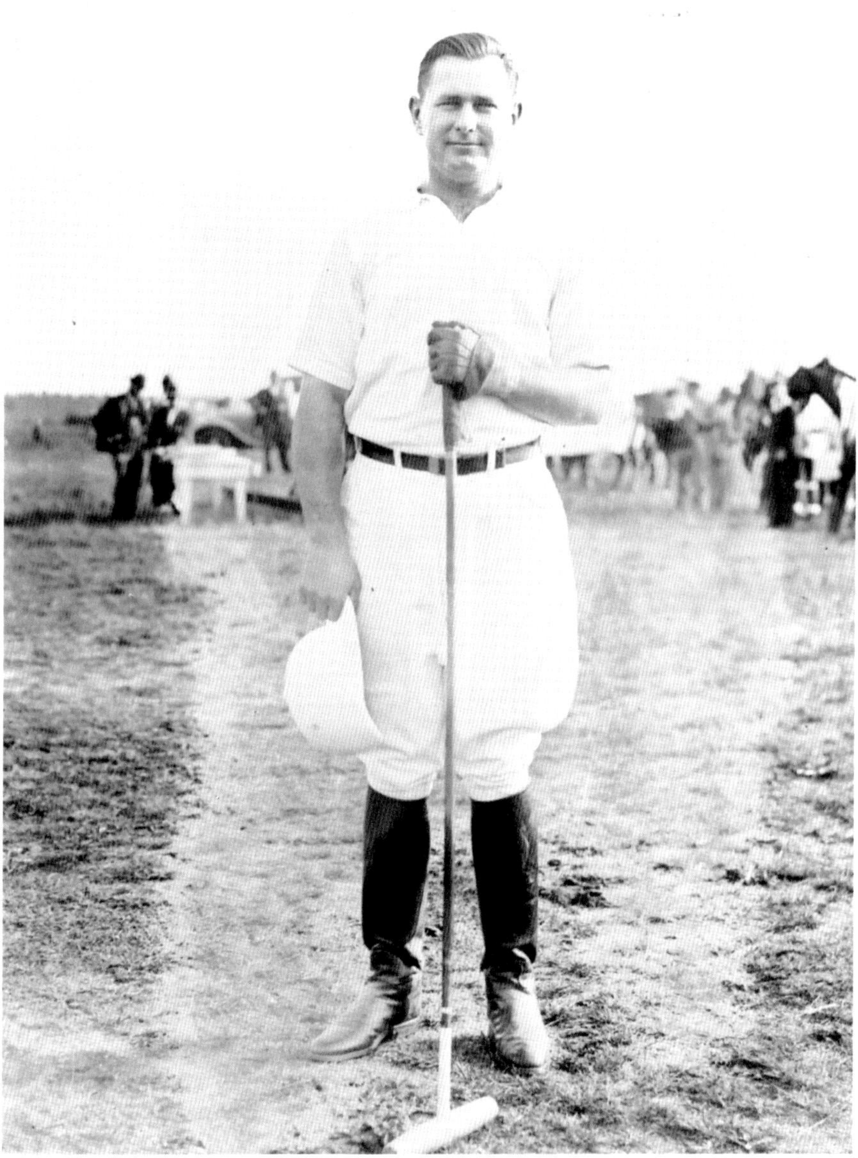

Cecil Smith in his polo uniform. *Courtesy of the Texas Sports Hall of Fame.*

in the mid-1940s before joining the Minneapolis Lakers in 1949. While still developing in 1950, Martin was already becoming known as one of the most fearsome defenders in professional basketball. In that year, Martin and the

Lakers would take on the Syracuse Nationals, beating them in Game 6 of the NBA Finals on April 23 by the score of 110–95 to claim the championship. Martin would continue to develop, becoming one of the most feared and respected defenders of the 1950s and helping lead the Lakers to three more titles before joining the St. Louis Hawks, with whom he won his fifth and final NBA title. A seven-time NBA All-Star and five-time All-NBA Second Team selection, Martin was inducted into the Naismith Memorial Basketball Hall of Fame in 1982 and is one of three Longhorn basketball players to have their number retired by the school.

April 24, 1994: Robinson's Scoring Spree

Of all Texas' great basketball players, one might stand above the rest—David Robinson. Originally from Florida, Robinson came to Texas after he was the first overall selection by the San Antonio Spurs in the 1987 NBA draft. One of the best centers to ever play the game, Robinson was a feared defender and rebounder. But that certainly didn't mean he couldn't score. On April 24, 1994, Robinson poured in an incredible seventy-one points as the Spurs defeated the Los Angeles Clippers, 112–97. Robinson is one of just five NBA players to have scored over seventy points in a game. Robinson won the regular-season scoring title, edging out Shaquille O'Neal, who had been leading the race before Robinson's big game.

April 25, 1993: Michael Strahan Is Drafted

Born in Houston, Michael Strahan moved with his family to Germany when he was just nine years old. By the time he reached high school, Strahan's athleticism was apparent, so his dad sent him back to Texas to play his final high school season at Houston's Westbury High School. In that one season, Strahan made such an impact that he earned a scholarship offer to Texas Southern, where he would become one of the greatest college football players of all time. He set a school record for career sacks with 41.5 while being named an Associated Press All-American and a two-time SWAC Player of the Year. On April 25, 1993, the New York Giants selected Strahan with their first pick. It proved to be a smart move, as Strahan would go on to generate 141.5 sacks, twenty-four forced fumbles and four interceptions over his NFL career while setting a single-season record for sacks, with 22.5 in 2001. Strahan spent his entire career with the Giants (1993–2007), making the Pro Bowl seven times, being named to an All-Pro team six times and helping the Giants to victory in Super Bowl XLII.

April 26, 1983: Dickerson Goes Pro

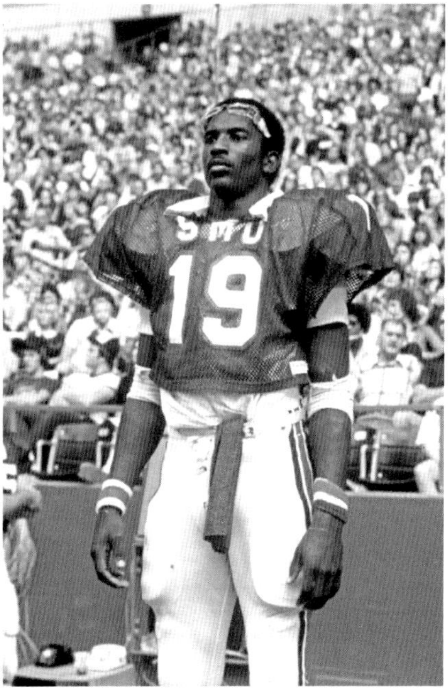

Eric Dickerson watches anxiously from the sidelines of a SMU game. *Courtesy of the Texas Sports Hall of Fame.*

Today, Texas football is known in large part for the incredible quarterbacks it produces. At the start of the 2016 NFL season, one-fourth of the league's starting quarterbacks hailed from the Lone Star State—twice as many as the next closest state, California. However, for much of its history, Texas football was known for producing elite running backs. From John David Crow and Earl Campbell to LaDainian Tomlinson and Adrian Peterson, Texas churned out running backs quicker than the wishbone formation scored touchdowns. One of those great backs was SMU's Eric Dickerson. At six feet, three inches and 220 pounds, Dickerson was a behemoth of a back noted for a combination of size and speed. He would briefly hold the Southwest Conference's career rushing record when he broke Earl Campbell's rushing total by 7 yards (4,450 yards for Dickerson compared to 4,443 for Campbell). Dickerson continued his onslaught in the NFL, rushing for 2,105 yards in 1984 while playing for the Los Angeles Rams. It remains a single season NFL record. A member of the Pro Football Hall of Fame, Dickerson played in six Pro Bowls, was named First Team All-Pro five times and was the NFC Offensive Player of the Year three times.

April 27, 1983: Ryan Breaks the Strikeout Record

Originally from Alvin, Texas, Nolan Ryan finally returned to the Lone Star State in 1980 after spending the first part of his professional baseball career on the East and West Coasts. An immediate fan favorite, Ryan delighted Houston spectators in 1983 when he broke a fifty-five-year-old MLB record, striking out the 3,509th batter of his career.

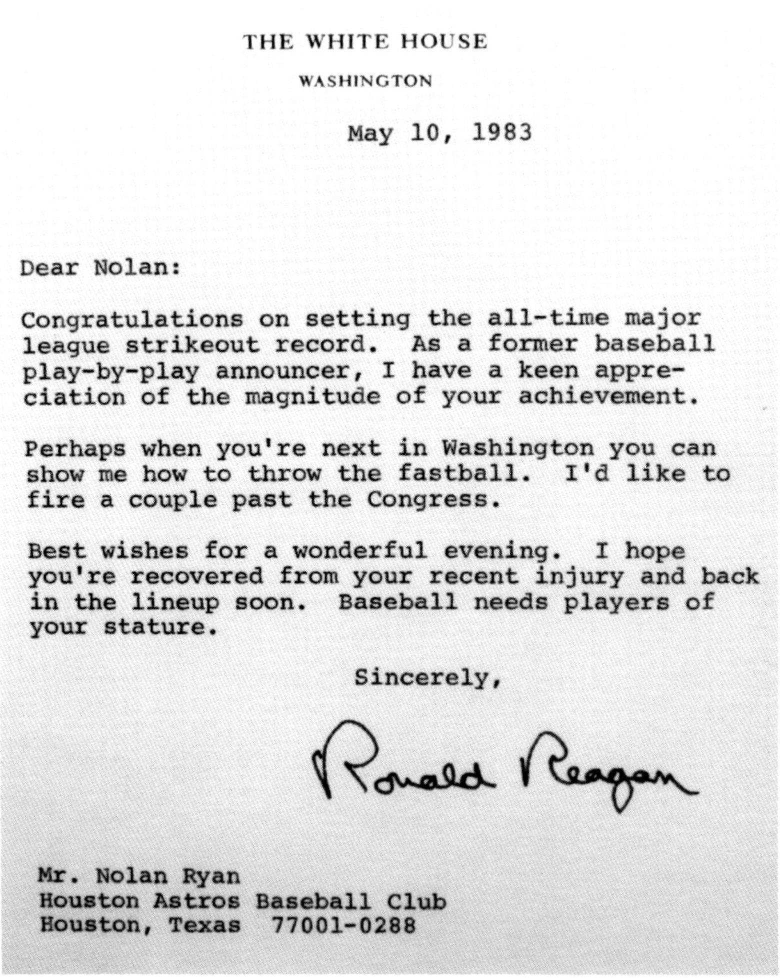

THE WHITE HOUSE

WASHINGTON

May 10, 1983

Dear Nolan:

Congratulations on setting the all-time major league strikeout record. As a former baseball play-by-play announcer, I have a keen appreciation of the magnitude of your achievement.

Perhaps when you're next in Washington you can show me how to throw the fastball. I'd like to fire a couple past the Congress.

Best wishes for a wonderful evening. I hope you're recovered from your recent injury and back in the lineup soon. Baseball needs players of your stature.

Sincerely,

Ronald Reagan

Mr. Nolan Ryan
Houston Astros Baseball Club
Houston, Texas 77001-0288

Letter from President Ronald Reagan to Nolan Ryan. It reads, in part, "Perhaps when you're next in Washington you can show me how to throw the fastball. I'd like to fire a couple past the Congress.…Baseball needs players of your stature." *Courtesy of the Texas Sports Hall of Fame.*

April 28, 2011: Face of the Franchise

There have been some pretty incredible drafts in the history of the NFL. For instance, 1989 was ripe with talent, including Troy Aikman, Deion Sanders and UT's Eric Metcalf. Another example is 1983, which featured future stars like John Elway, Dan Marino, Jim Kelly, Darrell Green, Bruce Matthews and Eric Dickerson. However, an argument can be made that the 2011 draft was one of the greatest ever—certainly one of the best in the twenty-first century. Texas stars Von Miller and Andy Dalton were selected in the first two rounds, along with Cam Newton, Patrick Peterson, A.J. Green and Julio Jones. For their part, the Dallas Cowboys selected Pro Bowl lineman Tyron Smith. Even in a class of this magnitude, the Houston Texans managed to find a pick with a little something extra: J.J. Watt. The Texans managed to get Watt with the eleventh overall pick, and he almost immediately became the face of the franchise. In his first five seasons, Watt was named First Team All-Pro and was a Pro Bowl selection four times. Even more impressive, Watt was named the NFL's Defensive Player of the Year in 2012, 2014 and 2015 making him one of only two players in league history to receive the distinction three times (Lawrence Taylor is the other).

April 29, 1981: Rockets Make the NBA Finals

After upsetting Magic Johnson and the defending NBA champion Lakers in the first round, followed by the San Antonio Spurs in the second round, the Houston Rockets beat the Kansas City Kings in Game 5 on April 29 to win the Western Conference. The win catapulted the Rockets to the NBA Finals, making Houston the first Texas team to reach the finals. It also marked the last time a team with a losing record in the regular season reached the finals. The Rockets stole a game from Boston to even the series at one game apiece, but the Celtics would eventually assert themselves, winning the series in six games, 4-2.

April 30, 1985: The Great Trade Robbery

On April 30, 1985, the NFL draft began. Sensing the end of the United States Football League (USFL), the Dallas Cowboys acquired the rights to

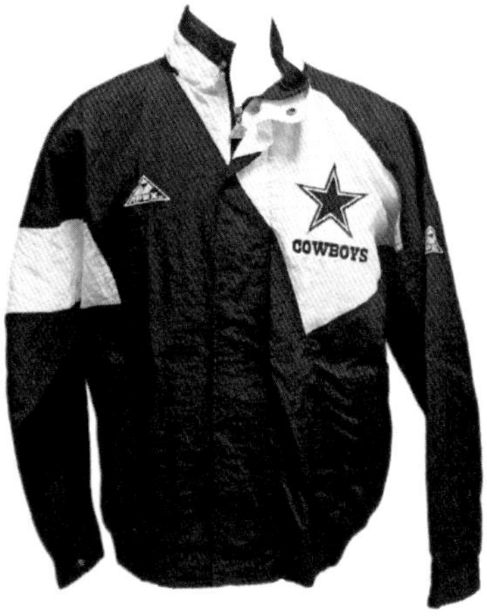

One of Jimmy Johnson's Dallas Cowboys coaching jackets. *Courtesy of the Texas Sports Hall of Fame.*

Herschel Walker, drafting him in the fifth round. After becoming only the tenth NFL player to amass over two thousand yards in a single season, Walker earned a Pro Bowl selection with the Cowboys in 1988. However, new head coach Jimmy Johnson began shopping players around to build more roster depth. When a trade opportunity with the Vikings presented itself, Johnson shipped Walker to Minnesota in 1989 for a first-round pick and five players. The five players came with conditions that if they were cut, Dallas would receive extra draft picks as compensation. Johnson cut all the players to gain the picks, using the picks and further trades to build the core of the great Cowboys teams of the 1990s, including Emmitt Smith, Russell Maryland, Kevin Smith and Darren Woodson. Over five years, Dallas traded fifty-one times—more than the rest of the NFL combined.

MAY

May 1, 1980: Mavs Join the NBA

The Dallas Mavericks officially became the twenty-third member of the NBA after owner Don Carter's Dallas National Basketball Association, Incorporated, was awarded an expansion by Commissioner Larry O'Brien. Carter was assisted by the Mavericks' first president and general manager, Norm Sonju, who was successful in lobbying the city of Dallas to build the 17,007-seat Reunion Arena downtown in 1979. Led by head coach Dick Motta, the Mavs won their first game, beating San Antonio, 103–92, but it would be a season of few bright spots. Dallas finished its inaugural season with a record of 15-67.

May 2, 1936: Max Hirsch's First Kentucky Derby

Born in Fredericksburg, Texas, in 1880, Maximilian Justice "Max" Hirsch was introduced to horse racing early, working as a jockey and a groom at the Morris Ranch. After he became too heavy to ride, Hirsch turned wholeheartedly to the job of trainer. For much of his career, Hirsch was the trainer at the famous King Ranch, where he was responsible for many horses, including Bold Venture, Assault and Middleground. Bold Venture would be his first Kentucky Derby winner, on May 2, 1936, at the sixty-second running of the event. In total, Hirsch would have three Kentucky

Derby winners. Assault would prove to be a Triple Crown winner, thanks in large part to a special steel spring, created by Hirsch, that allowed the animal to run without ill effects from a serious foot injury it suffered earlier in its career. Hirsch's abilities would be passed on to his children, as two of them went on to become trainers themselves, including his daughter Mary, who was the first woman to be granted a trainer's license by the Jockey Club.

May 3, 1903: Vandervoort Summoned by the King

Born in Corpus Christi, Robert B. Vandervoort became one of America's earliest daredevils and performers, going by the performing name "Diavalo." Vandervoort was the first man to successfully complete a loop the loop on a bicycle, and he was summoned before King Edward VII to do a command performance of the trick on May 3 in London, England.

May 4, 1946: Texas's Only Triple Crown

Bred at the iconic King Ranch, Assault won the 1946 Kentucky Derby by eight lengths (the largest margin of victory at the time). Due to his Texas heritage, many racing fans doubted his abilities. The best racing horses came from Kentucky, after all. Assault was favored going into the Preakness Stakes, but a close finish resulted in Lord Boswell being made the favorite for the Belmont Stakes. Not to be deterred, Assault overcame a slow start, pushing through the last two hundred yards to win the Belmont and become the seventh Triple Crown winner in history. Assault's victories boosted the King Ranch's national image, helped in no small part by the fact that his jockey, Warren Mehrtens, wore brown-and-white racing silks with the famous "running W" King Ranch brand.

May 5, 1995: Forty and Forty

Clyde Drexler scored a game-high forty-one points, and Hakeem Olajuwon added forty more, to lead Houston to a 123–106 win over visiting Utah in

Game 4 of the first round of the Western Conference playoffs. It marked the third time in NBA playoff history that a pair of teammates had scored forty or more points in the same game. Olajuwon hit fourteen of twenty-two shots, and Drexler was twelve of eighteen. They accounted for all but forty-two of the Rockets' points. It was the second time Olajuwon and a teammate both scored more than forty points in a playoff game. He had scored forty-one points, and Eric "Sleepy" Floyd scored forty-two, against Dallas in the 1988 playoffs. In the only other such double-forty playoff game, Elgin Baylor had forty-five and Jerry West forty-one for the Lakers in 1962.

May 6, 1914: The SWC

Led by the University of Texas's L. Theo Bellmont, leaders from seven colleges conferred at the Oriental Hotel in Dallas, Texas, to discuss collegiate athletics. It was the first organizational meeting of what would become the Southwestern Conference. Most of the representatives were from Texas, though some came from Oklahoma and Louisiana. After another meeting in December 1914, a group including Arkansas, Baylor, Southwestern, Oklahoma, Oklahoma A&M (now Oklahoma State), Texas and Texas A&M comprised the charter members of the Southwestern Intercollegiate Athletic Conference. The storied conference—known simply as the Southwestern Conference for most of its history—would last until May 18, 1996. It produced a strong Olympic tradition; 350 First Team All-Americans in football, basketball and baseball; five Heisman Trophy winners; five Outland Trophy winners; three Vince Lombardi Trophy recipients; and one Jim Thorpe Award winner.

May 7, 1955: The May Man

Without question, the Kentucky Derby is the crown jewel of American horse racing. The Belmont Stakes and Preakness Stakes are incredibly important, but for most Americans, the derby holds a special, often romanticized, place. The event is associated with men in seersucker suits and women in wide-brimmed hats. One of the most prolific Kentucky Derby riders of all time hails from the Lone Star State. Born in Fabens, Texas, Bill Shoemaker won his first American Classic race when he piloted Swaps to the 1955 Kentucky Derby crown on May 7, 1955. Shoemaker would go on to win the Kentucky Derby four times, the Preakness Stakes twice and the Belmont Stakes five times. In his career, Shoemaker won an astounding 8,833 races, which was a world record for almost three decades.

May 8, 1954: Segrest Wins Title

On the final day of the 1954 University Interscholastic League State Track Meet, many teams were ready to make a push for the title. However, one team was a little different from the others. Bangs High School had only one competitor, James Segrest. Despite overwhelming odds, Segrest won the state title running by himself, leading reporters to dub him the "One Man Gang from Bangs." After high school, Segrest chose to join the powerhouse Abilene Christian track team, where he would run on relay teams that set an amazing five world records. When his career was over, Segrest turned to coaching. He again enjoyed phenomenal success, including leading Odessa College to eleven National Junior College Athletic Association championships in indoor and outdoor track. While Segrest's UIL accomplishment remains one of the greatest track stories in the Lone Star State, he would be one-upped years later by a teenager named Bonnie Richardson. Richardson, like Segrest, was the lone representative for her school, Rochelle High School. Unlike Segrest, Richardson won the state title by herself not once, but twice. After high school, Richardson joined the Texas A&M track-and-field team.

May 9, 1985: Whitworth Sets the Mark

Kathy Whitworth, born in Monahans, Texas, began her quest to win the United Virginia Bank Classic golf tournament on May 9, its first day. Four days later, Whitworth won the tournament for her eighty-eighth and final career victory. Her total continues to be the most victories by any golfer on the PGA or LPGA tours. Whitworth won a total of six LPGA major tournament titles over her career while claiming the best scoring average on the LPGA seven times from 1965 to 1972.

May 10, 1979: Carter Makes Waves with Shot Put

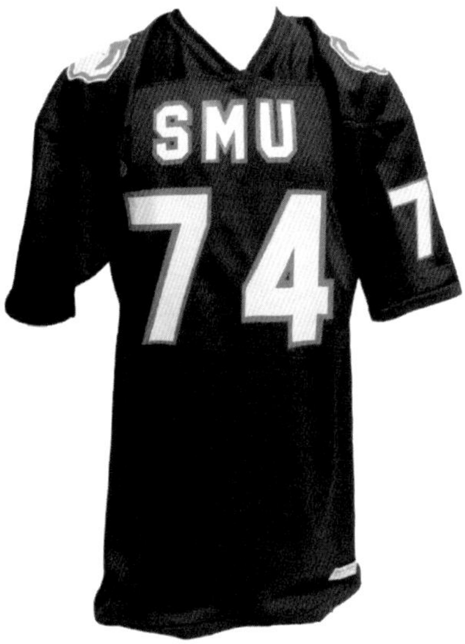

Michael Carter's 1983 SMU football jersey, worn in the Cotton Bowl. The Cotton Bowl logo is on the shoulders. *Courtesy of the Texas Sports Hall of Fame.*

On the first day of the UIL State Track Meet, Michael Carter of Dallas Jefferson sets the Texas state meet record for shot put: seventy-five feet, nine inches. As impressive as the throw was, it paled in comparison to his throw the following month. After graduating, Carter went to the Golden West Invitational (GWI) in Sacramento, California. The GWI continues to be one of the most prestigious track-and-field events in the country. Its slogan is "Where Olympic Careers Begin!" Carter didn't disappoint, throwing a monstrous eighty-one feet, three and a half inches—a national high school record. Since 1979, no one has gotten closer than within four feet of Carter's record. A standout nose tackle, Carter committed to SMU, where he roomed with Eric Dickerson. In 1984, Carter became the only person to win an Olympic medal and a Super Bowl ring in the same year. His NFL career spanned from 1984 to 1992, all with the San Francisco 49ers. He finished with three Super Bowl championships, three Pro Bowls and three First Team All-Pro selections. Following in her father's footsteps, Michelle Carter became a world-renowned athlete, winning gold at the 2016 Rio Olympics in shot put after a standout career at the University of Texas.

May 11, 1953: The Waco Tornado

An F5 tornado hit Waco, damaging hundreds of buildings, including historic Katy Park. Baylor and TCU were scheduled to play there the next day, May 12. The game, of course, was canceled. Katy Park had hosted many notable events and sports teams, including the world-champion New York Yankees, the Kansas City Monarchs and the first night baseball game in Texas.

May 12, 1970: Banks Goes Yard Again

Down 0-2 in the count, Ernie Banks hit a home run off the Atlanta Braves for his 500th career homer and 1,600th career RBI. Originally from Dallas, Banks is one of the greatest baseball players the Lone Star State has ever produced. He played for the Chicago Cubs his entire career (1953–71), finishing with a total of 512 home runs, 1,636 RBIs and 2,583 hits. Banks's blast on May 12 remains a piece of Cubs lore—some say you can't find a Cubs fan who wasn't there that day to witness the hit. In reality, heavy rains and poor weather held attendance to 5,264, one of the smallest crowds that season.

May 13, 2005: UIL Recognizes PVIL Records

Representatives from the Prairie View Interscholastic League (PVIL) Coaches Association met with University Interscholastic League (UIL) athletic director Dr. Charles Breithaupt and University of Texas vice president Dr. James L. Hill to discuss full recognition of all PVIL records. Later that year, the UIL began recognizing PVIL state championship records alongside all UIL records. The PVIL played a leading role in developing African American students in the arts, literature, athletics and music from the 1920s through 1967, as those students were barred from other state high schools due to segregation. The PVIL has a proud history of producing some of the greatest athletes, teams and coaches the Lone Star State has ever seen, including Gene Upshaw, Charley Taylor and "Mean" Joe Greene.

May 14, 1915: First SWC Track Meet

In Austin, Texas, the young Southwest Conference held its first conference championship track meet. Going into the final event, Texas and Oklahoma were tied for first, but the Longhorns won the event to take their first SWC track title. Oklahoma finished second, and Texas A&M came in third. One of UT's athletes at the 1915 meet was a student by the name of Clyde Littlefield. He won the 120-yard hurdles in a time of 15.6 seconds, then

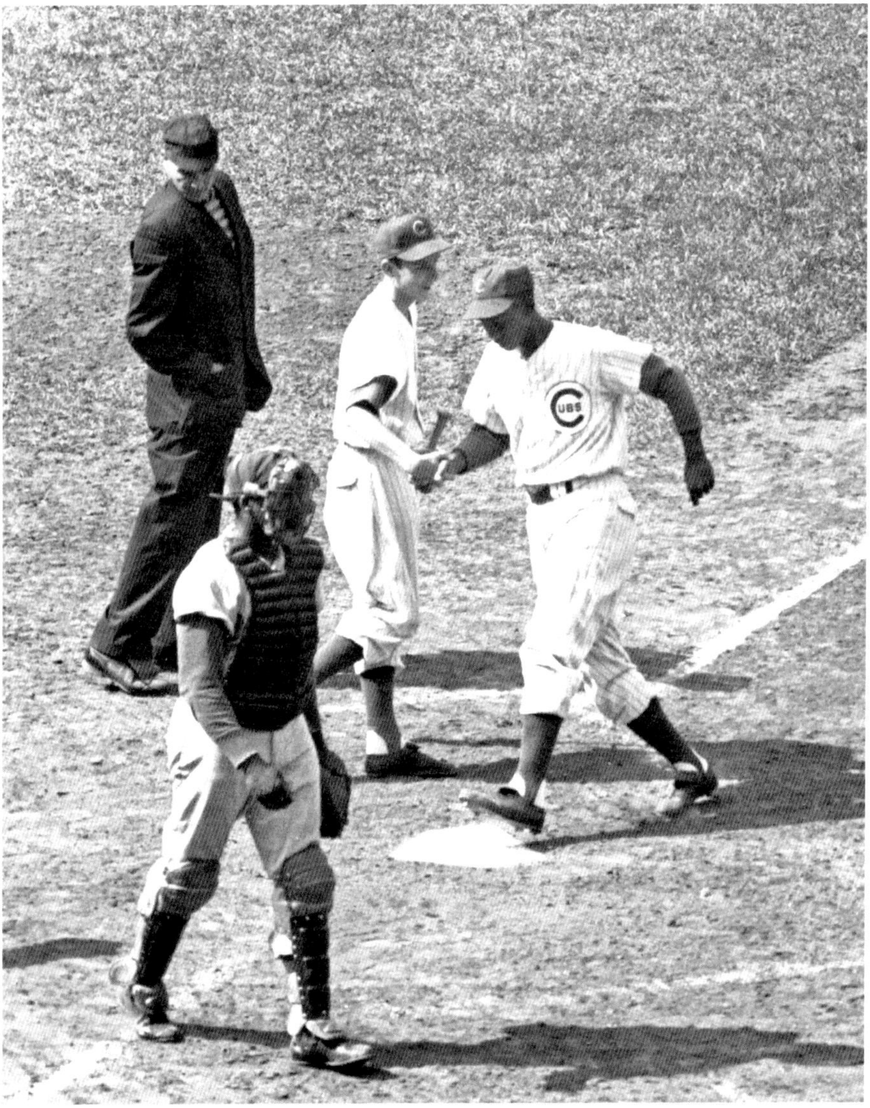

Ernie Banks taps home plate after recording his 500th home run. *Courtesy of the Texas Sports Hall of Fame.*

returned for the Longhorns in 1916 to record a meet-high eleven points as Texas defended its title, beating second-place Texas A&M. Interestingly enough, Oklahoma would win the next two SWC track meets, in 1918 and 1919, in dominating fashion before leaving the conference.

May 15, 1973: The Strikeout King's First No-Hitter

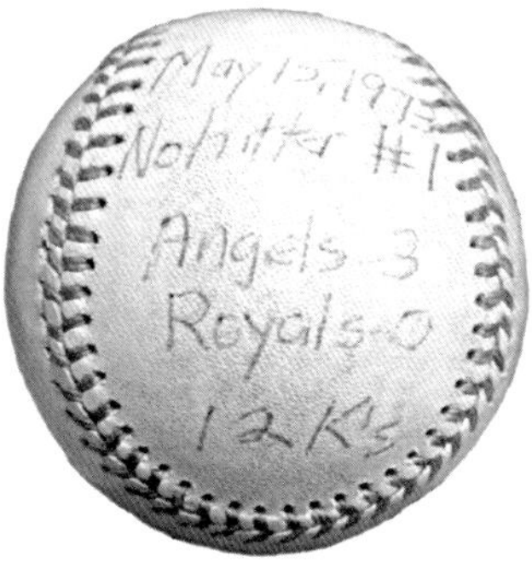

Final ball from Nolan Ryan's first no-hitter. Ryan's writing is present on the ball. *Courtesy of the Texas Sports Hall of Fame.*

Nolan Ryan threw his first no-hitter while playing for the California Angels, who won the game against the Kansas City Royals, 3–0. Just two months later, on July 15, Ryan would record his second no-hitter, striking out an impressive seventeen batters, as the Angels defeated the Detroit Tigers, 6–0. He would throw five more no-hitters in his career. His seven no-hitters (an MLB record) span three decades (1973 twice, 1974, 1975, 1981, 1990 and 1991). Ryan would accumulate ninety-four strikeouts and just twenty-six walks in those games for a strikeout-to-walk ratio of 3.6, nearly double his career ratio of 2.0.

May 16, 1943: Donny Anderson's Birthday

Born in Borger, Texas, Donny Anderson would go on to have one of the most prolific football careers in Texas Tech history. After playing for Stinnett High School, Anderson joined the Red Raiders. He earned All-American status twice (1964 and 1965) while being named All-SWC three times. Nicknamed the "Golden Palomino," Anderson finished fourth in the 1965 Heisman Trophy race and was selected seventh overall in the 1965 NFL draft by the Green Bay Packers in a draft that included Gale Sayers, Dick Butkus, Joe Namath and Fred Biletnikoff. It was reported that Anderson's initial contract with the Packers was for $600,000, edging out Joe Namath's record contract the year before. While Anderson never became a star for the Packers, he did help them to win Super Bowl I and Super Bowl II while inventing the concept of "hang time" on punts. In the past, punts had served solely as a means to kick the ball as far as possible. But this opened up space on the field for long kick returns. Instead, Anderson worked on shorter punts that went higher and hung longer in the air, allowing his kick coverage team to surround the punt returner. His new technique limited opposing teams to an average of just one-third of a yard on punt returns in 1967.

May 17, 2009: Baseball's Back

The Big Bend Cowboys played a double-header at Kokernot Field, bringing professional baseball back to the "Best Little Ballpark in the World" for the first time in forty-eight years. Constructed in 1947 for $1.25 million by generous and baseball-loving rancher Herbert Lee Kokernot Jr., the field has been covered by publications such as *Sports Illustrated* and *Texas Monthly*. Sparing no expense, Kokernot blasted a quarry on his ranch to provide the signature red rock for the outside of the stadium, placed individual wooden seats with season-ticket holders' names inscribed on them in the grandstand and brought in red clay for the infield by train from Georgia. Kokernot Field has hosted many exciting games, the most notable being a 1951 exhibition contest featuring Satchel Paige and the St. Louis Browns versus the Chicago White Sox.

May 18, 1933: First MLB All-Star Game

The first major-league All-Star Game was played as a part of the Chicago World's Fair. Longview native and St. Louis Browns outfielder Sam West was the lone Texan to appear in the game.

May 19, 1974: Aeros Win the WHA Championship

The Houston Aeros of the World Hockey Association won the championship after defeating the Chicago Cougars in four straight games. The unquestionable star of the Aeros was Gordie Howe. At age forty-five, he scored one hundred points during the season and won the league's MVP award. Also on the Aeros were Howe's sons Mark and Marty. This was the first father/son combination to play professional hockey together on the same team.

May 20, 1993: Goodbye to HemisFair

Although the stadium no longer exists, HemisFair Arena remains a piece of San Antonio culture. The Spurs' first home in San Antonio, HemisFair became an icon for the city and, during the NBA season, a focal point for the city's nightlife. On May 20, 1993, the Spurs played in HemisFair for the final time, losing their playoff series against the Phoenix Suns as Charles Barkley hit a last-second field goal, lifting the Suns to a 102–100 victory. The Spurs' home for two decades (1973–93), HemisFair was torn down in 1995 to expand the city's convention center.

May 21, 1962: The AFL Loses Antitrust Suit

In a case that many viewed as the American Football League's last chance to win Dallas, the $10 million antitrust suit filed by the AFL against the NFL was concluded with Judge Roszel Thomsen's dismissal of the suit. His thirty-seven-page decision stated that the NFL obviously didn't monopolize professional football. One year later, on May 23, 1963, Lamar Hunt made the Texans' move to Kansas City official. The team most responsible for bringing the NFL to "Big D" left Texas.

May 22, 1965: LeVias Inks Letter of Intent

When Hayden Fry interviewed to become the next head football coach at Southern Methodist, he had one request: he wanted to recruit and sign African American players. While there is no question that this was a noble act during the height of discrimination in the South, Fry would honestly say that another reason for his request was that he wanted to win football games. SMU leadership gave Fry its blessing, but he didn't rush out and sign every African American athlete he could find. Instead, he waited to make sure he selected the right person to bear that responsibility. A few years later, Fry thought he had found just the right player to break the barrier: Jerry LeVias. Although a small player, LeVias was an outstanding athlete from a solid background, and Fry thought he was the perfect person to become the first African American football player in the SWC. LeVias signed his letter of intent to SMU on May 22, 1965, and history was made. While LeVias endured unimaginable hardships and discrimination during his time at SMU, he also proved that athleticism, sportsmanship and teamwork transcended skin color. During his career, LeVias set multiple records, including receptions in a game (15 against Ohio State), receptions in a season (80), receptions in a career (155), yards in a season (1,131), yards in a career (2,275) and career touchdown receptions (22). LeVias was a First Team All-SWC selection and held most of the SWC's receiving records for nearly two decades. He was without question one of the greatest receivers in the country at the time.

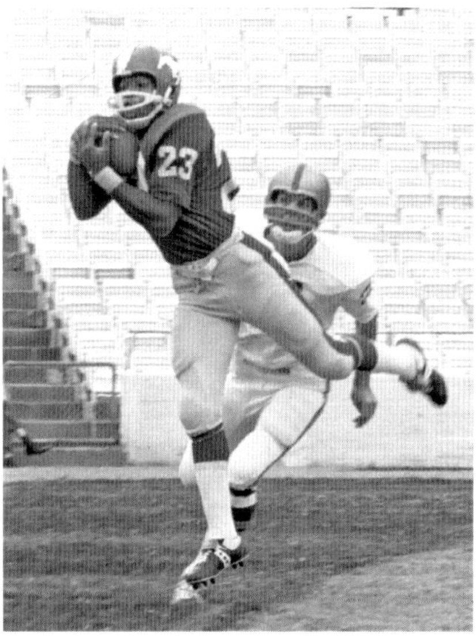

Jerry LeVias leaps for the catch while playing for SMU. *Courtesy of the Texas Sports Hall of Fame.*

May 23, 1995: Robinson's MVP

David Robinson, who received the NBA Most Valuable Player trophy on this day in 1995, was the first Spurs player to garner the prestigious award. Robinson was a gracious winner, congratulating the runner-up, Shaquille O'Neal, although the vote wasn't that close—Robinson won by sixty-one first-place votes. the "Admiral" averaged 27.6 points, 10.8 rebounds, 2.9 assists and 3.23 blocks over the course of the season while navigating the Spurs to the Western Conference finals. The award was bittersweet, as the 1994 MVP, Hakeem Olajuwon, and his Houston Rockets knocked the Spurs out of the playoffs on their way to winning the championship.

May 24, 1987: Texas A&M Wins the College World Series

After falling in the College World Series title game her sophomore and junior seasons, Shawn Andaya faced elimination her senior year. The Texas A&M Aggies were down one game to zero in the 1987 NCAA softball championship. In 1985, the Aggies lost a heartbreaker in thirteen innings to UCLA, despite Andaya striking out seventeen batters. In 1986, the Aggies lost in the title game again, this time to Cal State–Fullerton. In 1987, the Aggies looked poised to make it over the hump, having won thirty-six games that season. With an opening-game loss to UCLA, things looked dicey. The Ags would need to win both games of a double-header on May 24 to claim the crown. Texas A&M delivered, knocking off UCLA, 1–0 and 4–1. Andaya threw a perfect game in the first game. The Aggies also had All-Tournament Team players in second baseman Julie Smith and shortstop Liz Mizera.

May 25, 1980: Rutherford Wins the Indy 500

Johnny Rutherford III—also known as "Lone Star JR"—won his third and final Indianapolis 500 after leading for 118 laps, a race record. Rutherford had won the race's pole position and was a favorite to take the checkered flag. He did just that, winning by a commanding 29.92 seconds. Rutherford also won the prestigious race in 1974 and 1976, making him the sixth driver in history to win three Indy 500s.

May 26, 1993: The Canseco Header

In what is now considered a microcosm of his time with the Texas Rangers, Jose Canseco had a fly ball bounce off his head and over the outfield wall for a Cleveland Indians home run. Canseco lost the fly ball, hit by the Indians' Carlos Martínez, while he was crossing the warning track.

May 27, 1961: Jill Sterkel Is Born

Born in Hacienda Heights, California, Jill Sterkel would become well known as a swimmer and coach at the University of Texas. As a collegiate swimmer, Sterkel earned back-to-back Broderick Award National Swimmer of the Years (1980 and 1981), leading the Longhorns to Association for Intercollegiate Athletics for Women national championship titles in 1981 and 1982. From 1980 to 1983, she claimed sixteen individual national titles, including two in 1983, when the Longhorns debuted at the NCAA Swimming and Diving Championships. She led UT to a third-place finish. Sterkel swam in her first Olympics at the age of fifteen, winning a gold medal as a member of Team USA's 4x100 relay team. In all, Sterkel earned four Olympic medals during three Olympics. From 1992 to 2007, she was the head coach of the UT women's swim and dive teams, winning six Coach of the Year honors and multiple conference titles.

May 28, 1956: January Wins Dallas Open

In his rookie PGA season out of Texas State, Plainview's Don January hit an eagle on the eighteenth hole to win the Dallas Open with a score of 268. Over a PGA career that lasted from 1956 to 1999, January won ten PGA Tour tournaments and twenty-two Senior PGA Tour events, the latter tied for sixth all-time. In 1961, January entered an eighteen-hole playoff against Jerry Barber to decide the 1961 PGA Championship. Despite January's phenomenal playoff score of 68, Barber edged him by one stroke, shooting a 67. January's 68 remains the lowest losing score to be carded in an eighteen-hole playoff at a PGA major. He would have some vindication, winning the PGA Championship in 1967. It would be his only major victory.

May 29, 1993: Canseco Part II

Just three days after having a fly ball bounce off his head for a home run, Texas Rangers outfielder Jose Canseco convinced manager Kevin Kennedy to let him pitch in the eighth inning of a blowout loss to the Boston Red Sox. Canseco subsequently injured his arm pitching, requiring Tommy John surgery, and he missed the rest of the season. Canseco, who played for the Rangers from 1992 to 1994 (he played for seven teams in all), is probably best remembered for publicizing steroid use in Major League Baseball in his 2005 book, *Juiced*.

May 30, 1961: Foyt's First 500

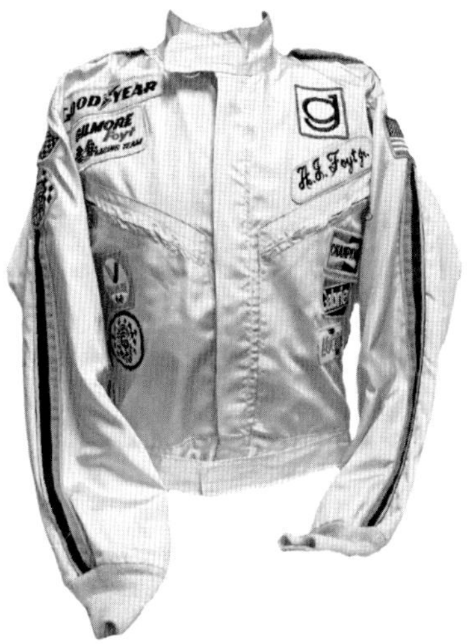

The top of A.J. Foyt's coveralls. *Courtesy of the Texas Sports Hall of Fame.*

Born in Houston, Anthony Joseph "A.J." Foyt is one of the most prolific automobile racers in history. One of Foyt's most notable accomplishments began on May 30, 1961, as he won the Indianapolis 500 for the first time. He would win again in 1964, 1967 and 1977, giving him four Indy 500 titles—the first driver to accomplish the feat. His career of achievements is perhaps best represented by the fact that he is the only driver to win the Indianapolis 500, the Daytona 500, the 24 Hours of Daytona and the 24 Hours of Le Mans. Such an accomplishment showcases his ability to adapt and succeed in a multitude of cars and driving styles.

May 31, 1994: Rockets to the Finals

The Houston Rockets dispatched the Utah Jazz four games to one to win the Western Conference finals. The victory sent the Rockets to their third NBA Finals and their first since 1986. Houston was matched against a New York Knicks team led by head coach Pat Riley. The 1994 Finals proved to be a classic, going the full seven games. Led by coach Rudy Tomjanovich and star player Hakeem Olajuwon, the Rockets proved to have just enough, winning Game 7, 90–84. It was Houston's first NBA title and Olajuwon was named the Finals MVP. The team would successfully defend its title the following year, winning the 1995 NBA championship.

JUNE

June 1, 1925: Hornsby Takes Over St. Louis

The St. Louis Cardinals announced that Rogers Hornsby of Winters, Texas, would be the team's new player-manager (he would be responsible for managing the team while also playing a position on the field). The move proved a successful one, as Hornsby led the Cardinals to their first National League pennant in 1926 and a shot at the World Series against a New York Yankees team featuring Babe Ruth and Lou Gehrig. While the Cardinals took a 2-1 series lead, the Yankees bounced back, winning the next two games to go up 3-2. With the Yankees needing just one more game to win the series, things looked dire for the Cardinals. Hornsby tabbed the team's star pitcher, Grover Cleveland Alexander, to start Game 6. The choice worked, as the Yankees offense was limited to two runs while the Cardinals exploded for ten. In game seven, the Cardinals were up by a score of 3–2, but their starting pitcher was beginning to wear down. Hornsby had to decide who he would turn to with the game on the line. Despite pitching a complete game the day before, Hornsby brought Alexander back to finish Game 7. It proved to be the right choice. Alexander shut down the Yankees after a shaky start, and Hornsby recorded the final out, tagging Babe Ruth at second after Ruth attempted to steal. Hornsby would later say that Ruth "didn't say a word. He didn't even look around or up at me. He just picked himself up and walked away." While Hornsby had proved himself a successful manager, he was an equally capable player, finishing his career with a .358 batting average, 2,930 hits and 301 home runs.

June 2, 1920: Tex Schramm's Birthday

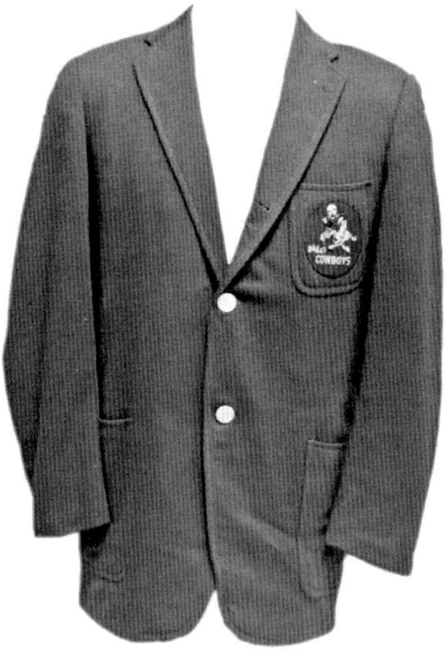

Tex Schramm's Dallas Cowboys booster jacket, featuring the team's original alternate logo on the pocket. *Courtesy of the Texas Sports Hall of Fame.*

Despite what his name implies, Tex Schramm was not born in the Lone Star State. He didn't even go to high school in Texas. In fact, the name came from his father, also named Tex (who was from Texas). The Lone Star State just happened to be where Schramm's parents met. After high school, Schramm made his way to Austin, where he attended the University of Texas. He earned a degree in journalism and headed back to California, his state of birth, to take a job with the Los Angeles Rams. Schramm served on the team's staff from 1947 to 1956. One of his most notable moves was hiring a young Pete Rozelle as the Rams' public-relations director. Rozelle, of course, would go on to become one of the most important commissioners in NFL history. When it became apparent that the NFL would be expanding to Dallas, Schramm immediately began working with his connections to get a job with the team. Cowboys owner Clint Murchison hired Schramm as his general manager. Among Schramm's first moves were hiring Tom Landry as head coach and the innovative Gil Brandt as chief scout. The three formed the core of the franchise. By the 1960s, they had built the Cowboys into an elite team. In the 1970s, the Cowboys appeared in five Super Bowls. While the 'Boys were only 2-3 in those games, the three losses came by a combined eleven points. Furthermore, Schramm helped promote the idea of the Cowboys as "America's Team."

June 3, 2006: Mavs Make Their First Finals

The 2005–6 Dallas Mavericks season marked the team's twenty-sixth as an NBA franchise. Under the leadership of coach Avery Johnson and behind the play of Dirk Nowitzki and Jason Terry, the team finished with an impressive regular-season record of 60-22 before advancing to the Western Conference finals. Facing the Phoenix Suns, the Mavs entered Game 6 with a 3-2 series lead. On June 3, the Mavs entered US Airways Center with a trip to the finals on the line. In the fourth quarter, Dallas showed who the better team was, pulling away to win, 102–93. The victory sent the Mavericks franchise to the NBA Finals for the first time. Although they lost to the Miami Heat in six games, the Mavericks were on the right path. And it was clear that new owner Mark Cuban understood how to build a winner. When Cuban bought the franchise in 2000, the team had won only 40 percent of its games in the previous two decades and had a paltry 21-32 record in the playoffs. By 2006, the team was in its first finals; in 2011, the team would win its first championship.

June 4, 1974: Ten-Cent Beer Night

Regardless of how you feel about baseball, there is one unquestionable truth about the sport: it knows how to promote itself. Baseball teams will try just about anything to fill seats, although those attempts can have mixed results. An example of a negative promotion was the now-infamous ten-cent beer night at Cleveland Stadium. The Indians were hoping to raise attendance at the stadium by lowering the price on a twelve-ounce beer from sixty-five cents to just ten cents. A limit was imposed on the number of beers that could be purchased at one time, but there was no limit on the number of beers a fan could purchase throughout the game. The results were predictable. Fans became heavily intoxicated, and this culminated in a riot during the game's ninth inning.

It all began when a nineteen-year-old Cleveland fan ran onto the field and tried to steal a cap from one of the Texas Rangers. Misinterpreting the action as an attack on the player, members of the Texas team immediately rushed the field to defend their teammate. This in turn led to more intoxicated fans running onto the field. Some Rangers players held bats, and fans began employing knives, chains and pieces of stadium seats as weapons. Sensing that the Rangers' lives might be in danger, Cleveland manager Ken Aspromonte ordered his players to grab bats and go to the defense of the Rangers—the Indians were put in the position of potentially attacking their own fans. Bottles and folding chairs were thrown at the players from the stands, and fans continued to try to attack players. Meanwhile, the players organized a retreat, backing through dugouts on their way to safety. The game was tied, 5–5. Umpire Nestor Chylak recognized that there was no chance order would be restored, so he called the game off. It was ruled a forfeit in the Rangers' favor.

After the game, differing opinions were expressed about what had happened. Aspromonte, for instance, blamed the umpires. Chylak called fans "uncontrollable beasts." American League president Lee MacPhail made the most obvious (and most accurate) statement: "There was no question beer played a part in the riot."

June 5, 1931: David Browning's Birthday

Just one of numerous decorated University of Texas athletes, David "Skippy" Browning Jr. was born in Boston before coming to the Lone Star State. While a student at UT, Browning was a member of Team USA at the 1952 Helsinki Olympics. Competing in springboard diving, Browning won a gold medal. In 1953, he earned his degree in business administration and, in 1955, became a pilot in the U.S. Navy. Browning was scheduled to be reassigned to Los Angeles to start training for the 1956 Melbourne Olympics, but he died when his plane crashed on a training mission over Kansas in March 1956.

June 6, 1969: Mills Burns Through the 440

In 1969, Texas A&M track-and-field coach Charlie Thomas signed Curtis Mills, Sidney Chachere and Edgar Harvey to compete for the Aggies. The trio would be the first African American athletes to compete for Texas A&M, and Mills would show what fans had been missing out on. He would set a world record in the 440-yard dash, running it in a blazing 44.7 seconds. Mills would set or help set eleven school records and win seven SWC championships while being named an All-American all four years he competed.

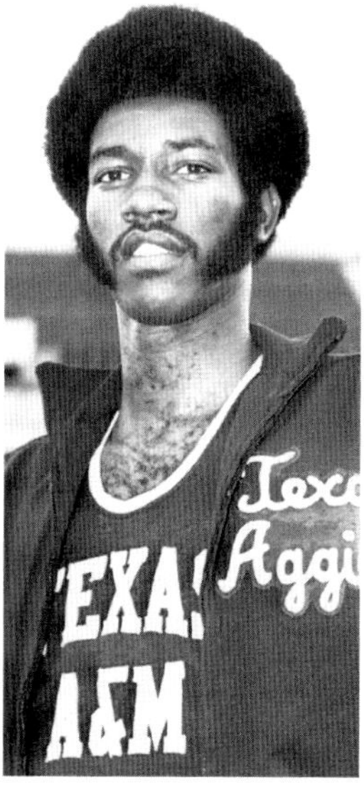

Texas A&M's first African American scholarship athlete, Curtis Mills showed the school just what it was missing by barring athletes of color. *Courtesy of the Texas Sports Hall of Fame.*

June 7, 1941: First Texas U.S. Open

The first U.S. Open to be held in Texas concluded on this day. The event, held at Colonial Country Club in Fort Worth, would be the last U.S. Open for five years, due to the outbreak of World War II. Craig Wood won the tournament, shooting a 284. Ben Hogan was the Texan with the best score, finishing tied for third.

June 8, 1966: AFL-NFL Merger

In a press conference, Pete Rozelle, Tex Schramm and Lamar Hunt announced the merger of the National Football League and the American Football League after several months of secret negotiations. Led mostly by the work of Hunt and Schramm, the merger would consist of an annual world championship game beginning after the 1966 football season and a combined draft in the spring of 1967. The leagues would officially combine, with two separate conferences, in 1970.

June 9, 1963: Sunday Night Baseball

After acquiring an exemption from MLB's commissioner, the Houston Colt .45s received permission to play Sunday night games. The main reason for the night games—and the reason the team was working to build the world's first domed stadium—was the oppressive Texas heat. After fans experienced severe medical issues during a day game, the Colt .45s appealed the ban on Sunday night games and were granted a temporary allowance to play in the cooler evening hours. The first night game was played between the San Francisco Giants and Houston as the Colt .45s won, 3–0. By 1990, ESPN had built Sunday Night Baseball into a weekly marquee matchup.

June 10, 2006: Aggies Win Track-and-Field Title

The NCAA Track and Field Outdoor Championships in Fayetteville, Arkansas, commenced on this date. Over the next three days, Texas A&M would separate itself from the pack, as the school's men's and women's teams both won national titles. The Aggies were led by legendary head coach Pat Henry. Although 2009 represented Henry's first national championship with the men's team at A&M, he had made a trend of turning track programs into national powerhouses. At Blinn College in Brenham, Texas, Henry won two NJCAA national titles. He then moved on to LSU, where he won twenty-seven national championships, fifteen SEC Coach of the Year awards and five national Coach of the Year awards. In 2004, looking for a new challenge, Henry moved to Texas A&M. Having coached at Blinn, Henry felt he understood the culture of the area and saw immense potential. Five years later, his hard work came to fruition when the men and women captured their respective outdoor titles. It was the first time in nearly twenty years that one school won both championships (Henry had done it nineteen years earlier with LSU). He would go on to repeat the feat, leading A&M to men's and women's outdoor titles in 2010 and 2011.

June 11, 1964: Yeoman and McVea

Bill Yeoman helped to break the color barrier for major Texas college football when he signed Warren McVea of San Antonio to a scholarship to the University of Houston. McVea had played for Breckenridge High School, earning the moniker "Wondrous Warren." His prolific play drew the attention of *Sports Illustrated*: "During his career at San Antonio's Brackenridge High School he was the most exciting, the most talked-about and the most ardently sought-after Texas player in 20 years. In three years against the state's best high school competition, McVea scored just under 600 points. As a senior he averaged better than a first down per carry and rushed for 1,332 yards." McVea would continue to dazzle in college, earning All-American status twice.

June 12, 1939: Byron at the U.S. Open

Byron Nelson won the 1939 U.S. Open in dramatic fashion. After the final round on Saturday, there was a three-way tie among Nelson, Denny Shute

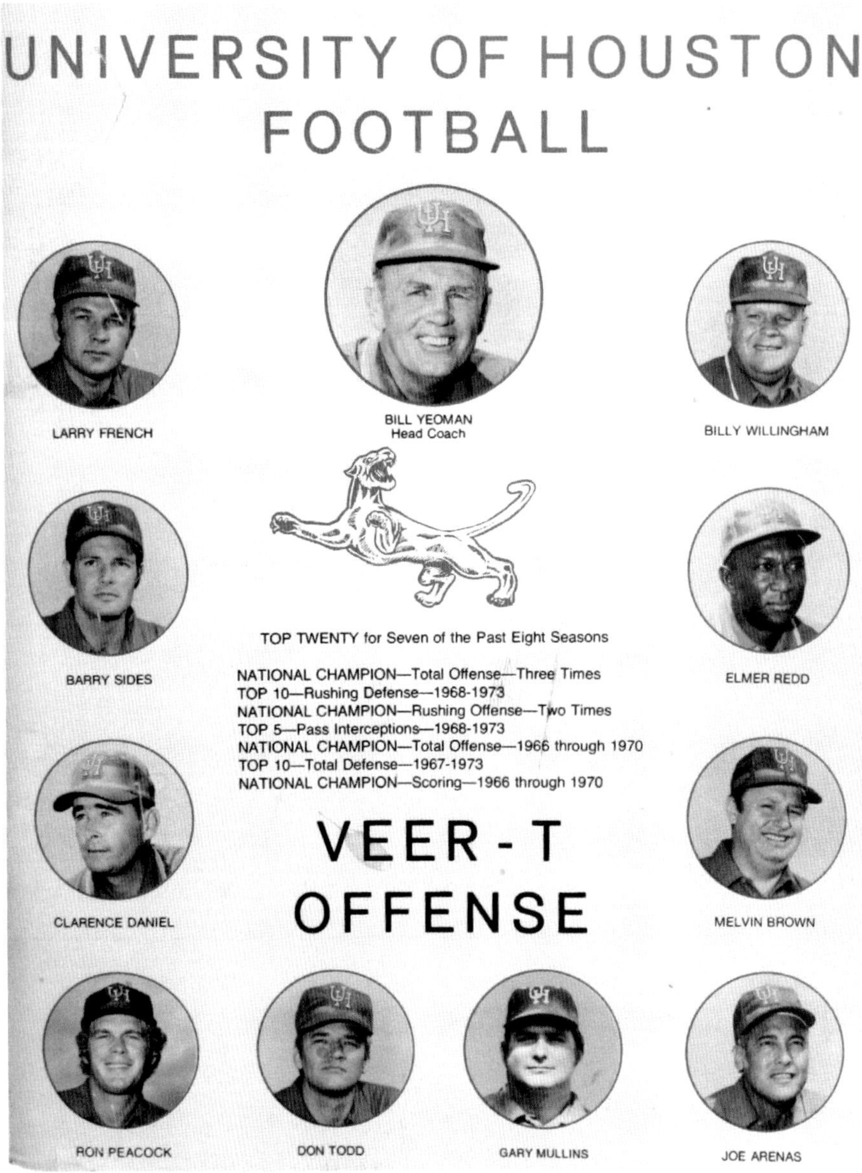

Houston coach Bill Yeoman's Veer-T offensive manual. *Courtesy of the Texas Sports Hall of Fame.*

and Craig Wood, leading to a playoff. After an eighteen-hole playoff on Sunday, Wood and Nelson were still tied. This led to another eighteen-hole playoff, on Monday, when Nelson's 70 beat Wood's 73. Nelson's eagle on the fourth hole of the final playoff, shot from two hundred yards out, was enough for him to ride to victory. The shot is still considered one of the best, if not the best, single shot in U.S. Open history.

June 13, 1968: Trevino Scores His First PGA Victory

On the first day of the sixty-eighth U.S. Open, Lee Trevino shot a 69. He would carry the momentum to win the tournament, shooting in the 60s all four rounds (a first for the U.S. Open). The tournament was his first PGA Tour victory, but far from his last. Trevino's total tournament score of 275 tied a U.S. Open record set by Jack Nicklaus the year before. Trevino would go on to win twenty-nine PGA Tour events over his career, including six majors. He never won the Masters, which he routinely boycotted.

June 14, 2007: Pop Leads the Spurs to Glory

Gregg Popovich and the San Antonio Spurs swept the Cleveland Cavaliers in the NBA Finals, defeating LeBron James in his first finals appearance. The Spurs dropped both regular-season contests to the Cavs (88–81 in San Antonio, 92–78 in Cleveland), but they played better when it mattered most. While the first two games, played in San Antonio, weren't particularly close, Games 3 and 4 were incredibly tight. Game 3 was the lowest-scoring finals game since 1955, as the Spurs edged Cleveland, 75–72, and San Antonio squeaked past the Cavs, 83–82, to win Game 4. Spurs point guard Tony Parker was named the finals MVP as the Spurs wrapped up their fourth NBA title—all of them coming under Popovich's leadership. Claiming NBA titles in 1999, 2003, 2005 and 2007, the Spurs made their fans wait awhile for the fifth championship, which Pop engineered in 2014.

June 15, 1976: The Astrodome Rainout

Ironically, the Astrodome suffered a rainout on June 15, 1976, as the Astros' scheduled game against the Pittsburgh Pirates was called off when massive flooding in the Houston area prevented all but a few fans from reaching the stadium. Both teams had arrived early for practice, but the umpires were several hours late. At 5:00 p.m. that day, with only a handful of fans and activities already several hours behind schedule, the umpires and teams agreed to call the game off. Tables were brought onto the field, and the teams ate dinner together. Although the Astros still had a home series with Pittsburgh in August, this game was made up in Pittsburgh in July.

June 16, 2014: Dempsey's Quick Strike

In one of the fastest goals in World Cup history, Clint Dempsey scored for the United States thirty seconds into a match against Ghana. It was the fastest goal in American World Cup history and the fifth fastest in World Cup history. The goal also made Dempsey the first American player to score in three consecutive World Cups. Dempsey, from Nacogdoches, Texas, remains one of the most prolific scorers in U.S. international soccer history, with fifty-two goals in 130 appearances.

June 17, 1976: NBA-ABA Merger

The National Basketball Association and the American Basketball Association came to final terms, merging America's two major professional basketball leagues into one. While Texas was represented in the NBA by the Houston Rockets, the NBA-ABA merger brought a second Texas team to the world's premier professional basketball association: the San Antonio Spurs. The Spurs had played in the ABA after the franchise moved from Dallas in 1973. The city of San Antonio had shown a strong interest in the team, posting high attendance numbers. This made the franchise more financially viable than it had previously been. The NBA, impressed by the city's support, selected the Spurs as one of the four ABA teams to join the league.

June 18, 1992: Kite's U.S. Open

From McKinney, Texas, Tom Kite paired with Ben Crenshaw at the University of Texas to make one of the most formidable collegiate golf teams in NCAA history. Both men would continue to have success when they turned professional. Kite's brightest moment came at the ninety-second U.S. Open, which began on June 18, 1992, at Pebble Beach. Kite made a surge in the tournament's third round, moving up to a tie for second. On the final day, he held steady, shooting an even par. As others struggled, Kite took the tournament by two strokes. Although the 1992 U.S. Open was Kite's only victory in a major championship, he was always competitive at golf's premier events, finishing second at the Masters three times, second at the Open Championship once and fourth at the PGA Championship twice. Kite would win nineteen tournaments on the PGA Tour before being inducted into the World Golf Hall of Fame in 2004.

June 19, 1999: Stars Win the Stanley Cup

Texas's lone representative in the National Hockey League, the Stars proved a force in professional hockey after the franchise relocated to the "Big D" from Minnesota. The Stars had their best season in 1998–99. The team broke fifty wins for the first time in franchise history while recording a franchise record of 114 points. In the Stanley Cup playoffs, the Stars moved quickly through Edmonton and St. Louis before facing their first real test: Colorado. Down three games to two, the Stars played nearly flawless hockey in Games 6 and 7, defeating the Avalanche in back-to-back games to reach the Stanley Cup Finals. The Stars faced the Buffalo Sabres and held a 3-2 lead in the series entering Game 6. As with all good finals games, Game 6 was a battle. When regulation time couldn't decide a winner, the Sabres and Stars headed to overtime. It turned out that wasn't enough, either. The teams played through two full overtime periods, locked at a score of 1–1. Then, at 14:51 of the third overtime period, Brett Hull scored off a rebound from Sabres goaltender Dominik Hasek. The goal ended the game, 2–1, and the Stars had their first Stanley Cup. The second-longest finals game ever played, Game 6 was the longest finals game to decide a Stanley Cup winner.

June 20, 1968: Hines's 9.9

A member of the Texas Southern track team, Jim Hines became the first athlete to record an official 9.9-second time in the 100 meters. Hines would later win two gold medals at the 1968 Olympics, where he recorded the first 100-meter race under 10.0 seconds with fully automatic timing.

June 21, 1969: Rice Runs the Mile

The 1969 NCAA Division I Mile Relay final took place on this date. Earlier in the season, Rice defeated the UCLA Bruins in Los Angeles, setting a new American record. However, on the day of the NCAA finals, Rice's legendary head coach, Emmett Brunson, had a stroke and was hospitalized. The Owls would go on to participate in one of collegiate track's most memorable races. Again battling the UCLA Bruins, the Owls would finish second, running a 3:04.7 to the Bruins' 3:03.4, which broke the Owls' record from earlier in the season. Texas teams did solid throughout the mile relay, as ACU finished fourth (3:06.6) and UT–Austin finished fifth (3:06.7). Rice tied with Texas A&M as the highest-finishing teams at the meet (tied for thirteenth overall).

June 22, 1949: Longhorns Win CWS

Led by coach Bibb Falk, the University of Texas defeated St. John's, 7–1, in the first round of the College World Series on June 22, 1949. The Longhorns would go on to win the tournament, giving Falk and the school their first CWS title. Falk would show it was no fluke, taking the Longhorns back the following year and successfully defending their title. Over the years, Texas has proven be one of the greatest collegiate baseball programs, winning a total of six CWS titles. After Falk won two, his successor, Cliff Gustafson, won two more (1975, 1983), followed by Augie Garrido, who won two more (2002, 2005). After having eight coaches in its first fifteen years of play, UT baseball has had just five coaches since 1911. One of those, Blair Cherry, served only three seasons (1943–45) as a wartime replacement for Falk.

June 23, 2003: Rice Wins First CWS

In the first game of the 2003 College World Series championship round, the Rice Owls defeated Stanford in a close game, 4–3. In Game 2, Stanford responded, winning by a score of 8–3. The Owls' head coach, Wayne Graham, wasn't fazed. He had been building toward this moment. In the third and final game of the championship series, Rice exploded, jumping to a 4–0 lead before tacking on seven more runs in the bottom of the sixth. With the final score 14–2, the Owls claimed their first College World Series title.

June 24, 1994: Bagwell Homers Twice

As the Astros stormed past the Los Angeles Dodgers, 16–4, Jeff Bagwell made a little history. He sent two pitches over the Astrodome's outfield wall in the sixth inning, becoming the twenty-eighth MLB player to homer twice in one inning. A four-time All-Star, Bagwell was also the National League's Rookie of the Year in 1991 before being named the NL MVP in 1994. Originally from Boston, Bagwell played his entire career (1991–2005) with the Astros. The team retired his number in 2007.

June 25, 1999: The Dynasty Begins

Over the years, it has become hard to pick just one Spurs moment as the greatest in franchise history. That's true for all great professional sports teams. In fact, the only NBA teams with more championships than the Spurs are the Boston Celtics, the Los Angeles Lakers and the Chicago Bulls. It just so happens the Spurs are the youngest franchise in that group. The Spurs' run to the top began in the waning years of the 1990s, as Sean Elliot, Tim Duncan, David Robinson and Greg Popovich led the team to its first NBA Finals, against the New York Knicks. With a 3-1 lead in the series, the Spurs traveled to storied Madison Square Garden for Game 5. If the Knicks were going to mount any kind of a comeback, it would start at the Garden. Instead, Avery Johnson hit an eighteen-foot jumper with forty-seven second left in the game to put the Spurs up, 78–77. After that, both teams' defenses clamped down, and neither offense scored. The Spurs had captured their first NBA title.

June 26, 1988: Biggio Debuts

One of the greatest Houston Astros, Craig Biggio made his MLB debut on June 26, 1988. He would play his entire career with the team, retiring in 2007 after making seven All-Star teams and earning four Golden Gloves and five Silver Sluggers. Biggio finished his career with a .281 batting average, 3,060 hits and 1,175 RBIs. The Astros retired his number in 2008, and the National Baseball Hall of Fame welcomed him in 2015.

June 27, 1952: Smith Helps USA to Gold

After winning both its opening heat and the semifinal race, Team USA lined up to run the 4x100 final at the 1952 Helsinki Olympics. The team counted on Dean Smith to do his part. From Breckenridge, Texas, Smith first gained fame as an athlete at the University of Texas. At the Helsinki games, he finished fourth in the 100-meter final, despite winning the event at the Amateur Athletic Union finals prior to Helsinki. He was looking to make up for that in the 4x100. At the starting gun, the United States charged out to a lead, which they held to the end, outpacing the Soviet Union's runners. Following his sports career, Smith turned to working in rodeos and as a stuntman in several Western films, including *The Alamo*, *El Dorado* and *How the West Was Won*.

June 28, 1987: Baylor Sets Record for HBP

Hailing from Austin, Texas, Don Baylor had options when it came to choosing a sports career. Coming out of Austin High School, he received football scholarships, including an offer from the University of Texas's Darrell Royal. Baylor turned that down, instead enrolling at Blinn Junior College to focus on a baseball career. He was rewarded when he made his MLB debut in 1970. Baylor experienced plenty of highs and lows throughout his playing career. Among the highlights are being named American League MVP in 1979 and earning a World Series championship in 1987. However, one achievement stands out as the most unusual. On June 28, 1987, Don Baylor was hit by a pitch (HBP) for the 244th time, setting the record for most times hit by a pitch in the modern era (1900–present). Baylor would finish his career with 267 HBPs.

June 29, 2005: Biggio Breaks Baylor's Record

Exactly eight years and one day after Don Baylor set the record for most times hit by a pitch (HBP), the Astros' Craig Biggio broke Baylor's record. Biggio would finish his career with 285 HBPs, which remains the modern-era record.

June 30, 1961: PVIL All-Star Game

The first East-West All-Star football game sponsored by the Prairie View Interscholastic League was held in Beaumont on this date.

JULY

July 1, 1989: Nickel Hot Dogs

A baseball promotion in 1989 turned out a little differently than the ten-cent beer night (see June 4). Two Texas League teams played for three hours and forty-five minutes on a night when hot dogs were being sold for a nickel. During the contest, seventeen thousand hot dogs were sold. The home team, El Paso, looking to increase attendance, promoted its offer of five-cent dogs. But the team did not anticipate such a long game. Almost four hours after the game began, the home team scored four runs in the bottom of the tenth inning to beat San Antonio, 13–12.

July 2, 1999: Zimmermans Square Off

Texas Christian graduate and pitcher Jeff Zimmerman beat his brother, Jordan Zimmerman, as the Texas Rangers defeated the Seattle Mariners, 7–6. Jeff earned a berth in the MLB All-Star Game that year, as he had an eye-popping 0.76 ERA and an 8-0 record with three saves through mid-July.

July 3, 1983: Rangers Score Record Runs

The Texas Rangers tied a major-league record for the most runs scored in a single extra inning when they plated twelve runners in the fifteenth inning for a 16–4 win over the Oakland Athletics. The Rangers earned the runs with eight hits, four walks, a wild pitch and an error. Bob Jones doubled twice in the inning.

July 4, 1932: Reynolds-Dickey Incident

In a game against the New York Yankees, LaRue native Carl Reynolds scored from third base after a wild throw by Yankees catcher Bill Dickey. Thinking he had overrun the plate, Reynolds walked back to touch home when Dickey punched him in the face, breaking his jaw. For his actions, Dickey received one of the harshest punishments in league history up to that time: a $1,000 fine and a one-month suspension.

July 5, 1930: Fiftieth Wimbledon

Second-seeded Bill Tilden defeated unseeded Wilmer Allison, 6–3, 9–7, 6–4, in the men's championship match at Wimbledon. To reach the final, Allison defeated the tournament's eighth seed, fourth seed and first seed. Allison, from San Antonio, attended the University of Texas, where he was the intercollegiate national champion in 1927.

July 6, 1918: Work or Fight

The Texas League season ended prematurely, a result of the government's "work or fight" mandate, which ordered all able-bodied men to join the military or work for a defense-related industry.

July 7, 1990: Garrison Fights in Wimbledon

After knocking off the world's No. 1, Steffi Graf, in a stunning upset, Houston native Zina Garrison moved on to the Wimbledon finals to face Martina Navratilova. Unfortunately, Garrison proved to be overmatched, and Navratilova won, 6–4, 6–1, capturing her record ninth Wimbledon women's singles title.

July 8, 1988: Ritter's High-Jump Record

Jumping at the University of Texas, Dallas native Louise Ritter set the American women's record for high jump, at six feet, eight inches. Just a few weeks later, Ritter matched the mark in a jump-off to claim gold at the 1988 Seoul Olympics. At thirty years of age and having received five surgeries, Ritter stunned the world when she defeated top-ranked Stefka Kostadinova of Bulgaria to claim gold. Kostadinova held the world record at the time.

July 9, 2013: Texans at the Gold Cup

The United States opened the 2013 CONCACAF Gold Cup with a 6–1 obliteration of Belize. Texans Brek Shea (Bryan–College Station), Omar Gonzalez (Dallas) and José Francisco Torres (Longview) helped the U.S. men's team to the championship of the Confederation of North, Central American and Caribbean Association Football. Shea scored his first international goal in the tournament to beat Costa Rica, 1–0. It was the fifth CONCACAF Gold Cup title for the United States.

July 10, 1971: 100th Open Championship

Held at the Royal Birkdale Golf Club, the 1971 Open Championship entered its final day on July 10, 1971. Lee Trevino had moved into a tie for first in the opening round and held steady throughout, shooting a final-round 70 to win by a stroke. Having won the U.S. Open less than a month earlier, Trevino became just the fourth golfer to win the U.S. Open and the Open Championship in the same year. The others were Bobby Jones, Gene Sarazen and Ben Hogan.

July 11, 2007: Tomlinson Named Male Athlete of the Year

LaDainian Tomlinson won the ESPY Award for Male Athlete of the Year, over the likes of LeBron James, Peyton Manning and Tiger Woods. In the 2006 season, Tomlinson set an NFL record for most touchdowns in a season and most points in a season. Originally from Waco, Tomlinson—also known as "LT"—played for TCU, where he was a consensus All-American, a two-time WAC Player of the Year, the Doak Walker Award winner and the Jim Brown Trophy winner.

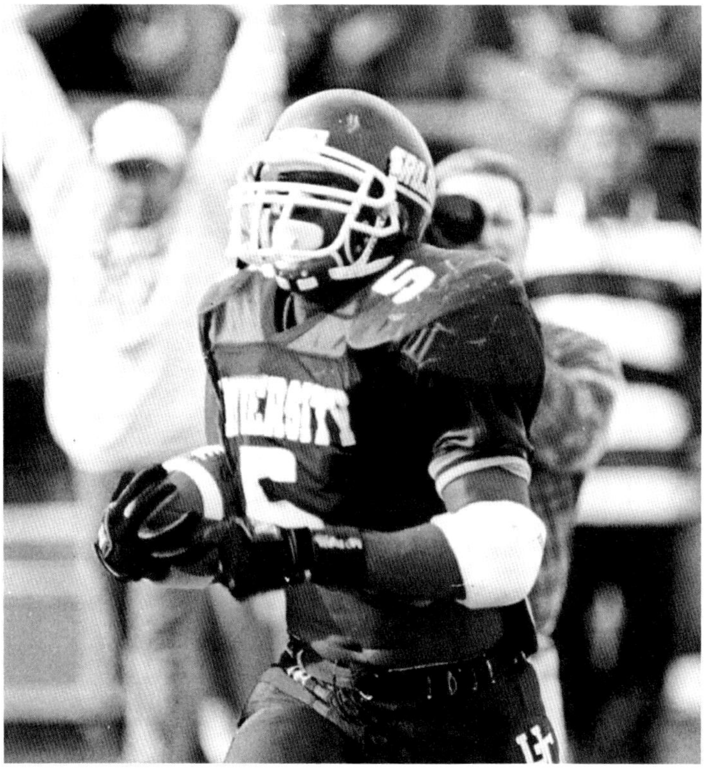

LaDanian Tomlinson races for a touchdown while playing at University High School in Waco. *Courtesy of the Texas Sports Hall of Fame.*

July 12, 1963: The Thousand Oaks Cowboys

The Dallas Cowboys hosted their first training camp at California Lutheran College in Thousand Oaks. The team would continue to train at the site until 1989. The location became one of the more famous NFL training camps while it was associated with "America's Team."

July 13, 2005: NHL Lockout Ends

The NHL and the NHLPA (the league's players' association) reached an agreement to end the 2004–05 NHL lockout. It had been the first time a major American sports league missed an entire season due to a labor dispute. It was also the first time since 1919 that the Stanley Cup wasn't awarded. The Dallas Stars came out of the lockout on fire, working to a 53-23-6 record and a No. 2 seed in the Western Conference playoffs. While some thought the Stars might make a run for another Stanley Cup, the team stumbled out of the gate, losing to Colorado in the first round.

July 14, 1967: Mathews Hits No. 500

In his one season with the Astros, Texarkana native Eddie Mathews hits his 500th career home run, in a game against the San Francisco Giants. A twelve-time All-Star and a two-time World Series champion, Mathews was one of the most feared hitters of his day. He led the National League in home runs in 1953 and 1959. Mathews would finish his career with 2,315 hits, 512 home runs and 1,453 RBIs before being inducted into the National Baseball Hall of Fame in 1978.

July 15, 1986: Clemens Named All-Star MVP

The 1986 MLB All-Star Game was about as Texan as you can get. The first pitch was thrown out by President George H.W. Bush, and the contest was held in the Astrodome. So it was fitting that the game would have a native Texan as the MVP. Roger Clemens, in his first All-Star Game, allowed no hits and no walks. He threw twenty-one strikes and just three balls while shutting down the National League over the game's first three innings. Meanwhile, his American League teammates scored two runs, good enough for the victory as the AL held on to win, 3–2. Clemens pitched in the major leagues from 1984 to 2007, being named to eleven All-Star Games and winning two World Series titles and seven Cy Young Awards.

July 16, 1936: Stinson Flying School

Windburn Field in San Antonio was renamed Stinson Field. First opened in 1915, Stinson Field is the second-oldest general aviation airport in continuous operation in U.S. history. Stinson's long history is indicated by its unusual identifying code, SSF, which stands for Stinson School of Flying. The airfield was opened by Katherine Stinson. She became just the fourth woman in the United States to receive a pilot's license, which she used to start a career as a touring pilot. Among her achievements, Stinson was the first woman to perform the loop the loop and fly for U.S. Mail. To operate the school, Katherine was joined in San Antonio by her sister Marjorie and brother Eddie. Marjorie and Katherine served as instructors, while Eddie worked as lead mechanic. While training pilots for the war effort, Katherine was twice refused by the army when she applied to be a fighter pilot. Stinson Field remains open today and includes a branch of the Texas Air Museum.

July 17, 1979: Morgan Wins Fiftieth All-Star Game

Played at the Kingdome in Seattle, Washington, the fiftieth MLB All-Star Game had plenty of Texas star power, including Nolan Ryan and Don Baylor. However, it would be Bonham native Joe Morgan who ended up with the game's winning play. A reserve player, Morgan came off the bench and drew a walk with one out in the top of the ninth inning. After a balk and two more walks, Morgan was standing on third base. Another walk allowed him to stroll home. The run gave the National League a 7–6 lead, which they would maintain through the bottom of the ninth. A standout player from the 1960s to the early 1980s, Morgan would enter the National Baseball Hall of Fame on his first ballot.

July 18, 1974: Haynie at the U.S. Women's Open

Hailing from Fort Worth, Sandra Haynie entered the twenty-ninth Women's Open golf championship as one of the favorites to win. However, it would take an incredible final-round effort to see that goal realized. Down with just a few holes to play, Haynie hit a seventy-foot putt on the seventeenth hole for birdie, followed by a fifteen-foot putt on eighteen to gain another stroke. It would prove just enough, as Haynie won the tournament by one stroke. It was her second major championship in a row, having won the LPGA Championship a month earlier. Haynie competed on the LPGA Tour from 1961 to 1989, winning forty-two LPGA tournaments and four major championships.

July 19, 1966: Outfield AstroTurf Installed

The outfield portion of AstroTurf was installed in the Astrodome in 1966 while the Astros were away on an extended road trip. Prior attempts at using natural grass had been unsuccessful. Groundskeepers dressed as astronauts kept the turf clean with vacuum cleaners between innings. The infield dirt retained the traditional design, with a large dirt arc, similar to that on natural grass fields.

July 20, 1954: Brinker's Tennis Career Ends

Maureen Connolly Brinker's tennis career ended after she suffered a tragic accident, being pinned between her horse and a truck. A native of San Diego, Brinker won nine Grand Slam singles titles while reaching a world ranking of No. 1 in 1952. Eventually, Brinker and her family moved to Dallas, where she became an undergraduate at SMU in 1964. In 1968, she and her close friend Nancy Jeffett cofounded the Maureen Connolly Brinker Tennis Foundation to provide tennis clinics and aid to promising juniors who could not afford to compete nationally. In 1969, just thirty-four years old, Brinker lost her battle with cancer. The foundation continues to operate in Dallas today.

July 21, 1952: Hooper Wins Silver

A native of Fort Worth, Darrow Hooper graduated from North Side High School before joining the Texas A&M track-and-field team. While competing for the Aggies, Hooper won the 1951 national championship in shot put. In 1952, she competed for Team USA at the Helsinki Olympics in the same event. During the Olympic trials, Hooper had bested fellow American Parry O'Brien by nearly an inch to win the event. In the Olympic finals, O'Brien flipped the script, edging Hooper by a nearly identical margin. O'Brien won gold and Hooper won silver, and both athletes easily passed the world-record holder at the time, Jim Fuchs. O'Brien would go on to win an unprecedented 116 consecutive meets, a gold medal in the 1956 Melbourne Olympics and a silver medal in Rome in 1960.

July 22, 1984: Whitworth Wins Eighty-Fifth Event

Kathy Whitworth of Monahans, Texas, won her eighty-fifth LPGA Tour event on this date, further extending her record of most all-time tour victories.

July 23, 1996: Strug Guarantees U.S. Gold

Originally from Tucson, Arizona, Kerri Strug moved to Texas in 1991 to start training full time with the Károlyis. Béla and Márta Károlyi defected to the United States from Romania in 1981 before making Texas their home base to train U.S. gymnasts. The pair led a transformation in American gymnastics. That success first came to light when Strug responded to an emotional speech from Béla and nailed her vault at the 1996 Atlanta Olympics despite an injured ankle. The vault guaranteed the United States its first gold medal in women's team gymnastics.

July 24, 1967: January Wins PGA Championship

Tied for fifth place after the third round of the 1967 PGA Championship, Don January was looking at a steep climb if he was going to win his first major. However, the Plainview native showed he had what it took. Shooting a 68 in the final round, January moved into first. Don Massengale shot a 66 to tie January and force a playoff. The two squared off the following day, July 24, to decide the winner. While both played solid rounds, January edged Massengale, 69 to 71, claiming his first and only major title.

July 25, 1964: Hansen Sets World Record

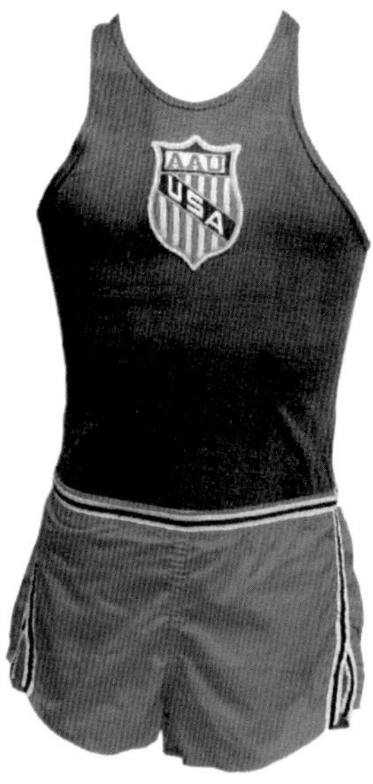

Fred Hansen's USA track uniform, worn while competing for the AAU. *Courtesy of the Texas Sports Hall of Fame.*

A native of Cuero, Fred Hansen attended Rice University, graduating in 1963. Hansen, a pole-vaulter, began preparing for the 1964 Tokyo Olympics by competing in trials in the United States. On July 25, 1964, in a match against the USSR at the Los Angeles Coliseum, Hansen jumped seventeen feet, four inches, breaking his own world record. The jump would prove inspirational heading into the Olympics, as competition in pole vaulting was stiff in 1964. While all athletes at the Olympics face pressure, Hansen experienced more than most. The United States had never lost a pole-vault competition at the Olympics, and it was expected that the streak would continue. The finals began, and the field narrowed to Hansen and German athlete Wolfgang Reinhardt. Both men failed twice at sixteen feet, eight and three-quarters inches, but on the third attempt, Hansen sailed clear while Reinhardt did not. Hansen won the gold and continued the U.S. streak, which would last until 1972.

July 26, 1939: Bob Lilly's Birthday

Born in Olney, Texas, Bob Lilly would move with his family to Oregon while he was in high school because of a severe drought that hampered Texas farming. Lilly didn't waste much time moving back south, opting to play college football for TCU, where he was a two-time All-SWC player and a consensus All-American in 1960. In the 1961 NFL draft, the Dallas Cowboys traded up with the Cleveland Browns to select Lilly thirteenth overall. It was the first draft pick in Dallas Cowboys history. The move proved to be smart one. Lilly would go on to eleven Pro Bowls and seven First Team All-Pro selections while anchoring the Cowboys' defensive line for a decade. A fan favorite, Lilly was known by his nickname, "Mr. Cowboy." He was the first player to be ushered into the Dallas Cowboys Ring of Honor.

July 27, 1897: "Biz" Mackey's Birthday

Hailing from Eagle Pass, Texas, James Raleigh "Biz" Mackey was one of the greatest catchers to ever play the game of baseball. Although he never played in the major leagues, Mackey was a star in the Negro leagues. While many people know the names of Negro league stars like Josh Gibson and Satchel Paige, Mackey has somewhat faded from history. "Cool Papa" Bell once said that, despite his respect for Gibson and Roy Campanella, "I believe Biz Mackey was the best catcher I ever saw." Hall-of-fame pitcher Hilton Smith was equally gushing, stating, "I've pitched to some great catchers, but my goodness, that Mackey was to my idea the best one I pitched to. The way he handled you, the way he just built you up, believing in yourself. He was marvelous."

July 28, 1998: McCombs Purchases Vikings

On July 28, 1998, the NFL approved Red McCombs's purchase of the Minnesota Vikings. It was far from McCombs's first foray into sports; the mogul was one of the primary parties responsible for bringing the Spurs to San Antonio. McCombs sold the team to current owner Zygi Wilf in 2005, but he continues to be one of the primary patrons of sport in Texas. Along with multiple generous gifts to the University of Texas's athletics program, McCombs was the primary backer of Austin's new Formula 1 track, the Circuit of the Americas.

July 29, 1996: Lewis's Fourth Long-Jump Gold

Originally from Birmingham, Alabama, Carl Lewis chose to attend the University of Houston under coach Tom Tellez. Tellez would help Lewis's jump technique, and the two worked to attain the 1980 NCAA long-jump national title. They missed out on the 1980 Olympics, however, as the United States boycotted the Moscow games. Lewis would keep Tellez on as his coach for the rest of his career, and the duo got its first crack at the Olympic games in 1984. What followed was one of the most dominate streaks in Olympic history. Lewis won the gold medal in the long jump in 1984, 1988 and 1992. He lined up on July 29, 1996, in an attempt to achieve a four-peat. Going into his final attempt, Lewis trailed the leader by two inches. On his third attempt, he sailed past the first-place mark by a foot, securing his fourth gold in the event and further cementing his place as one of the greatest Olympians of all time.

July 30, 1932: Zaharias Stars in Los Angeles

The 1932 Los Angeles Olympics had several firsts. It was the first time an Olympic village was constructed for athletes. It was the first time a winner's podium was used. It also happened to be Mildred "Babe" Didrikson Zaharias's first and only Olympics. Of course, being one of the greatest athletes to ever live, she made the most of it. Zaharias won three Olympic medals: a gold in the hurdles, a gold in the javelin and a silver in the high jump. It could have been a gold medal sweep, but Zaharias's final high jump was deemed illegal, and she was relegated to second place.

She would never compete in another Olympics, but this was far from the end of Zaharias's athletic career. The Port Arthur native excelled at just about all sporting events, competing in basketball, pool, baseball, diving, bowling and other sports. However, the one sport for which Zaharias is most remembered is golf. The list of her golf accomplishments is long, including

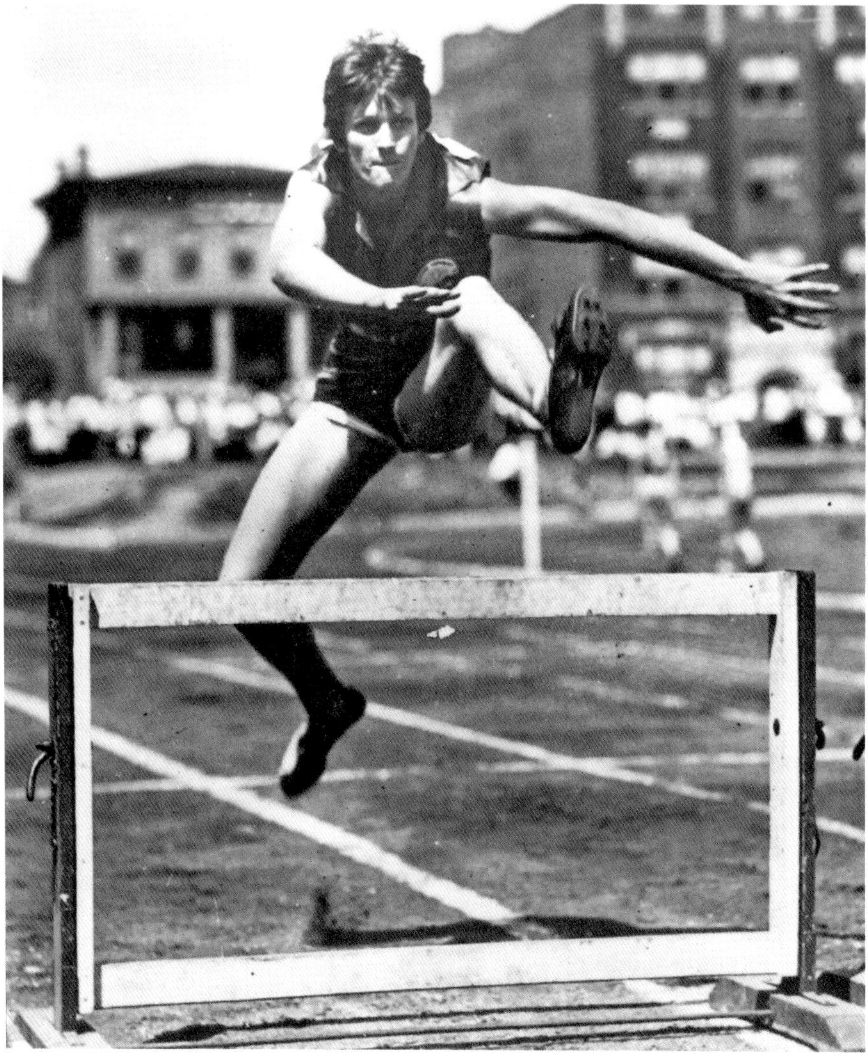

Babe Zaharias running hurdles. *Courtesy of the Texas Sports Hall of Fame.*

forty-one LPGA Tour wins and ten LPGA major championships. But one fact encapsulates her golf prowess. To date, Zaharias is the only female golfer to make a cut at a PGA event. She first entered a PGA tournament in 1938, missing the cut. But she had been golfing for only about three years at the time. Once she gained more experience, she entered another PGA tournament and made her first cut at the 1945 Los Angeles Open. She would make the cuts again at the Phoenix Open and the Tucson Open. Her

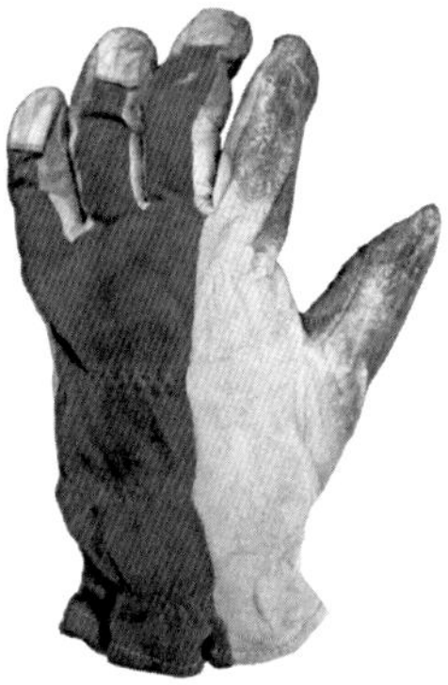

One of Babe Zaharias's golf gloves. The left side is red, and the right side is cream. *Courtesy of the Texas Sports Hall of Fame.*

best PGA finish was thirty-third place. In 1948, Zaharias applied to compete in the U.S. Open, but the USGA rejected her application, stating that the event was intended for men only.

In 1956, Zaharias passed away from colon cancer at the age of forty-five. When ESPN ranked the top athletes of the twentieth century, Zaharias was in tenth place—the highest rank for a woman on the list. In an article about Zaharias for the *New York Times*, Charles McGrath wrote, "Except perhaps for Arnold Palmer, no golfer has ever been more beloved by the gallery." Legendary sports journalist Grantland Rice commented, "The Babe is without any question the athletic phenomenon of all time, man or woman." In a separate piece, Rice wrote: "She is beyond all belief until you see her perform. Then you finally understand that you are looking at the most flawless section of muscle harmony, of complete mental and physical coordination, the world of sport has ever seen."

July 31, 1914: Claude Gilstrap's Birthday

The great head football coach at the University of Texas–Arlington, Claude "Chena" Gilstrap, was born in Granger, Texas. Gilstrap coached the Mavericks football team from 1953 to 1965, with his most notable seasons 1956 and 1957. Those teams won consecutive Junior Rose Bowl titles, the equivalent of a junior college national title. The 1957 team went undefeated. In 1959, he guided the program from a two-year school to a four-year college, with impressive results. In his final season, Gilstrap led the team to a 6-3 record in the Southland Conference and was named the conference's Coach of the Year. He took the opportunity to retire gracefully and served as the school's athletic director until 1975. His coaching record at UT–Arlington was 85-40-3.

AUGUST

August 1, 1990: Arkansas Leaves the SWC

Arkansas, a founding member of one of the country's oldest athletic conferences announced their intent to leave the Southwest Conference and join the Southeastern Conference (SEC). The SWC, begun as a regional conference, had shrunk to a group that consisted of only Texas schools with the departure of Arkansas. By March 1994, other SWC schools Texas, Texas A&M, Baylor and Texas Tech announced they would be joining members of the Big 8 Conference to create the Big 12.

August 2, 1973: A Welcome Distraction

Constitutional law expert Charles Alan Wright composed a letter to Dave Campbell, thanking him for the distraction of *Dave Campbell's Texas Football*, which Wright read while representing President Richard Nixon during the Watergate hearings. A Texas sports staple, *Dave Campbell's Texas Football* was first published in 1960. It previews all professional, college and high school football in Texas. A sports reporter for the *Waco Tribune-Herald*, Campbell worked with his wife to produce the first issue on their own. Today, the magazine is operated by Sports in Action, a company owned by Drayton McLane.

THE WHITE HOUSE

WASHINGTON

August 2, 1973

Mr. Dave Campbell
Sports Communications, Inc.
P. O. Box 95
Waco, Texas 76703

Dear Dave:

I appreciate enormously your letter of July 31st and the copies of the magazine you enclosed. As it happened, I was in Austin last weekend for the first time since June 3rd. Mail of various kinds was stacked very high on top of my filing cabinet. I did not have time to look at it all, but when I happened to see the summer edition of Texas Football was in one of those stacks, I pulled it out and brought it back up on the plane with me. Thanks to your kindness, I now have a copy at the hotel and another copy that I can dip into at the office on those rare occasions when I get a minute or two without seven things to do.

Thank you also for sending the extra copies to that great football fan who is now my client. I am sure that he does have fond memories of that great game in 1969. Let's hope that the article by Mr. Cook comes true. If it does come true, the President might well want to see the Longhorns in action once again.

I just hope that my duties here won't cause me to miss any of the Texas games this fall. My very best to you.

Sincerely,

Charlie

Charles Alan Wright

Letter from Charles Alan Wright to Dave Campbell, which reads, in part, "when I happened to see the summer edition of Texas football…I pulled it out and brought it back up on the plane with me.…I now have a copy at the hotel and another copy that I can dip into at the office on those rare occasions when I get a minute or two without seven things to do.…I just hope that my duties here won't cause me to miss any of the Texas games this fall." *Courtesy of the Texas Sports Hall of Fame.*

August 3, 1984: Retton Wins All-Around

Mary Lou Retton, a native of West Virginia, moved to Texas to train with Béla and Márta Károlyi. With their help, Retton would win the American

Cup in 1983 and place second at the U.S. Nationals that same year. On August 3, 1984, Retton competed in the final day of the women's individual all-around at the Los Angeles Olympics. In second place with two events left, Retton earned perfect scores on the final two events and moved into first. She became the first U.S. woman to win the individual all-around gold medal. Retton won four more medals at the same Olympics, two silver and two bronze. Today, Retton lives with her husband, former University of Texas quarterback Shannon Kelley, and their children in Houston.

August 4, 1993: Ryan vs. Ventura

In one of modern baseball's most memorable moments, the Robin Ventura of the Chicago White Sox charged Nolan Ryan on the pitcher's mound. Ventura had been hit by one of Ryan's pitches and came at Ryan in retaliation. Ryan, two decades older than Ventura, calmly placed Ventura in a headlock and hit him several times as both benches cleared. When order was finally restored, Ventura was ejected and Ryan—who had basically held his ground—was allowed to remain in the game. Chicago's manager strongly protested the decision to leave Ryan in, leading to his ejection as well. Ryan, for his part, threw hitless baseball the rest of the game.

August 5, 1936: Meadows Sets Record in Pole Vault

One of Texas's greatest pole vaulters, Earle Meadows began his career in Fort Worth for Central High School. He won the city title all four years he competed and won the state championship in 1933 with a record vault of thirteen feet, one and one-half inches. That mark would stand for twenty-five years, until fiberglass poles were introduced. Since Texas schools did not offer scholarships to track-and-field athletes at the time, Meadows opted to attend the University of Southern California. He set an Olympic record in the pole vault at the 1936 Olympics, also known as the "Nazi Games," in Berlin, Germany. His jump, fourteen feet, three inches, edged out those of two Japanese competitors, who came in second and third. Meadows missed two opportunities to compete in the Olympics, in 1940 and 1944, as World War II led to the cancelation of the games.

He attempted to return in 1948, but just missed making the team. The United States still won gold as Texas-born Guinn Smith won a competition remembered more for rain than the height of the jumps.

August 6, 1960: Dallas Cowboys' First Game

The Dallas Cowboys played their first game, against the San Francisco 49ers, in a preseason contest at the University of Washington's Husky Stadium. The 'Boys lost, 16–10.

August 7, 1943: Baylor Withdraws from SWC Gridiron

On the morning of August 7, football fans across the state opened their newspapers to see an Associated Press report that the Baylor Bears would not be playing football in the 1943 season. Many Bears players and many Baylor male students had gone off to war, so the school chose to withdraw from competition for the season. Baylor was the only major Texas program to cancel the season, although the Texas College of Mines (now the University of Texas–El Paso) also canceled its season. The Bears would cancel again in 1944.

August 8, 1984: Lewis Wins 200-Meter Final

Originally expected to focus on the long jump, it became apparent early in his collegiate career that Carl Lewis was also a very competent sprinter. Soon he was being compared to Jesse Owens, who had dominated sprints and long jumps in the 1930s. Lewis won gold in the 200-meter final at his first Olympics, in 1984. He won additional gold medals in the 100 meters and the 4x100 meters in Los Angeles before winning gold in the 1988 100-meter final and the 1992 4x100 meters. In his final games, in 1994, Lewis earned a silver medal in the 200-meter final, bringing his career Olympic medal total to ten. He is one of just three Olympic athletes to win four golds in a single event.

August 9, 1965: Big 33

On this date, the second "Big 33" high school all-star game was held in Hershey, Pennsylvania. It was the first win by the Texas team. The game began in 1964 and was named for the size of the team's rosters. Featuring high school players headed to college teams, the first "Big 33" game saw Pennsylvania win, 12–6. That victory was short-lived, as Texas would win the next four Big 33 games by a margin of 105–26. The series was ended after the 1967 game.

August 10, 1989: Stewart Wins PGA Championship

In the seventy-first PGA Championship, Payne Stewart didn't appear in the top ten until the third round. Even then, he was only tied for tenth. The SMU legend would shoot a final-round 67, moving into first place and winning his first major tournament. He would go on to win the U.S. Open in 1991 and 1999 before dying tragically at the age of forty-two, just one month after leading the American team to a come-from-behind victory at the Ryder Cup. Stewart won a total of eleven PGA tournaments over his career and was inducted into the World Golf Hall of Fame in 2001.

August 11, 1994: Bagwell's Lost Season

Major League Baseball players walked away from the game over a labor dispute with owners in 1994. The strike led to the first time in eighty-nine years that an MLB champion wasn't crowned. The strike proved especially hurtful to the Houston Astros, as Jeff Bagwell was in the midst of his most impressive individual year. Bagwell set club records for home runs, batting average and slugging percentage despite the abbreviated schedule. The effort earned him the National League MVP, making him the first and only Astro to win the award. Despite a less-than-impressive record of 52-62, the Texas Rangers were leading the American League West when the strike started.

August 12, 1957: Parker Resigns

After leading the Detroit Lions to NFL championships in 1952 and 1953, Raymond "Buddy" Parker abruptly resigned. Catching almost everyone off guard, the Slaton, Texas native merely remarked, "When you get to a situation where you can't handle football players, it's time to get out." He also said, "We've got good boys but there has been no life…no go… it's a completely dead team." The Lions would go on to win another NFL championship that year (1957) under new coach George Wilson and veteran quarterback Bobby Layne. Parker would later join the Pittsburgh Steelers, coaching that team from 1957 to 1964 and producing, at best, mixed results. His final NFL head-coaching record was 104-75-9.

August 13, 1948: Robinson Leads U.S.A. to Gold

Jackie Robinson of Baylor lore led Team USA to the 1948 London Olympic basketball gold medal. The team defeated France, 65–21, in the championship game. Afterward, Robinson met the British royal family. With typical Texas brashness, he corrected the king on his misconception on the sizes of California and Texas. The moment is immortalized in a BBC recording that is still available for listening.

August 14, 1959: First AFL Meeting

Led by Texan Lamar Hunt, the American Football League held its first organizational meeting in Chicago. Hunt worked with other individuals around the country who were interested in bringing professional football to their cities. All of these people had been turned down by the NFL when they applied for expansion franchises. Hunt, always a big thinker, decided that, rather than waiting on the NFL, he would start his own league. When the members of the new league met for the first time, they had no commissioner, no president, no public relations staff or any other official personnel. Since the league was his idea, Hunt led the meeting and collected $25,000 from each of the owners present to start a league treasury.

AUGUST 15, 1958: ALL-STARS UPSET THE LIONS

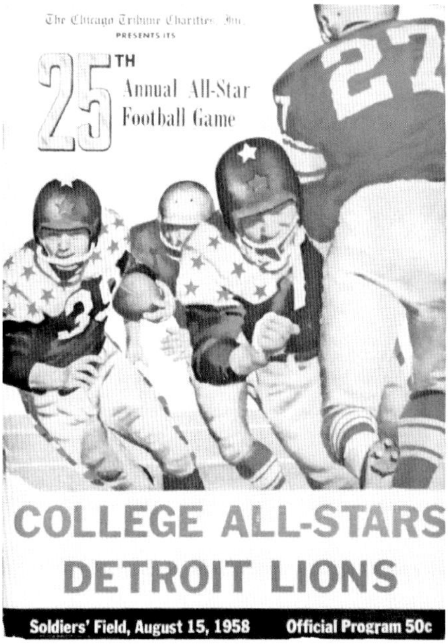

25th Annual All-Star Football Game program. The game was held at Chicago's Soldier Field. The College All-Stars would knock off the NFL champion Lions. It was just one of nine times the college team won the game. *Courtesy of the Texas Sports Hall of Fame.*

In a rare instance of a college all-star team defeating the reigning NFL champions, the 1958 Annual Chicago College All-Star Game featured five Texans who helped lead the college team to victory. The collegiate squad scored the most points by their side in a 35–19 victory over the Detroit Lions. The Texans were Aggies John David Crow, Bobby Conrad and Charles Krueger, Rice quarterback King Hill and TCU halfback Jim Shofner. The Detroit Lions had routed the Cleveland Browns in the NFL championship game, 59–14, and were expecting to make similar work of the college all-stars. With a crowd of seventy thousand on hand at Chicago's Soldier Field, the game had the atmosphere of a major professional game. Conrad kicked four field goals (a record) and three extra points to lead the scoring. He also dazzled defensively, with six tackles and five pass breakups. Krueger put a devastating hit on the Lions' Bobby Layne, leading to one of Detroit's five interceptions to go along with one lost fumble. It was the twenty-fifth Chicago College All-Star Game. The game was played annually from 1934 to 1976 (the only exception being 1974, when it was canceled due to the NFL strike), but the college team managed to win only nine of those games.

AUGUST 16, 2004: OSTERMAN'S FIRST OLYMPICS

Houston native Cat Osterman pitched her first Olympic game, throwing eight scoreless innings. USA and Japan were tied, 0–0, after seven innings, but the Americans scored three runs in the top of the eighth. Osterman combined with pitchers Lisa Fernandez, Jennie Finch and Lori Harrigan to lead Team USA to a 7-0 record and the gold medal while allowing no runs. Osterman started her softball career at the University of Texas, where she was the Big 12 Pitcher of the Year as a freshman in 2002. She ended her career with records in wins, strikeouts, ERA, shutouts, strikeout ratio and opponent's batting average.

August 17, 1951: McFadin Named MVP

University of Texas tackle Bud McFadin was named the first MVP from Texas in the Chicago College All-Star Game. The all-star team lost to the Cleveland Browns, 33–0, but McFadin would go on to a successful professional career, making the Pro Bowl twice while playing with the Los Angeles Rams and being named to three AFL All-Star Games while a member of the Denver Broncos.

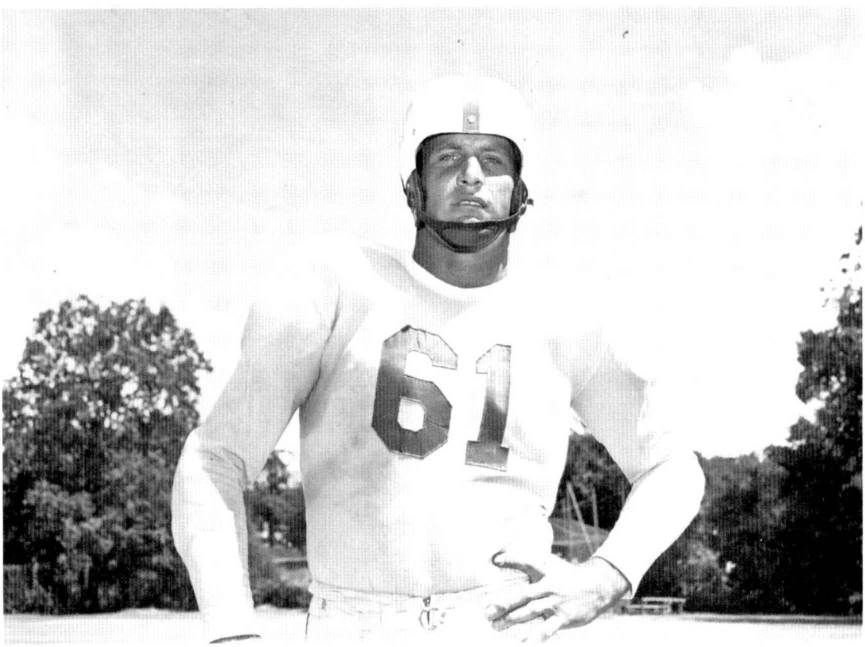

University of Texas tackle Bud McFadin in his Longhorn uniform. *Courtesy of the Texas Sports Hall of Fame.*

AUGUST 18, 1962: RILEY LEADS UNITED STATES IN CURTIS CUP

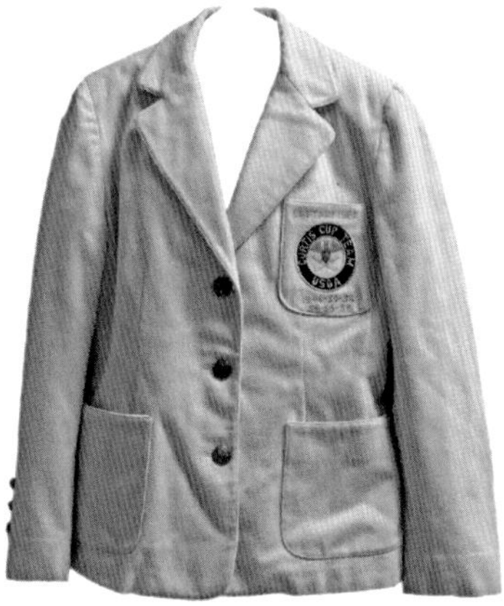

Polly Riley's Curtis Cup jacket. *Courtesy of the Texas Sports Hall of Fame.*

Under captain Polly Riley, a native of Fort Worth, the United States won the Curtis Cup (the female counterpart to the Ryder Cup) by a score of 8–1. Riley was a distinguished golfer, winning the first LPGA event, the 1950 Tampa Open, as an amateur. Her 1962 team posted the most lopsided finish in the history of the Curtis Cup, a seven-point differential.

AUGUST 19, 1960: FIRST SALESMANSHIP GAME

In what would become an icon of every new Dallas Cowboys season, the first Salesmanship Club game was played on August 19, 1960. The first match pitted the Cowboys against the Baltimore Colts and their star quarterback, Johnny Unitas. The Colts had strong ties to Dallas; the Colts technically purchased the city's first franchise, the Dallas Texans, which became the new team in Baltimore. The team changed its name to the Colts, but it kept the colors, blue and white. (Today, the Colts call Indianapolis home.) In front of a crowd of forty thousand at the Cotton Bowl, the Cowboys fell to Unitas and the Colts, 14–10.

AUGUST 20, 1920: NFL ORGANIZED IN CANTON

Originally called the American Professional Football Association, the NFL was organized at a meeting in Canton, Ohio. One of the league's early stars was Benny Boynton, of Waco, Texas. Boynton first made a name for himself as the "Purple Streak" while playing for Williams College in Massachusetts. In 1921, on just the second All-Pro team ever selected, Boynton was a First Team selection at quarterback. One of the league's early owners, Leo Lyons, said that Boynton was the second-greatest football player of all time, behind only Jim Thorpe.

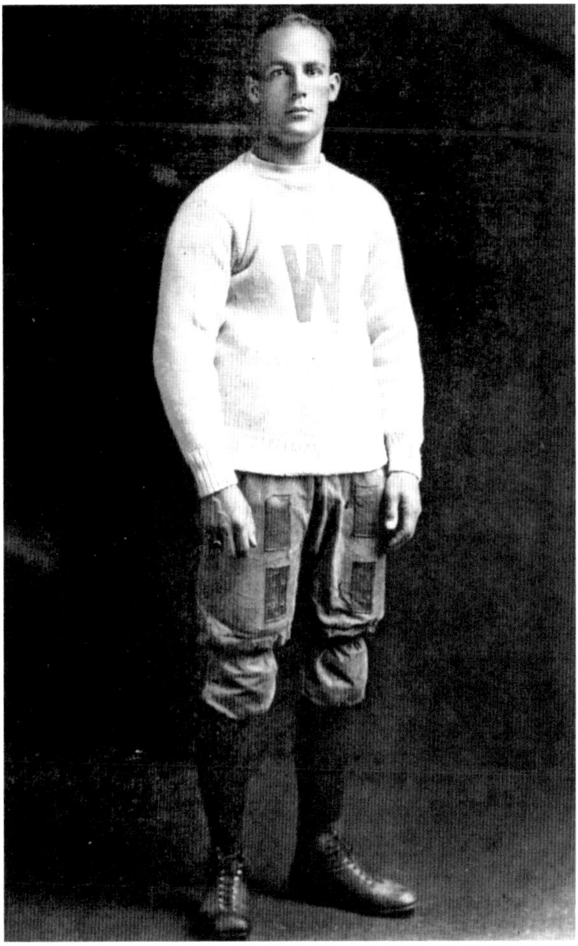

The "Purple Streak," Benny Boynton, in his Williams College gear. *Courtesy of the Texas Sports Hall of Fame.*

August 21, 1926: Lyons's No-Hitter

Baylor university baseball star Ted Lyons threw a no-hitter for the Chicago White Sox, defeating the Red Sox, 6–0, at Fenway Park. The game took just one hour and forty-five minutes to complete. On offense, Lyons had a hit and one RBI. A member of the National Baseball Hall of Fame, Lyons's number was retired by the White Sox in 1987.

August 22, 1989: Strikeout No. 5,000

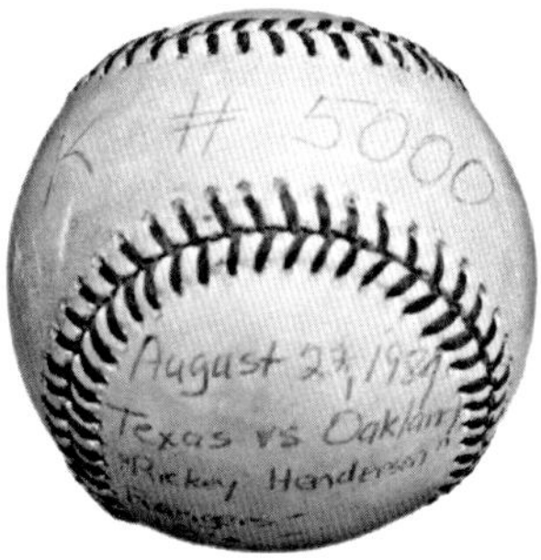

The "Strikeout King" did it again. Nolan Ryan took down future hall of famer Rickey Henderson to record his 5,000th career strikeout. Henderson was a good sport, saying afterward, "If you haven't been struck out by Nolan Ryan, you're nobody." The only person to reach 5,000 strikeouts, Ryan finished his career with an astounding 5,714.

Final ball from Nolan Ryan's 5,000th strikeout against Rickey Henderson. Ryan's writing is present on the ball. *Courtesy of the Texas Sports Hall of Fame.*

August 23, 1942: Hughson Wins Eleven Straight

Pitcher Cecil "Tex" Hughson, from Buda, Texas, earned his eleventh straight win. His streak began on June 30 and lasted almost two full months. Hughson recorded an AL-leading twenty-two wins in 1942 as the Red Sox went 93-59 and finished second in the American League. Over his career, Hughson was named a three-time All-Star and finished in the top fifteen in MVP voting three times.

August 24, 2004: Sanya Richards-Ross's First Olympic Final

Sanya Richards-Ross ran in her first Olympic final, the 400 meters in Athens, finishing sixth. She would return to the Olympics in 2008, earning a bronze medal in the 400 meters and a gold in the 4x400 relay. She returned in 2012, adding two more gold medals to her career count with victories in the 400 meters and the 4x400 relay.

August 25, 1979: First Annual Armadillo Races

Held in New Braunfels, Texas, the first International Armadillo Race presented one of the oddest events in the history of Lone Star State racing.

The festival featured "armadillo jockeys," working to coax their armored athletes from the starting line to the finish line. Between races, attractions included a beauty contest, a freckle contest and a beer-chugging contest.

August 26, 1939: Jameson Wins Golf Championship

Betty Jameson won the finals of the National Women's Golf Championship. Born in Norman, Oklahoma, Jameson moved with her family to Dallas, where she graduated from Sunset High School. After playing at the University of Texas, Jameson turned professional in 1945, winning thirteen LPGA Tour events, including three major championships.

August 27, 2013: Beaty Passes Away

On this date, early Texas basketball star Zelmo Beaty died in Bellevue, Washington, after a battle with cancer. A widely respected player, Beaty was inducted into the Naismith Basketball Hall of Fame in 2016.

August 28, 2004: Wariner Runs for Gold

Hailing from Irving, Texas, Jeremy Wariner made a name for himself running at Baylor University. He was another product of the Bears' "400 U"—a nickname given to Baylor for its dominance in the 400 meters. On August 28, 2004, Wariner helped lead the United States to a gold medal in the 4x400 relay while winning gold in the 400 meters at the same Olympics. Wariner would return to the games in 2008, winning gold in the 4x400 relay and placing second in the 400-meter final.

August 29, 1970: Oilers Beat Cowboys

In the Houston Oilers' first season as a part of the NFL, they played the Dallas Cowboys in a preseason matchup. The Oilers defeated the Cowboys,

37–21, behind Jerry LeVias's three scores. The Oilers would go on to win their first NFL regular-season game, defeating the Pittsburgh Steelers, 19–7. However, the remainder of the team's first season in the league would be less inspiring. The Oilers finished 3-10-1, including a 52–10 loss at the hands of the Cowboys in the final game of the regular season.

August 30, 1997: Comets Win WNBA Title

To conclude the first season of the Women's National Basketball Association, the Houston Comets won the title. Their star player, Cynthia Cooper, was named MVP. The Comets would go on to establish the first dynasty in women's professional basketball, winning the league's title four consecutive years (1997, 1998, 1999 and 2000). Cooper, the league's MVP in 1997 and 1998, was named the WNBA Finals MVP all four years. Her teammate Sheryl Swoopes was named the league's MVP for the 2000 season.

August 31, 1996: First Big 12 Football Game

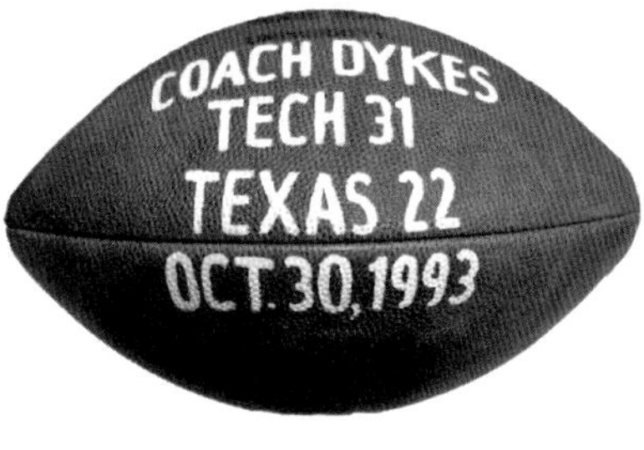

One of Coach Sonny Dykes's game balls from a Texas–Texas Tech game. Dykes would beat the Longhorns six times in thirteen tries. *Courtesy of the Texas Sports Hall of Fame.*

After the fall of the SWC, four Texas schools—Baylor, Texas, Texas A&M and Texas Tech—joined with the schools of the Big 8 Conference to form the Big 12. The new conference's first football game was played on August 31, 1996, as Texas Tech, led by Spike Dykes, traveled to Manhattan, Kansas, to play Kansas State. The Wildcats were ranked No. 21, but they got a fight from the Red Raiders. Kansas prevailed by just one score, 21–14. Tech would finish that first Big 12 season in second place in the Southern Division, while the division's first-place team, Texas, upset No. 6 Nebraska, 37–27, in the conference title game.

SEPTEMBER

September 1, 1954: Junction Boys

When head coach Paul "Bear" Bryant arrived in College Station from Kentucky, he had a clear vision for the football program. Convinced that most of the players on the team were weak or poorly trained, Bryant planned to start his first season at a training camp in Junction, Texas. The Hill Country was experiencing a record-setting drought at the time, and on many days of the camp, temperatures topped one hundred degrees. Practices began before dawn and lasted all day. Compounding the players' exhaustion, Bryant prohibited water breaks, a common practice at the time to toughen up players. While the exact number of players who went to Junction is unknown, reports go as high as one hundred. When the camp ended ten days later, only thirty-seven remained. The group included two men who would go on to coaching distinction in their own right: Gene Stallings and Jack Pardee. The team went 1-9 in the 1954 season (its only victory was over Georgia), but it was clear that a new culture was expected. In 1955, the team went 7-2-1, and in 1956, the Aggies went 9-0-1 and won the SWC.

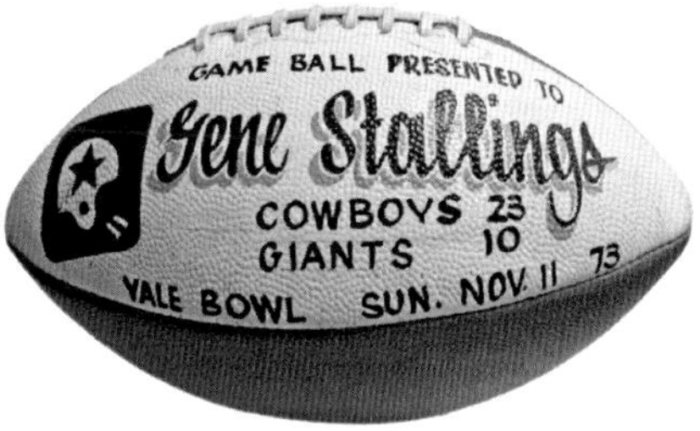

Gene Stallings's game ball from the Cowboys' victory over the Giants in the Yale Bowl. The Giants played in the Yale Bowl while Yankee Stadium was being renovated from 1973 to 1974. The Cowboys won both games played there. *Courtesy of the Texas Sports Hall of Fame.*

September 2, 2011: Turnaround

In the first game of their season, the Baylor Bears stunned No. 14 TCU in an instant classic. Led by Robert Griffin III, Terrance Williams and Kendall Wright, the unranked Bears knocked off the Horned Frogs, 50–48, when kicker Aaron Jones hit a thirty-seven-yard field goal. The Bears would suffer some setbacks during the season, including blowout losses to Texas A&M and Oklahoma State, but they would take down No. 5 Oklahoma on an incredible pass from Griffin to Williams with eight seconds left. The Bears went to the Alamo Bowl, winning their first bowl game since 1992. Griffin won the Davey O'Brien Award, was named the AP Player of the Year and took home the Heisman Trophy—Baylor's first player to win the Heisman.

September 3, 1972: Heidenreich Pushes Spitz

A standout for SMU's swim team, Jerry Heidenreich entered the 1972 Munich Olympics in the shadow of an all-time great, Mark Spitz. The two faced off in the 100-meter freestyle final on September 3, with Spitz edging Heidenreich. Spitz swam the race in 51.22 seconds, a world record, and Heidenreich finished at 51.65 seconds. At Munich, Heidenreich also earned a bronze medal in the 100-meter butterfly and claimed two gold medals in relay events.

September 4, 1966: The Oilers Stifle the Broncos

In one of the more impressive defensive showcases in professional football history, the Houston Oilers took down the Denver Broncos, 45–7. The craziest part of the victory was that Houston kept Denver from gaining a single first down. The strong start to the season proved illusory, as Houston went 3-11 over the regular season.

September 5, 2001: Clemens Makes History

Roger Clemens became the second pitcher in major-league history to win nineteen of his first twenty decisions in a season, leading the New York Yankees over the Toronto Blue Jays, 4–3.

September 6, 1960: Rafer Johnson Wins Decathlon

Rafer Johnson, from Hillsboro, Texas, claimed gold in the decathlon at the 1960 Rome Olympics. He had placed second in the event at the 1956 Melbourne games. Johnson would retire from competition after the meet, but his story was far from over. In 1968, he joined Robert F. Kennedy's campaign and ended up using his athleticism to run down and tackle Kennedy's assassin, Sirhan Sirhan. Interestingly enough, Johnson's brother Jimmy would enjoy a career in athletics. He is a member of the Pro Football Hall of Fame.

September 7, 1992: SWC Discusses Expansion

Officials of the Southwest Conference met in 1992 to discuss expansion. One plan was to create a merger with the Big 8 Conference and become the Big Southwest. Another proposal called for an alliance with an "Eastern Seaboard League" that would consist of Miami, Syracuse, Boston College, Pittsburgh, Rutgers, Temple, Virginia Tech and West Virginia. It was an ambitious plan, but the merger with the Big 8 would prove more realistic.

September 8, 2002: Texans' First Game

The expansion Houston Texans played their first NFL regular-season game, beating the Dallas Cowboys, 19–10. Houston became just the second NFL expansion team to win its opening game. The two Texas teams would not meet again in a regular-season game until 2006. The Cowboys exacted revenge, winning 34–6.

September 9, 1972: Bellard's First TAMU Game

Widely credited with inventing the wishbone formation, Emory Bellard coached his first game at Texas A&M on this date. Bellard had come from the University of Texas, where he first implemented the formation as an assistant coach. Bellard and the Aggies would struggle in his first year, going 3-8, but the team produced back-to-back ten-win seasons in 1975 and 1976. While there is no doubt that Bellard was the first to use the wishbone to run a devastating triple-option attack, there is some debate over whether he was the first to implement the unique formation. A variation of the split-T offense, the wishbone may have started with Texas junior high school coach Spud Cason. Over twenty-one years, beginning in 1952 (well before Bellard's offense was unveiled in 1968), Cason utilized an offensive formation almost identical to the wishbone. Cason's teams would use the formation to devastating effect. They once won forty-two straight games. When he retired, Cason's record was 137-20. Of course, Cason would readily admit that his teams never ran a triple option out of the set; that was all Bellard's invention.

September 10, 1966: Westbrook Breaks Barrier

John Hill Westbrook became the first African American football player to play in the SWC, entering a game just one week before SMU's Jerry LeVias. Westbrook and the Bears handed seventh-ranked Syracuse its worst loss since 1954.

September 11, 1965: Cougar Firsts

The Houston Cougars play their first game in the Astrodome, losing to Tulsa, 14–0. Exactly eleven years later, on September 11, 1976, the Cougars played their first SWC game. That would go a little better, as Houston dismantled Baylor, 23–5, in Waco.

September 12, 1962: "Why Does Rice Play Texas?"

In a speech given at Rice's historic football stadium, President John F. Kennedy gave his unbending support of the space program. While many doubted the validity of the program or questioned the wisdom of pouring financial resources into its creation, Kennedy argued that people often do things that are hard or seem silly. "But why, some say, the moon? Why choose this as our goal? And they may well ask why climb the highest mountain? Why, 35 years ago, fly the Atlantic? Why does Rice play Texas?" Kennedy answered his own questions. "We choose to go to the moon in this decade and do the other things, not because they are easy, but because they are hard, because that goal will serve to organize and measure the best of our energies and skills, because that challenge is one that we are willing to accept, one we are unwilling to postpone, and one which we intend to win."

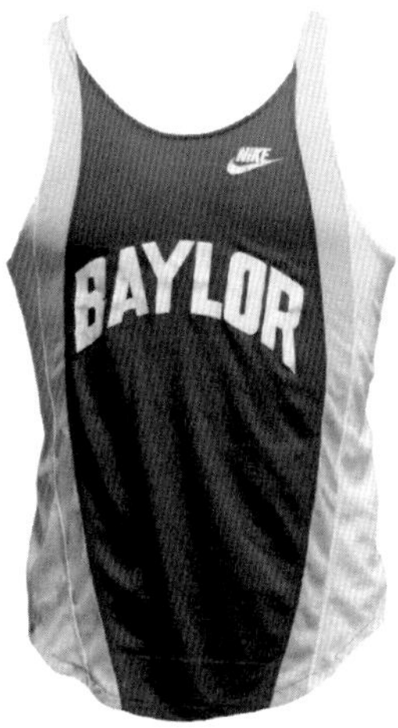

Michael Johnson's Baylor University track top. *Courtesy of the Texas Sports Hall of Fame.*

September 13, 1967: Michael Johnson's Birthday

Born in Dallas, Michael Johnson would go on to become one of the most prolific sprinters of all time. A graduate of Skyline High School, Johnson opted to attend Baylor University to work with legendary track coach Clyde Hart. Johnson would go on to win multiple national titles with the Bears in sprints and relays before entering his first Olympic competition in 1992, helping the United States to a gold-medal finish in the 4x400 relay. In 1996, he earned two more gold medals, winning the 200-meter and 400-meter events. Johnson finished his Olympic career in 2000, winning a final gold medal in the 400 meters.

September 14, 1985: Aggies Surge Under Sherrill

After years of mediocrity, Texas A&M opened the 1985 season with a trip to Legion Field in Birmingham to play No. 20 Alabama. In front of a national television audience, the Aggies fell, 23–10. But they rebounded to win their next four games before a showdown with Grant Teaff and No. 14 Baylor. Again, the Aggies came up just short, losing 20–15. Head coach Jackie Sherrill rallied his players, and the team went undefeated for the rest of the season. Wins over No. 19 SMU and No. 9 Arkansas propelled the Aggies into the national rankings, and a 42–10 pummeling of No. 18 Texas to end the regular season earned TAMU its first SWC crown in eighteen years. The Aggies maintained momentum in the postseason, limiting Heisman Trophy winner Bo Jackson enough to defeat No. 16 Auburn, 36–16, in the Cotton Bowl. The Aggies finished the season ranked sixth in the nation. Jackie Sherrill and Texas A&M would go on to defend their SWC titles in 1986 and 1987.

September 15, 1958: Vaught's Rebels in the Top Ten

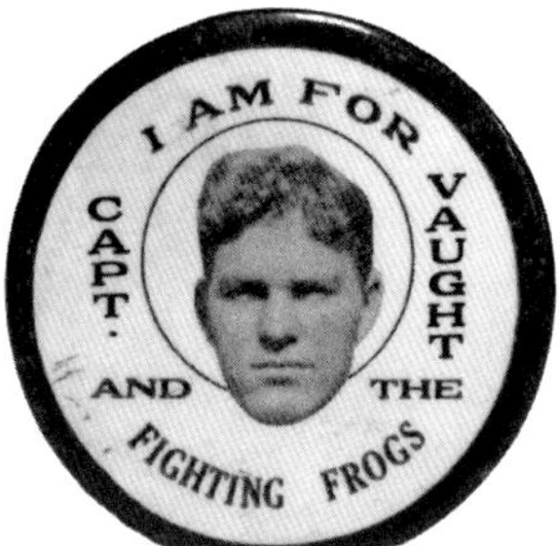

Pinback button for fans to wear supporting TCU's Captain Johnny Vaught and the "Fighting Frogs." *Courtesy of the Texas Sports Hall of Fame.*

The 1958 college football Preseason AP Poll had the Ole Miss Rebels ranked sixth. Led by Fort Worth native and TCU alum Johnny Vaught, the Rebels were on the brink of greatness. Unfortunately, a 14–0 loss to No. 1 LSU and an upset by Tennessee derailed the season, and the Rebs finished with a record of 8-2 before defeating Florida in the Gator Bowl. Vaught and Ole Miss would use the offseason to fine-tune their strategy. It worked, as the team won three national titles in the next four years (1959, 1960 and 1962).

September 16, 1973: Bethea's Best Season

The Houston Oilers began their season on this date. The 1973 season would prove to be a rough one for the team, but it would be a great season for their star player, Elvin Bethea. The Oilers would finish 1-13 that year, but Bethea would record a career-best seventeen sacks. He would play his entire career with the Oilers (1968–83), making eight Pro Bowls.

September 17, 1916: Breckenridge Opens

The first public eighteen-hole course in Texas, Breckenridge Golf Course, opened in San Antonio on this date. Designed by A.W. Tillinghast, who was also responsible for Bethpage Black and Winged Foot, Breckenridge was the original host of the Texas Open. Today, the course is also home to the Texas Golf Hall of Fame and Museum.

September 18, 1978: Washington Leads Baltimore

A native of Port Arthur, Texas, Joe Washington had his greatest professional football performance on this date, scoring three touchdowns in the fourth quarter of a *Monday Night Football* game between the Baltimore Colts and the New England Patriots. Washington started the fireworks with a fifty-four-yard pass to Roger Carr, followed by a twenty-three-yard touchdown catch. He finished the magnificent quarter with a ninety-yard kickoff return for a touchdown in the final seconds. Baltimore won, 34–27.

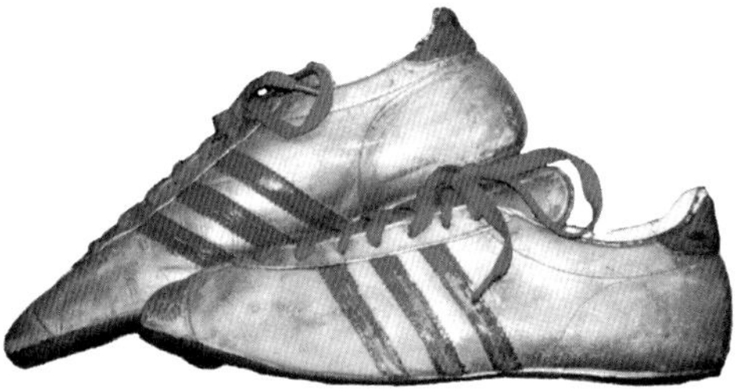

A pair of Joe Washington's cleats, which he wore while playing for the Oklahoma Sooners. Washington would hand-paint his cleats silver, while the stripes, laces and heel are red. *Courtesy of the Texas Sports Hall of Fame.*

September 19, 1953: Kelly Plays for San Angelo

In September 1953, Benjamin Kelly walked onto the football field for San Angelo College (today Angelo State University), becoming the first African American player to suit up for a previously all-white school south of the Mason-Dixon line. A graduate of San Angelo's Blackshear High School, Kelly would earn All-Pioneer Conference honors as a player. In 2014, the school renamed its Center for Human Performance in Kelly's honor.

September 20, 1973: Battle of the Sexes

Several tennis matches have carried the title "Battle of the Sexes," but to most people, the title refers to exactly one event: the September 20, 1973 contest between Billie Jean King and Bobby Riggs. Technically, this could be called the "Battle of the Sexes II," as Riggs had previously played a professional female tennis player, Margaret Court. He had defeated her, 6–2, 6–1. Things would go a little differently when Riggs met King in the Astrodome. King fell behind, 4–2, in the first match, but she rebounded to win four consecutive games and go up in sets, 1–0. King would take care of business in the next two sets, winning 6–3, 6–3 to sweep Riggs, three sets to zero. More than thirty thousand people were in attendance, and ninety million viewers tuned in to watch on television. While some would point to the age difference (King was twenty-six years younger than Riggs) rather than a mismatch in skills as the reason for the outcome, there is no doubt that this was an important event in King's movement to achieve equality in the treatment of female tennis players.

September 21, 1968: Wishbone

After being developed by offensive coordinator Emory Bellard, the wishbone offense of the University of Texas was rolled out against the University of Houston. The Longhorns managed only a tie against the Cougars, 20–20. But the UT backfield, with players like Chris Gilbert, Ted Koy, Steve Worster, James Street and Bill Bradley, quickly mastered the offense. Texas lost the next game, but utilizing the formation, the school went on to win thirty-six straight games, including two national titles.

September 22, 1979: Green and the Ags Stun Penn State

Texas A&M traveled to University Park, Pennsylvania, to face No. 6 Penn State. The Aggies would win, 27–14. A&M's star defensive end, Jacob Green, would finish the season with 134 tackles and a school record of 20.0 sacks. For his individual efforts, Green was an All-America selection before being drafted by the Seattle Seahawks. He would record 97.5 sacks for the Seahawks, third in NFL history at the time of his retirement.

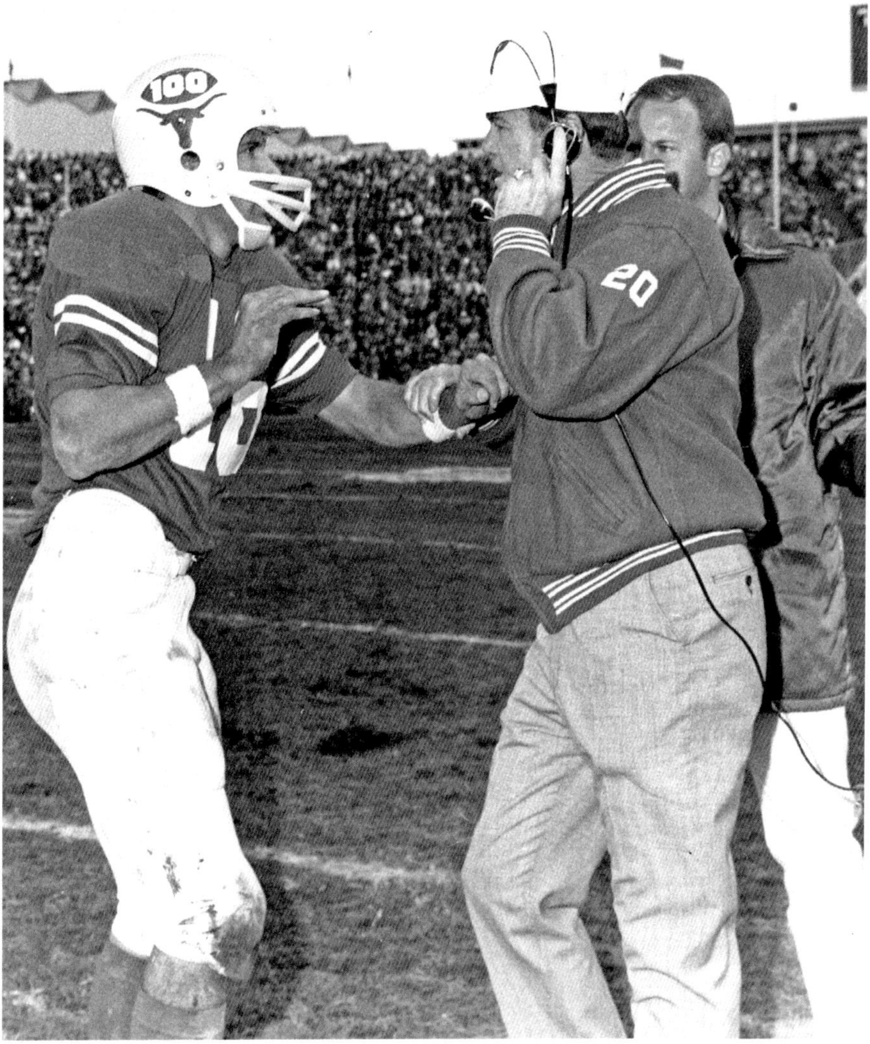

James Street (*left*) and Darrell Royal (*right*) have a brief discussion on the sideline of the 1970 Cotton Bowl as the Longhorns down Notre Dame, 21–17. *Courtesy of the Texas Sports Hall of Fame.*

September 23, 1989: Ware's Season

In the second game of their 1989 season, the Houston Cougars defeated Arizona State, 36–7, in Tempe, Arizona. The win was unusual, as the Cougars committed eight turnovers and were penalized twenty-three times for 236 yards. Houston was coached by Texas A&M graduate Jack Pardee, in his final season before joining the Houston Oilers. The Cougras were led on the field by quarterback Andre Ware. The team, under NCAA sanctions, couldn't reach a bowl game or play on television. Despite this, the Cougars were intent on putting together one of the greatest offensive seasons college football had ever seen. Despite a four-point loss to the Aggies and a six-point loss to the Razorbacks, the Cougars did just that. Ware threw for 4,699 yards and forty-four touchdowns, and the team set twenty-six NCAA records, finishing 9-2. Ware would win the Heisman Trophy and the Davey O'Brien Award before being drafted seventh overall by the Detroit Lions.

September 24, 2000: Wilkinson's Dive

When the women's 10-meter platform dive competition ended at the Sydney Olympics, Houston native Laura Wilkinson won the gold, becoming the first female American since 1964 to win a gold medal in the event. Her accomplishment was made more impressive due to the fact that she had a broken foot, which had kept her from training for the Olympics.

September 25, 1960: Cowboys and Texans Debut

Following the debut of the Dallas Cowboys the night before, the AFL's Dallas Texans played their inaugural game at the Cotton Bowl, beating the Los Angeles Chargers, 17–0, in front of a crowd of forty-two thousand, considerably larger than the crowd that had come to watch the Cowboys. On September 24, the Cowboys made their official debut as members of the NFL, playing before a crowd of thirty thousand. The 'Boys fell to hometown hero Bobby Layne and the Pittsburgh Steelers, 35–28.

September 26, 1933: Mancuso Leads Giants

In previewing the 1933 World Series, first-year New York Giants manager Bill Terry predicted that catcher Gus Mancuso would be the most

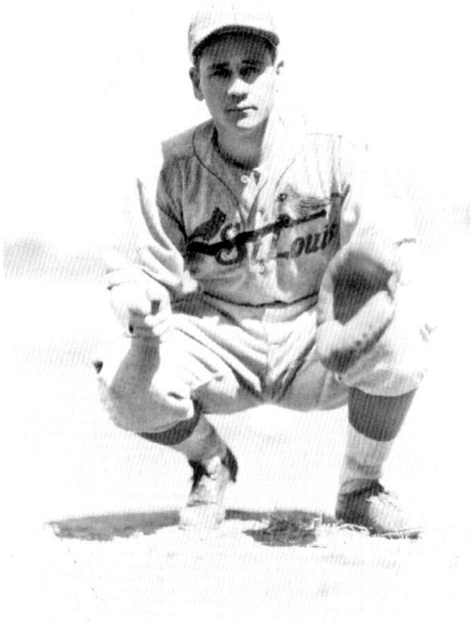

important factor of the series. Terry credited Mancuso's handling of the pitching staff for the turnaround of the Giants' fortunes from the 1932 season to the 1933 campaign. Terry was on point, as the Giants easily won the 1933 series over the Washington Senators, 4-1. A Galveston native, Mancuso was responsible for guiding a Giants' pitching staff that allowed only eleven runs over the five games of the World Series.

Gus Mancuso with his rookie team, the St. Louis Cardinals. *Courtesy of the Texas Sports Hall of Fame.*

September 27, 1942: Koy's Final Appearance

The patriarch of one of Texas's greatest sporting families, Ernie Koy Sr. made his final major-league appearance on this date. Koy quit baseball to join the navy. Prior to entering the majors, Koy was one of the first superstar athletes at the University of Texas, where he was a multisport athlete. A fullback for the football team and an outfielder for the baseball team, Koy was voted team captain in both sports. He signed with the Yankees in 1933, but he didn't have his MLB debut until being traded to the Dodgers in 1938. All three of Koy's children continued the family's sports lineage. Sons Ted Koy and Ernie Koy Jr. played for UT's national championship football teams in 1963 and 1969, and his daughter Margaret Koy is credited with being the first female sports reporter in the state of Texas. Her first assignment was covering Big Spring High School and the school's head coach, Spike Dykes. Koy Sr. once defeated Jesse Owens in a 100-yard dash, although Owens gave Koy a five- to ten-yard head start, depending on which report you read.

September 28, 1952: The NFL's Dallas Texans

The first NFL franchise in Texas, the Dallas Texans, played its first game on this date, losing 24–6 to the New York Giants at the Cotton Bowl. Only about seventeen thousand fans attended the game, foreshadowing the franchise's constant poor attendance. The team was formed when a group based in Dallas purchased the assets of the New York Yanks from the NFL. Unfortunately, with no professional sports management experience, the franchise hemorrhaged money and never gained support from the city. The team went 0-7 in 1952 before moving to Hershey, Pennsylvania. At the end of the 1952 season, the franchise was canceled. It was the last time an NFL franchise failed.

September 29, 1974: Nobis Notches Fifteen

Tommy Nobis had fifteen solo tackles, including eight that saved touchdowns, while playing for the Atlanta Falcons in a game against the New Orleans Saints. Originally from San Antonio, Nobis was one of the University of Texas's first defensive stars. From 1963 to 1965, he averaged nearly twenty tackles a game and was one of the only sophomores to start on the Longhorns' 1963 national championship team. In his final collegiate game, the 1965 Orange Bowl, Nobis led a UT defensive charge that halted Alabama's Joe Namath from scoring on fourth and inches, preserving the Longhorns' 21–17 victory. Nobis was drafted first overall by the Atlanta Falcons and played for the team from 1966 to 1976.

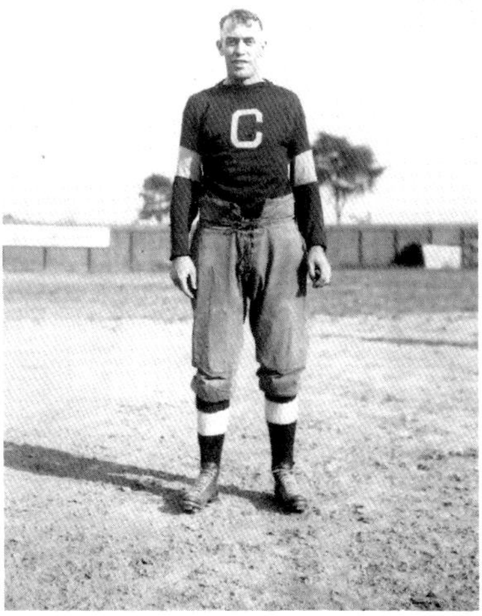

Cecil Grigg sports his Canton Bulldogs uniform. *Courtesy of the Texas Sports Hall of Fame.*

September 30, 1923: Bulldogs Start the Season with a Win

The Canton Bulldogs begin their season with a 17–0 victory over the Hammond Pros. Canton is helped to its second consecutive NFL championship that year by former University of Dallas star Cecil "Tex" Grigg. He played for Canton from 1919 to 1923 before returning to Texas to coach. He served a thirty-year stretch as Jess Neely's backfield coach at Rice (1936–66). In college, Grigg led Dallas in every offensive category all four years he played for the team.

OCTOBER

October 1, 1938: O'Brien's Heisman Season

TCU opened its Southwest Conference schedule with a game against Arkansas, winning 21–14. It was the only game TCU didn't win by double digits in the regular season. Led by Davey O'Brien, the Horned Frogs rolled through the schedule, earning a berth in the Sugar Bowl against No. 6 Carnegie Tech. TCU would win, 15–7, claiming the national championship. For his individual exploits, O'Brien won the Heisman Trophy, the first Texan to be so honored and the shortest recipient ever, at five feet, seven inches.

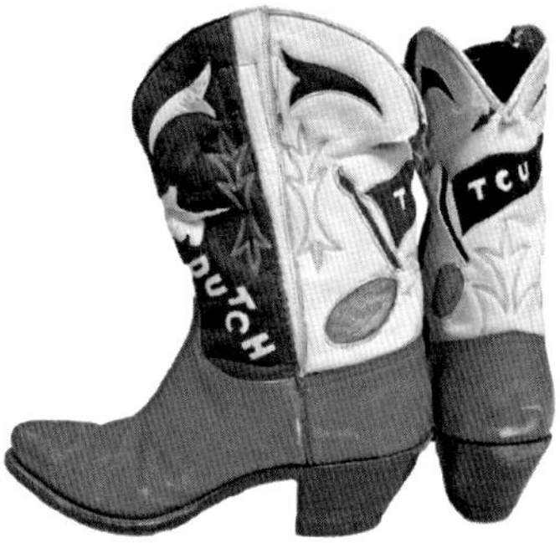

Custom-made boots by Justin Boots and presented to TCU head coach Dutch Meyer. The fronts are purple with white-horned frogs and the word "Dutch," and the backs are white with purple TCU pennants and gray footballs. *Courtesy of the Texas Sports Hall of Fame.*

October 2, 1988: Olympics Close

When the 1988 Olympics came to an end, the U.S. swim team had earned eighteen medals, including eight gold medals, second only to East Germany. The men's and women's teams were coached by Richard Quick, who first made a name for himself in high school at Highland Park before joining SMU and becoming an All–Southwest Conference swimmer. As good an athlete as he was, Quick was an even better coach. From 1976 to 2009, he was the head coach at five different schools, capturing twelve NCAA national titles and five Coach of the Year Awards. In international swimming, Quick coached at six different Olympics, including his role as head coach of men's and women's teams in 1988, the women's team in 1996 and the women's team in 2000. In 2008, Quick was diagnosed with an inoperable brain tumor, and he passed away in June 2009. His impact on others is incalculable, and his mantra, "Believe in Belief," continues to empower people today.

October 3, 1970: Elmendorf a Bright Spot for Ags

For the third game in a row, Texas A&M, on the road, faced a team ranked in the top fifteen. In the first game, A&M upset No. 12 LSU in Baton Rouge, 20–18, when Hugh McElroy (the first African American player to start a game for TAMU) caught a seventy-eight-yard touchdown pass with thirteen seconds left. The team's second game on the road trip was against No. 1 Ohio State in Columbus. The Aggies were walloped, losing 56–13. Finally, on October 3, the Aggies went to Ann Arbor to face No. 9 Michigan. Despite a hard-fought game, TAMU fell, 14–10. From there, the season only got worse. Gene Stallings and the Aggies finished a paltry 2-9. But A&M safety Dave Elmendorf earned All-American honors.

October 4, 1940: Higgins Shines in Game 3

In Game 3 of the World Series, Michael "Pinky" Higgins of Red Oak, Texas, led the Detroit Tigers to a win. Higgins posted a game-high three RBIs as the Tigers won, 7–4, to take a 2-1 series lead against the Cincinnati Reds. The 1940 World Series proved to be a good one, as the teams alternated wins until the Reds won back-to-back in Games 6 and 7 to claim the title.

October 5, 1993: Stars' First Game in Dallas

The Dallas Stars played their first game in Dallas on this date, beating the Detroit Red Wings, 6–4. The franchise had played in Minnesota for twenty-six seasons as the North Stars. When it moved to Dallas, the name was shortened as a nod to the Lone Star State and the sheriff's star.

October 6, 1999: Houston Awarded Franchise

The NFL awarded its thirty-second franchise to Houston with a $700 million entrance fee in 1999. In March 2000, the Houston Texans broke ground on Reliant Stadium (now NRG Stadium). Reliant would be the first NFL stadium with a retractable roof.

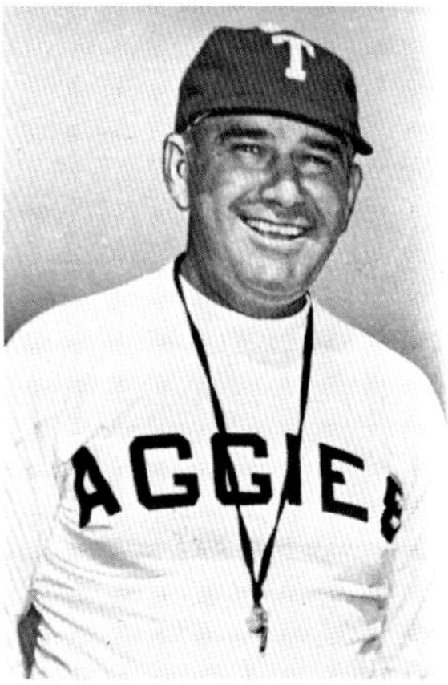

Texas A&M's Homer Norton. *Courtesy of the Texas Sports Hall of Fame.*

October 7, 1939: Aggies Down Santa Clara

Texas A&M played its most daunting nonconference opponent, Santa Clara, in October 1939. Santa Clara had won the 1937 and 1938 Sugar Bowls and would be the home team against the Aggies. A&M won, but just barely. The 7–3 victory showed that this TAMU team was the real deal. The only other team that would play the Aggies this closely in the regular season was No. 13 SMU. A&M won that game, 6–2. After a 14–13 victory over Tulane in the Sugar Bowl, Texas A&M officially won the season's national championship.

October 8, 1915: First SWC Football Game

Rice and Baylor met in Houston in the first Southwest Conference football game. Baylor won, 26–0. The team finished with a 3-0 conference record that year. However, the Bears would forfeit their claim to a co-championship after using an ineligible player. Instead, Oklahoma would claim the SWC's first title after beating Texas, Arkansas and Oklahoma State to go 3-0 in conference play.

October 9, 1960: Glenn Passes Away

In one of the most regrettable events in American Football League history, Howard Glenn passed away after sustaining a broken neck in a game against the Oilers in Houston. He would be the only player to die of injuries suffered during an AFL game.

October 10, 1957: Mathews Leads Braves

Eddie Mathews hit a double to bring in two runs, setting off a four-run third inning for the Milwaukee Braves. The Braves never looked back, winning Game 7 of the World Series, 5–0, and defeating the New York Yankees. From Texarkana, Texas, Mathews played with the Braves from 1952 to 1966, seeing the team move from Boston to Milwaukee and then to Atlanta. Between 1954 and 1966, Mathews paired with teammate Hank Aaron to hit 863 home runs (Mathews 421, Aaron 442) to move ahead of Babe Ruth and Lou Gehrig for most home runs by teammates in MLB history. Mathews appeared on the cover of the first issue of *Sports Illustrated*.

October 11, 1963: SMU Upsets Navy

The SMU Mustangs upset No. 4 Naval Academy, 32–28. Led by Roger Staubach, the Midshipmen would see the game lost when SMU's Billy Gannon plunged into the end zone from one yard out with only forty-seven seconds left on the clock. It was the first victory over a ranked opponent for head coach Hayden Fry, who had taken over in 1962.

October 12, 1963: Red River Rivalry

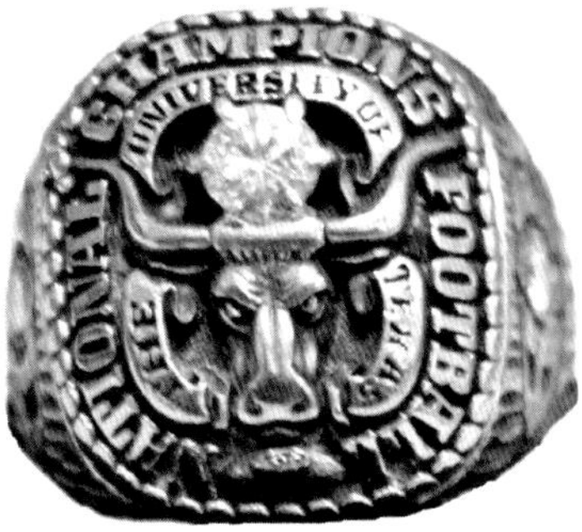

Emory Bellard's University of Texas 1969 national championship ring. *Courtesy of the Texas Sports Hall of Fame.*

In one of the most anticipated Red River Rivalry games ever player, No. 2 Texas met No. 1 Oklahoma in the Cotton Bowl. Despite the rankings, it turned into a lopsided affair as the Longhorns cruised to a 28–7 victory, putting them in prime position to win their first national championship. Under the direction of head coach Darrell Royal, despite some close calls, the Longhorns would do just that. With a 15–13 victory over rival Texas A&M, the Longhorns locked up their undefeated regular season and the Southwest Conference crown. The 'Horns headed to the Cotton Bowl to face No. 2 Navy, whose only blemish on the season came at the hands of SMU. UT shut down Heisman Trophy winner Roger Staubach on its way to winning, 28–6.

October 13, 1916: Neutral Site

In one of the Southwest Conference's earliest neutral-site games, the Texas Longhorns played Oklahoma State in San Antonio. The University of Texas won the matchup, 14–6.

October 14, 1969: Renfro to Court

The Dallas Cowboys' Mel Renfro petitioned U.S. District Court judge Sarah T. Hughes to order the Executive Duplex Apartments to stop discriminating against African Americans. Fully supported by Tex Schramm and the Cowboys organization, Renfro and his family eventually won $1,500 in damages and a new duplex.

October 15, 2009: Kershaw's First Playoff Game

Just twenty-one years old, Clayton Kershaw became the third-youngest pitcher to start a playoff series opener when he led the Los Angeles Dodgers against the Philadelphia Phillies. Kershaw had a legendary high school career at Highland Park, eventually being selected as *USA Today*'s "High School Baseball Player of the Year." After committing to play for Texas A&M, Kershaw turned down his scholarship to turn pro.

October 16, 1976: Sixty-Nine-Yard Field Goal

Abilene Christian's Ove Johansson set a record for longest field goal in football history when he booted a sixty-nine-yard kick against East Texas State. Originally from Sweden, Johansson's athletic career started in soccer before he joined the Wildcats football team.

October 17, 1869: Ad Toepperwein's Birthday

Adolf "Ad" Toepperwein is the type of figure whose achievements could fill books. Born in Boerne, Texas, Toepperwein was first introduced to guns while working in his father's gunsmith in Leon Springs. When his father passed away, he moved on to other jobs. Among these pursuits, Toepperwein worked as a cartoonist at the *San Antonio Express*. The skills he learned in this job would later apply to his shooting. In 1889, Toepperwein headed to New York in search of work in a vaudeville act to display his shooting. By 1901, he had entered a partnership with Winchester Repeating Arms Company. The partnership would last fifty years. Toepperwein received an unexpected benefit from his work with Winchester—he met his wife. While touring a Winchester factory, Toepperwein met a young worker from New Haven, Connecticut, named Elizabeth Servaty. The couple would marry in 1903. Although Elizabeth—later known as Plinky—had never fired a gun, the two started touring together in 1905 when she showed an immediate knack for shooting. Among Toepperwein's achievements was shooting 19,999 out of 20,000 blocks over a three-day period in 1906 and his world record in

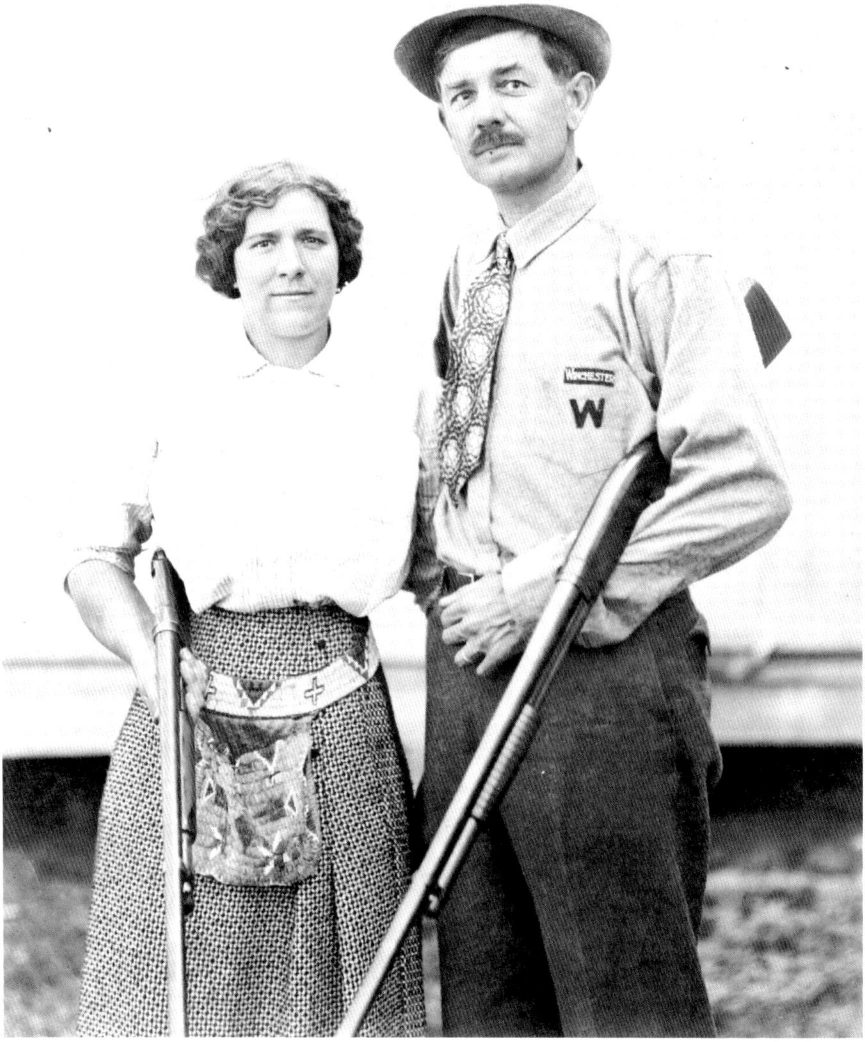

Plinky (*left*) and Ad (*right*) Toepperwein. Plinky's unusual nickname came when she told Ad the targets made a "plinky" noise when they were hit. Ad would start using the term as his affectionate nickname for her, and it stuck. *Courtesy of the Texas Sports Hall of Fame.*

San Antonio in 1907, when he shot 72,5000 wooden blocks, missing only 9. He managed that feat in just eight and a half hours, rotating guns to keep them from overheating or losing accuracy due to dirtiness.

October 18, 1968: Beamon Sets World Record

University of Texas–El Paso athlete Bob Beamon set the world record and Olympic record for long jump when he achieved a distance of twenty-nine feet, two and a half inches. The record was set on Beamon's third attempt. His first two attempts were scratched as faults. The previous world record was twenty-seven feet, four and three-fourths inches—Beamon shattered the record by almost two full feet.

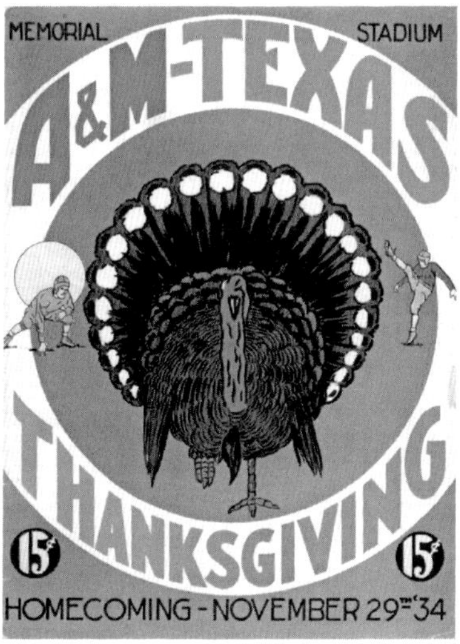

Thanksgiving Day program for the University of Texas–Texas A&M game in 1934. *Courtesy of the Texas Sports Hall of Fame.*

October 19, 1894: First UT–TAMU Football Game

By far the most storied rivalry between two Texas schools began on this date, when the University of Texas and Texas A&M first met each other on the gridiron. The Longhorns won the game, 38–0. In 1901, the game was played for the first time on Thanksgiving Day; this would become a tradition for the rivalry. In 2006, Wheaties announced that it would make a special cereal box honoring the series, marking the first time a rivalry series, rather than an individual or a team, was put on the cereal's box.

October 20, 1923: Baylor's Twelfth Man

Baylor traveled to play Arkansas. With a driving rainstorm limiting visibility, Baylor coach Frank Bridges deployed twelve defenders throughout the game (the officials didn't notice the extra man, due to the poor conditions). The tactic worked, and Baylor won, 14–0. It wasn't the only time that season that Bridges deployed, at best, unusual tactics. On November 10, the Bears played the University of Texas in Waco. After the two teams battled to a 7–7 tie, Texas players were upset, complaining that Bridges intentionally overinflated the balls to make them more difficult to use. Bridges supposedly responded by saying, "Show me in the rulebook where that isn't allowed." The Bears would finish the season 5-1-2.

October 21, 1956: Howton's Big Day

Former Rice University receiver Billy Howton had one of the greatest receiving days in NFL history. He hauled in seven catches for 257 yards as the Green Bay Packers defeated the Los Angeles Rams, 42–17. It remains one of the NFL's top twenty-five receiving games in history.

October 22, 1975: Morgan Helps Reds Win the World Series

Pete Rose, Ken Griffey Jr. and Bonham native Joe Morgan led the Cincinnati Reds to a Game 7 win over the Boston Red Sox, 4–3, at Fenway Park. Batting second behind Rose, Morgan recorded two hits, one RBI and one walk. He helped the Reds repeat as World Series champs in 1976, sweeping the New York Yankees four games to zero. Morgan made his debut for the Houston Colt .45s in 1963 before being traded to the Reds in 1972. Bill James, the influential baseball historian, once ranked Morgan as the greatest second baseman of all time, followed by Eddie Collins and fellow Texan Rogers Hornsby.

October 23, 1982: Rivera Leads Texas Tech

With a record of 3-3, no one thought Texas Tech had a shot to defeat the No. 1 Washington Huskies. Well, maybe no one besides Gabe Rivera. A defensive tackle for the Red Raiders, Rivera had made news a few weeks earlier when he recorded an astounding fourteen tackles against Air Force. That statistic would be impressive for a linebacker, but it was unheard of for a defensive lineman. Rivera made the news again when he fought to keep Tech in the game, which the Red Raiders lost, 10–3. Rivera would be named a consensus All-American for the season, as well as the SWC Defensive Player of the Year.

October 24, 1971: Cowboys Move to Texas Stadium

The Dallas Cowboys played their first game in Texas Stadium after residing in the Cotton Bowl from 1960 to 1971. The Cowboys defeated the New England Patriots, 44–21, in the contest, christening their new home in the best way possible.

October 25, 1930: Gig 'Em

At a yell practice before the 1930 TCU game, Texas A&M regent Pinky Downs (class of 1906) shouted, "What are we going to do to those Horned Frogs?" His muse did not fail him as he improvised, borrowing a term from frog hunting. "Gig 'em, Aggies!" he said as he made a fist with his thumb extended straight up. And with that, the first hand sign in the Southwest Conference came into being.

October 26, 1923: The Aerial Circus

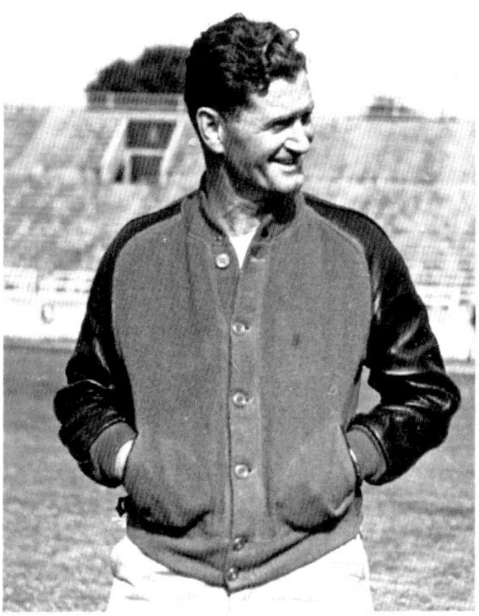

SMU head coach Ray Morrison. *Courtesy of the Texas Sports Hall of Fame.*

Led by head coach Ray Morrison, the Southern Methodist Mustangs headed to College Station to face Texas A&M. While the Aggies had never lost on Kyle Field, the Mustangs would be utilizing a new offense that just might be enough to make history. Morrison had returned to SMU in 1922 and revitalized the Mustang offense using the forward pass. The Mustangs were known to throw on early downs, regardless of distance—an unusual ploy at the time. While many teams threw fewer than ten times a game, SMU's pass attempts numbered between thirty and forty. This strange philosophy led reporters to name the SMU offense the "aerial circus"; some even called Morrison the "father of the forward pass." Morrison was on to something—SMU beat Texas A&M, 10–0. It was the Aggies' first ever loss at Kyle Field. The Mustangs rolled to a 9-0 season and the first football conference title in school history.

October 27, 1899: A Rivalry Begins

Two of the top universities in the Lone Star State, Baylor and TCU, have a long history. Baylor was chartered in 1845 by the Republic of Texas in Independence, Texas, and TCU began as AddRan College in 1873 in Thorp Springs. Baylor would move to Waco in 1885, and AddRan would move to Waco in 1895. With two leading Christian universities in the same town, a rivalry was destined to follow. The two teams would first play each other in football in 1899, concluding in a 0–0 tie. They wouldn't play each other again until 1901, when the Bears beat the Frogs twice, 36–0 and 42–0. In fact, TCU would not beat Baylor until the eleventh time they played. The Bears won seven of the first ten games; the other three contests resulted in ties.

October 28, 1962: Tittle Ties Record

From Marshall, Texas, Y.A. Tittle becomes the fourth NFL quarterback to throw for seven touchdown passes in a game, tying an NFL record. Tittle's record day leads the New York Giants to a 49–34 victory over the Washington Redskins. Not surprisingly, this passing record has lots of Texas ties. As of 2015, eight NFL quarterbacks have thrown for seven touchdowns in a single game. Five of them have Texas ties. Texas natives did it four times: Adrian Burk in 1954, Tittle in 1962, Nick Foles in 2013 and Drew Brees in 2015. Houston Oilers quarterback George Blanda accomplished the feat in 1961.

October 29, 1921: The Impossible Formula

Led by several players from Texas, the Centre Praying Colonels of Kentucky defeated Harvard, 6–0. The play of the game (executed by the player of the year) was a thirty-two-yard touchdown run by Bo McMillin. McMillin

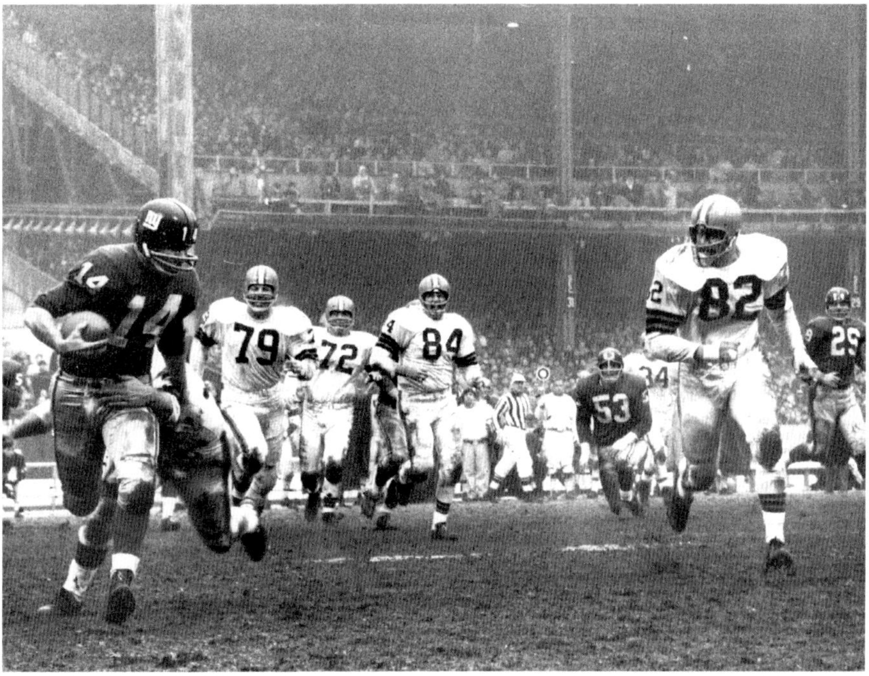

Y.A. Tittle (14) scrambles for the New York Giants against the Cleveland Browns at Yankee Stadium. *Courtesy of the Texas Sports Hall of Fame.*

had arrived at Centre via Fort Worth and became an instant football star. However, for all his success, his touchdown against Harvard would make him a national sensation. The game was played in Boston at Harvard Stadium, where a reported forty-five thousand fans had shown up to cheer on the home team. Instead, McMillin and his teammates handed the Crimson their first loss since 1916. Centre students dubbed the game the "Impossible Formula," painting the final score all over town in the form "C6H0." The *New York Times*, the *Associated Press* and ESPN have all named the game the greatest or one of the greatest upsets in college football history.

October 30, 2001: Bush Throws First Pitch

After the shock and horror of September 11, 2001, President George W. Bush signaled a resumption of American life by throwing out the first pitch at a New York Yankees game. The unbelievable acts of terrorism had caused MLB to postpone all games—the first time in over fifty years that all games had been canceled for a reason other than a work stoppage. Leaders decided to use the "social institution" of baseball as a mechanism of national healing, resuming the season on Monday, September 17. Support was immediate, as fans around the country made signs with messages such as, "We are all Yankees." Boston's Fenway Park played "New York, New York." Bush, following President Franklin D. Roosevelt's example of saying "Let's play ball!" during World War II, decided to make a symbolic throw at Yankee Stadium before a World Series game. While some were worried for President Bush's safety, he would later say, "You can't send a signal to people, 'Let's get on with our lives,' if the president is worried about his own life." Before Bush, a former governor of Texas, headed onto the field, Derek Jeter stopped by to give him a few words of encouragement, including, "Don't bounce the pitch—they'll boo you." Bush walked out to the mound and threw a perfect strike, leading to chants of, "USA! USA! USA! USA!" With a single pitch, a single symbol, Bush helped show the American public how we would move forward in a way that no speech could have ever done.

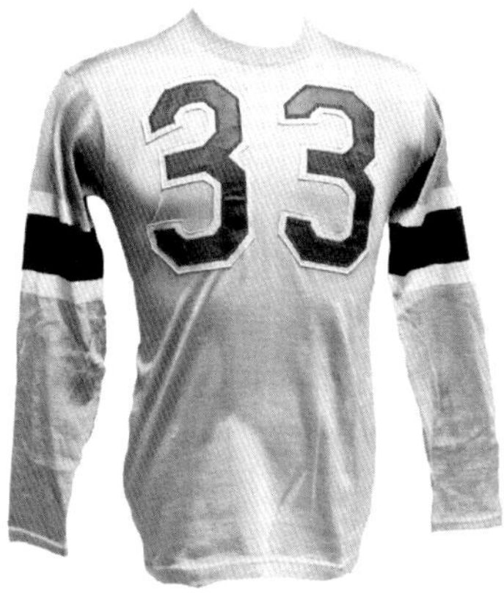

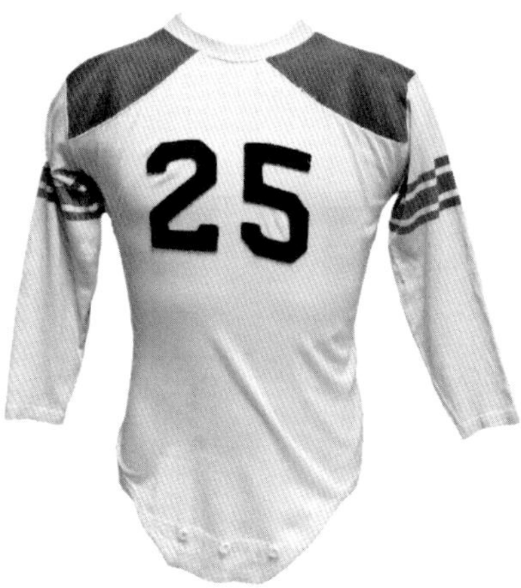

Top: One of Sammy Baugh's Washington Redskins jerseys. The jersey is gold, while the numbers and sleeve stripes are burgundy. *Courtesy of the Texas Sports Hall of Fame.*

Bottom: Dick Todd's 1938 Texas A&M football jersey. *Courtesy of the Texas Sports Hall of Fame.*

October 31, 1948: Baugh Sets Passing Record

Sammy Baugh set the NFL record for passing yards, completing seventeen of twenty-four passes for 446 yards (the previous record was set by Sid

Luckman, with 433). Baugh and the Redskins beat the Boston Yanks, 59–21, setting another team record with 59 points. Interestingly enough, Texas A&M star Dick Todd helped Baugh set the record with receptions of seventy-eight yards and thirty-eight yards, both touchdowns.

NOVEMBER

November 1, 1898: Jack Johnson's Debut

A native of Galveston, Texas, Jack Johnson had his professional fighting debut on November 1 in the city of his birth. Johnson knocked out Charley Brooks in the second round of a fifteen-round fight in what was called the "Texas State Middleweight Title." Johnson would go on to have one of the greatest boxing careers in history. Arguably his most famous fight came in 1910, when Johnson fought James Jeffries. Johnson dominated the fight before Jeffries's team threw in the towel, ending the fight to prevent a knockout loss. While some pointed to Jeffries's age as the reason for Johnson's victory, Jeffries himself said, "I could never have whipped Johnson at my best….I couldn't have hit him. No, I couldn't have reached him in 1,000 years." Johnson, an African American, proved with his victory over the white Jeffries that African Americans were every bit the equal of whites. The outcome incited race riots throughout the country; white people had dubbed Jeffries "the great white hope" and were humiliated when he lost. Riots took place in more than twenty-five states and in cities such as New York, Pittsburgh, Philadelphia and Houston. Whites—making further fools of themselves after having derided Johnson's abilities—attacked African Americans during these riots. Across the country, more than twenty people were killed and hundreds injured. Johnson would finish his career with a record of 73-13-10, with forty of his wins coming by knockout.

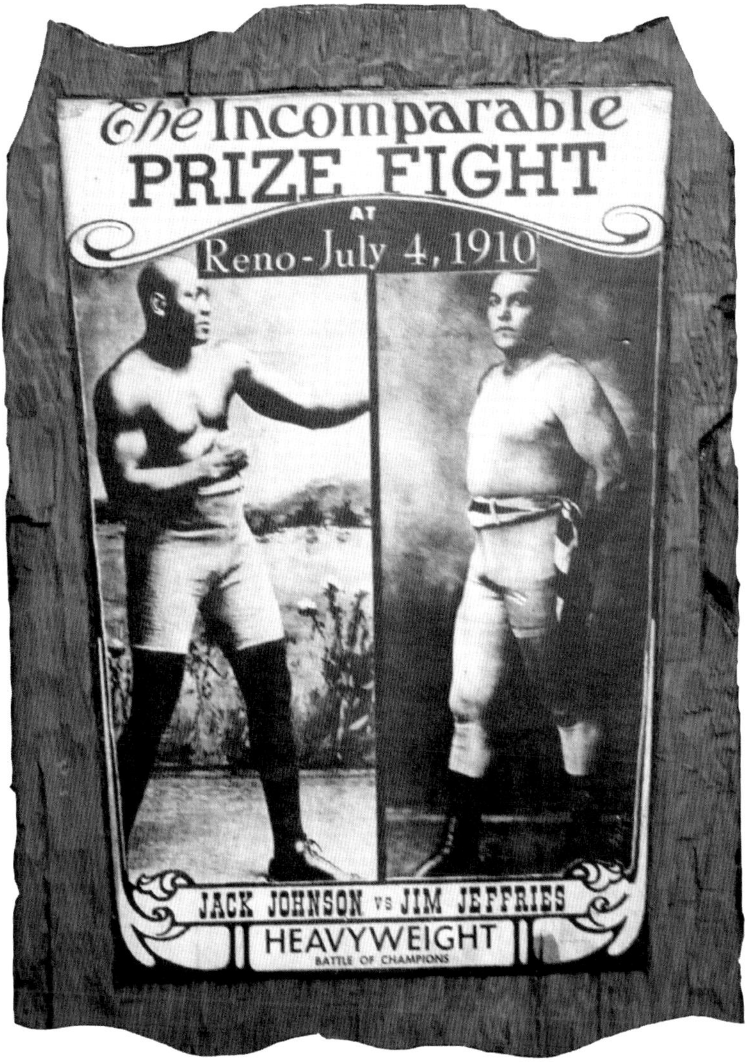

Poster from Jack Johnson's prizefight against Jim Jeffries. *Courtesy of the Texas Sports Hall of Fame.*

November 2, 1974: Rice Upsets Tech

Rice (0-5-1) stunned No. 13 TTU, 21–7. Led by Tommy Kramer and a two-touchdown second quarter, the Owls got their first win of the season. Kramer had set multiple passing records in high school while leading San

Antonio Lee before being thrust into the starting position as a freshman at Rice. He would proceed to lead the Owls in passing all four years. While Kramer was a bright spot, earning consensus All-SWC and All-American status in 1976, the Owls struggled mightily as a team. The victory over Tech was their only win against a ranked opponent. A 24–20 upset over Texas A&M in 1973 gained more attention for the Rice MOB (Marching Owl Band) than it did for the football team. Kramer would go on to be selected in the first round of the 1977 NFL draft and spend fourteen seasons in the NFL.

November 3, 1951: Bears Upset

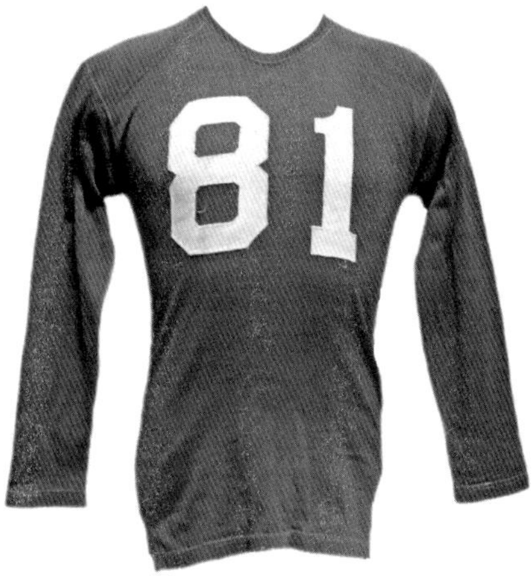

Stanley Williams's 1950 Baylor football jersey. *Courtesy of the Texas Sports Hall of Fame.*

A week after a disappointing 21–21 tie against No. 16 TAMU in College Station, No. 8 Baylor was upset in stunning fashion by unranked TCU, 20–7, in Waco. Fortunately for the Bears, they rebounded the next week, beating No. 10 Texas in Austin and regaining their top-ten status, which they didn't relinquish for the rest of the season. The Bears were led by four All-American selections, including quarterback Larry Isbell and end Stanley Williams. TCU would go on to win the SWC following a wildly inconsistent season. The Horned Frogs started 1951 with a 27–13 loss to Kansas, only to defeat No. 12 Nebraska in Lincoln, 28–7, the very next week. TCU lost to unranked Texas Tech in week four, to No. 6 Southern Cal in week six and to No. 15 UT in week eight. However, the Frogs beat No. 6 TAMU in week five, No. 8 Baylor in week seven and No. 18 Rice in week nine. Both Baylor (in the Orange Bowl) and TCU (in the Cotton Bowl) lost their bowl games.

November 4, 1950: Texas Edges SMU

No. 7 Texas edged No. 1 SMU, 23–20, in Austin. The Longhorns went on to win the SWC and finish the season ranked third by the Associate Press. Despite the successful season, the Longhorns' head coach, Blair Cherry, retired at the end of the year. Over four seasons, Cherry led UT to a record of 32-10-1 with two top-five finishes, but harsh criticism by fans and media led Cherry to suffer from ulcers and insomnia, so he stepped down. Cherry was replaced by Ed Price, who, despite some early success, would lead the team to a disastrous 1-9 record in 1956.

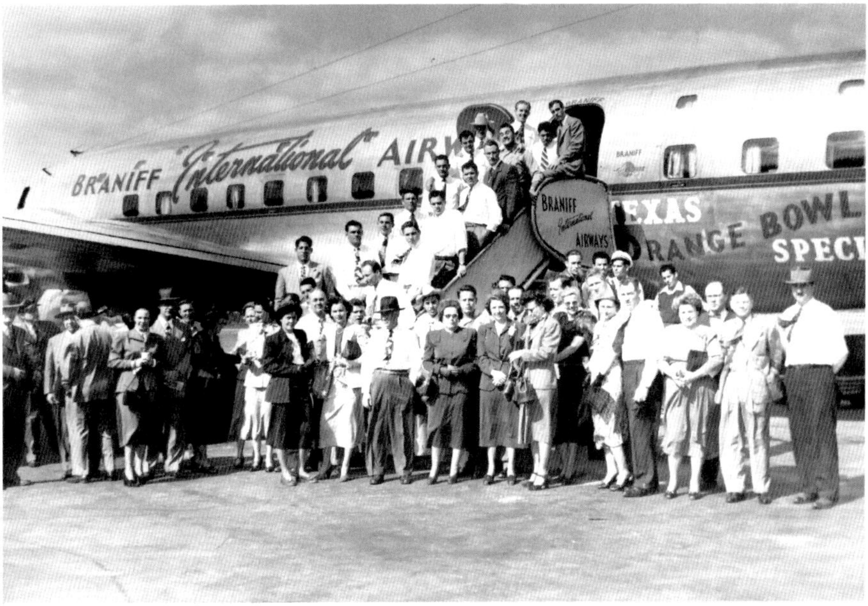

"The Orange Bowl Special," a Braniff Airways plane, flies Blair Cherry and the 6-3-1 Longhorns to the Orange Bowl to play the Georgia Bulldogs. *Courtesy of the Texas Sports Hall of Fame.*

November 5, 1967: Bubbles Cash

Local dancer Bubbles Cash put on an impromptu performance on her way back from the concession stand during a Dallas-Atlanta football game. She almost immediately became a news topic, covered by local TV and radio stations. Never one to miss a promotional opportunity, Dallas general manager Tex Schramm got Cash tickets to every Cowboys home game. She is often credited with being the inspiration for the iconic Dallas Cowboys Cheerleaders.

November 6, 1960: Repeat

For his second consecutive game, Raymond Berry hauled in three touchdown receptions for the Baltimore Colts. The first game was on October 30 against Dallas, and the second was on November 6 against Green Bay. Berry would finish the 1960 season with career highs in receptions (seventy-four), receiving yards (1,298) and yards per game (108.2). But despite his two games with multiple touchdown receptions, he only finished the year with ten—four less than his career high of fourteen, set in 1959.

November 7, 1988: Childress's Big Night

Ray Childress received the game ball for leading the Houston Oilers to a 24–17 victory over the Cleveland Browns. Childress had been a standout for Texas A&M, earning All-American status twice, before joining the Oilers as the third overall pick in 1985.

November 8, 1924: War Memorial Stadium Opens

After successful athletic campaigns in the early 1920s, Texas athletic director L. Theo Bellmont led the charge to replace the wooden stands of Clark Field with a more permanent concrete stadium. That dream was realized with the opening of War Memorial Stadium in Austin. Touted as "the largest sports facility of its kind in the Southwest," War Memorial seated twenty-seven thousand fans. The opening game wouldn't go as expected, as Baylor defeated the Longhorns, 28–10. Today, of course, the stadium is known as Darrell K. Royal–Texas Memorial Stadium.

November 9, 1946: Mr. Inside

Army and Navy fought to a 0–0 tie at Yankee Stadium, representing the only blemish on the careers of Mr. Inside (Doc Blanchard) and Mr. Outside (Glenn Davis) at Army (27-0-1). Blanchard would retire to Bulverde, Texas, after a lengthy military career. Blanchard is buried at Fort Sam Houston National Cemetery in San Antonio.

November 10, 1957: Berry's Big Day

In one of his many outstanding performances, Raymond Berry hauled in twelve catches for 224 yards. Berry had only thirty-three receptions at Southern Methodist before joining the Baltimore Colts in 1955. In his second pro season, Berry would break his college receiving total, with thirty-seven catches for 601 yards.

November 11, 1978: Tackling Machine

Mike Singletary registers an unheard-of 33 tackles as Baylor falls to Arkansas, 27–14. Just a sophomore, Singletary would finish that season with a school record of 232 tackles before registering another 188 as a junior and 145 as a senior.

November 12, 1955: Swink Runs Hard

Texas Christian's Jim Swink, a native of Sacul, Texas, carried the ball fifteen times against the University of Texas for an incredible 235 yards and four touchdowns. Not surprisingly, the Horned Frogs defeated the Longhorns, 47–20. Swink would lead TCU to back-to-back conference titles in 1955 and 1956, including a 28–27 upset of Jim Brown's No. 8 Syracuse. Swink opted to forgo a NFL career after being picked in the second round of the 1957 draft, instead heading to medical school.

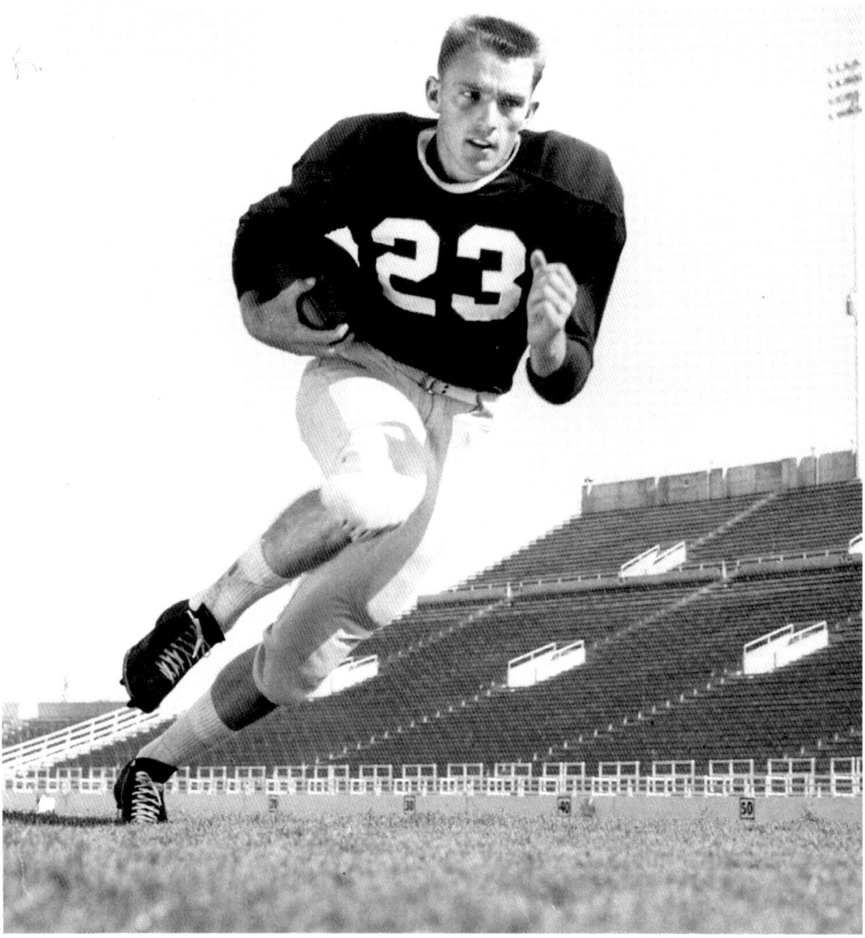

TCU's star halfback Jim Swink poses for a picture. *Courtesy of the Texas Sports Hall of Fame.*

While he played one season with the AFL's Dallas Texans in 1960, Swink ultimately focused on his career as a surgeon in Fort Worth.

November 13, 1982: Miracle on Fourth Avenue

With just seventeen seconds left to play, SMU's Blaine Smith picked up a Texas Tech kickoff and lateralled it to teammate Bobby Leach. With the game tied, 27–27, it looked like the Mustangs' perfect record would be lost.

Instead, Leach raced ninety-one yards to score, giving SMU a 34–27 win. The game was nicknamed the "Miracle on Fourth Avenue," a nod to the location of Tech's Jones Stadium. SMU would finish the year 10-0-1 after the Mustangs tied No. 9 Arkansas, 17–17, the following week.

November 14, 1954: Landry's Picks

Although remembered for his days as a coach in Dallas, Tom Landry was no slouch as a player in the NFL. On November 14, Landry intercepted the Philadelphia Eagles three times in a single game in his first year as a player-coach with the New York Giants.

November 15, 1930: Stafford Leads Texas

Harrison Stafford, from Wharton, Texas, was one of the state's earliest gridiron stars. Stafford would pair with Ernie Koy to make one of college football's best backfields in the 1930s. He was mostly counted on as a blocking back, but on November 15, 1930, Stafford slammed through the Horned Frog defensive line to give the Longhorns a 7–0 victory. Texas would finish the season 8-1-1 and claim the SWC title.

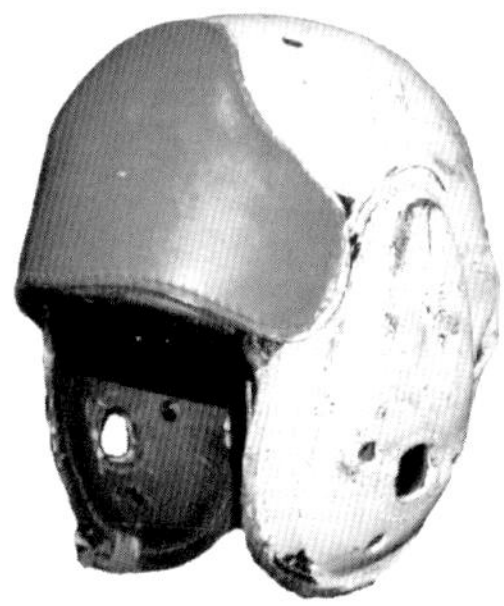

Harrison Stafford's University of Texas football helmet. The front portion of the helmet is burnt orange, and the rest is white. *Courtesy of the Texas Sports Hall of Fame.*

November 16, 1957: Upset of the Decade

Rice has played football since 1912, the first year the school held classes. But in all the subsequent decades, perhaps the biggest win in school history was the 1957 Rice–Texas A&M game. In 1957, Texas A&M was led by legendary head coach Paul "Bear" Bryant. The team was filled with exceptional players, headed by future Heisman winner John David Crow. From the beginning of the 1956 season to the match versus Rice, Texas A&M was an astounding 17-0-1. Over that same period, Rice was a mere 8-9.

Not surprisingly, with the Aggies working on a second straight undefeated season, they were ranked as the number-one team in the country. Fortunately, the Rice Owls were also led by a great coach, Jess Neely, and had their own star player, dynamic quarterback King Hill.

Midway through the first quarter, the Owls moved to the one-yard line before Hill punched the ball in for a touchdown on a quarterback keeper. He then kicked the extra point, and Rice was up on the number one team in the nation, 7–0. As expected, A&M fought back. The Aggies went on to score in the third quarter, but missed the extra point and remained down, 7–6 (Texas A&M was kicking into a twenty-eight-mile-per-hour wind).

The teams battled back and forth until midway through the fourth quarter, when some drama began to unfold. Faced with a fourth-and-one at the Texas A&M thirty-yard line, Coach Neely ignored the Rice fans cheering for the team to go for it. Instead, Neely had Hill punt, pinning TAMU at its own one-yard line. The stage was set. A&M would have to drive ninety-nine yards to save its perfect season and hopes for a national title.

While Texas A&M's Crow had been contained for most of the day, Bryant and the Aggie offense leaned on him with the game on the line. Their faith paid off. On the very first play of the drive, Crow broke through the line and scampered for eighteen yards. If not for a one-on-one tackle in the Rice secondary, Crow would have scored. With one minute to go, A&M was on the verge of field-goal range. On the Owls' twenty-three-yard line, a decision loomed about whether to attempt a field goal or to go for a first down. However, at the time, goalposts were considerably narrower than they are today; by no means was a field goal a certainty from that distance. Coach Bryant opted to go for it with his passing quarterback, Jim Wright. As Wright dropped back, Rice's all-SWC guard and co-captain Matt Gorges burst through the A&M line and threw Wright to the ground. A&M turned the ball over on downs, and the Owls easily ran out the clock, claiming a 7–6 victory.

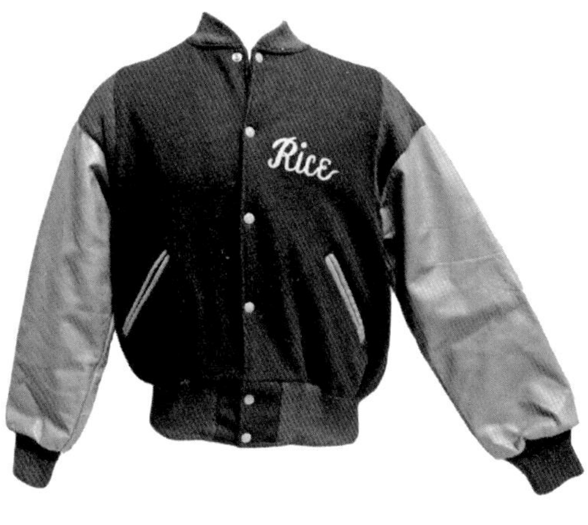

Jess Neely's Rice coaching jacket. *Courtesy of the Texas Sports Hall of Fame.*

Coach Neely proudly said of his star player, Hill, "There's not a better college football player in America than that boy right there. I don't care who it is. He does everything, and does everything well."

A few days later, Bryant was interviewed for TV and briefly summed up his feelings: "Well, I may be smiling on the outside, but I guarantee you I'm bleeding on the inside."

Rice's upset also allowed the Owls to win the SWC outright and play Navy in the Cotton Bowl. The Wednesday before the Rice game, Bryant announced his intentions to leave A&M to return to Alabama. The Aggies' glorious season came completely unraveled. After losing to Rice, the Aggies lost to Texas in the next game, 9–7, before dropping their bowl game against Tennessee, 3–0.

November 17, 1991: Hamm Scores

Just nineteen years old, Mia Hamm scored her first World Cup goal, in the sixty-second minute of the United States' first World Cup match. Hamm's goal put the Americans up, 3–2, and proved to be the match winner. The United States would go on to win the 1991 World Cup. The child of a military family, Hamm moved frequently, spending time in San Antonio and her first two years of high school at Notre Dame Catholic School in Wichita Falls.

November 18, 1907: Aggie Bonfire

Texas A&M held a bonfire on campus to celebrate a football victory over Tulane. The traditional Aggie Bonfire would begin two years later, in 1909, and continue in an official capacity until 1999, when tragedy struck. On November 18, the bonfire collapsed, killing twelve students and injuring twenty-seven more. A week later, the school held a candlelight vigil for those who passed away, with over forty thousand people in attendance. The next day, before the Aggies took the field against the Longhorns in their annual rivalry game, F-16 fighter jets piloted by former A&M students flew over Kyle Field in the missing man formation. The Aggie football team would rally to defeat the No. 5 Longhorns, 20–16.

November 19, 1966: Texans Lead Michigan State

Led by four Texans—lineman Alton Owens (Fort Worth), defensive back Jess Phillips (Beaumont), defensive end Charles "Bubba" Smith (Beaumont) and wide receiver Gene Washington (La Porte)—Michigan State battled Notre Dame to a 10–10 tie. It was the first game broadcast to Vietnam. ABC wasn't going to broadcast the game, but viewers signed a petition, and the network reconsidered. The game received a higher rating than the first Super Bowl just a few months later, in January 1967.

November 20, 1978: Luv Ya Blue

The Oilers took on the Miami Dolphins on *Monday Night Football.* In an attempt to boost team spirit, the Oilers gave each fan a blue-and-white pompom before the game. With over seventy thousand fans waving the pompoms, the Oilers went on to win, 35–30, behind Earl Campbell. After the game, Campbell stated, "The display of 'Luv Ya Blue' was a chance for people of all races and backgrounds to come together as a city. More than that, it was a feeling that the players and fans shared without even talking."

November 21, 1916: Southwestern Leaves

After recording a 0-4 record in SWC football games from 1915 to 1916, Southwestern played its final SWC football game, a 17–3 loss to the University of Texas.

November 22, 1973: Leaks Leads Longhorns

No. 11 Texas defeated Texas A&M, 42–13, in College Station. The victory was the exclamation point on the Longhorns' regular season, in which they went undefeated against SWC opponents and won their twenty-first SWC title. The star of the season was Roosevelt Leaks, who became the Longhorns' first African American player to earn All-American status. Leaks set multiple school records, including for most rushing yards in a career, most rushing touchdowns and most rushing yards in a game. Leaks's 342 yards against SMU remains a school record for rushing yards in a road game and was just eight yards shy of setting the NCAA record at the time. Along with earning All-American status, Leaks finished third in Heisman voting, tied for the highest finish in school history at the time.

November 23, 1929: TCU Downs Baylor

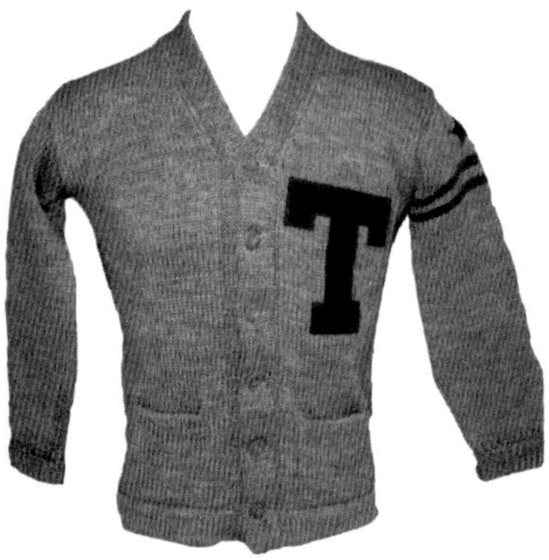

Howard Grubbs's TCU letter sweater. *Courtesy of the Texas Sports Hall of Fame.*

In its penultimate game of the year, TCU defeated Baylor, 34–7, in Waco behind the play of a brilliant young quarterback, Howard Grubbs. TCU would win its first Southwest Conference title that year with a 9-0-1 record, its only blemish coming on a 7–7 tie to SMU in the final game of the season. While Grubbs was the first in a long line of great TCU signal callers, his future lay outside of football. He would eventually become the SWC commissioner from 1950 to 1973.

November 24, 1966: Cowboys on Thanksgiving

The Dallas Cowboys played their first Thanksgiving Day game, beating the Cleveland Browns, 26–14. The Cowboys would join the Detroit Lions as the only two clubs guaranteed to play on Thanksgiving, although the Lions began the tradition in 1934.

November 25, 1909: First Homecoming

In 1909, Baylor alumni received an interesting postcard from the school, asking the graduates to return to campus in order to "renew former associations and friendships, and catch the Baylor spirit again." The postcard was sent to announce the first Baylor homecoming, a weekend of festivities ending with the football game against TCU on November 25. Baylor beat TCU, 6–3, but the weekend had much larger repercussions. This may have been the first homecoming game ever. Many schools claim to have hosted the first homecoming—Baylor is joined by Missouri, Illinois and Southwestern in claiming credit. While Missouri earned early credit for its call to "come home" in 1911, Baylor seems the more likely candidate. In fact, many historians, including some at the Smithsonian, eventually gave credit to Baylor's game against TCU in 1909. After a break from 1910 to 1915, the Bears have held a homecoming weekend every year since.

NOVEMBER 26, 1978: GREY CUP GLORY

In the sixty-sixth Grey Cup, the Edmonton Eskimos won, 20–13. A young quarterback, Warren Moon, happened to be playing in his first Grey Cup. Moon had joined Edmonton after going undrafted out of the University of Washington, but he used his time in the CFL to become one of game's most prolific passers. Moon would take Edmonton to five consecutive Grey Cups (1978, 1979, 1980, 1981 and 1982), winning the Grey Cup MVP in 1980 and 1982. The success propelled Moon to the NFL, where a bidding war for his services ensued. The Houston Oilers, led by ex-Edmonton coach Hugh Campbell, won the war, and Moon became an Oiler. The acquisition of Moon, a twenty-eight-year-old rookie, paid off. He became a nine-time Pro Bowler and led the NFL in passing twice (1990 and 1991). Moon retired as the franchise leader in passing yards, passing attempts, pass completions and passing touchdowns, all of which remain atop the Tennessee Titans lists.

NOVEMBER 27, 1924: BRIDGES' BEARS

Coached by Frank Bridges, the Baylor Bears defeated Rice, 17–9, in Houston to claim their second SWC title in three years. From 1922 to 1924, the Bears outscored their opponents 538–233 while compiling a 20-6-3 record. Of course, it would be the Bears' last conference title until 1974.

November 28, 1966: Cokes Defends the Belt

Curtis Cokes, a native of Dallas, began boxing professionally in 1958. After winning the world welterweight crown in August 1966, he had to defend his title for the first time in November of that year. Fighting at Municipal Auditorium in Dallas, Cokes defeated Frenchman Jean Josselin in fifteen rounds to retain his title. Cokes would continue successfully defending his title until 1969. His career boxing record was 62-14-4, with 30 wins coming by knockout.

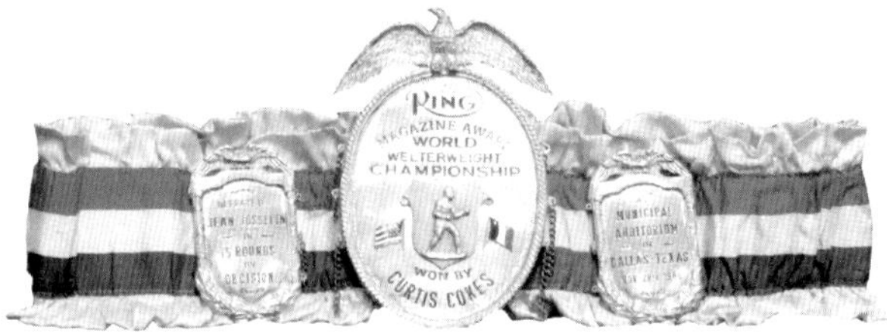

Curtis Cokes's Welterweight Champion of the World prize belt. *Courtesy of the Texas Sports Hall of Fame.*

November 29, 1958: SMU Plays Spoiler

After cruising through SWC play with a perfect record, SMU, led by Don Meredith, spoiled No. 7 TCU's season, beating the Horned Frogs, 20–13. The Frogs, led by head coach Abe Martin, would still win the SWC, earning a bid to the Cotton Bowl, where they tied No. 8 Air Force, 0–0. Martin played for TCU from 1928 to 1930 before entering high school football as a coach in 1932. In an eleven-year stint as a high school coach, Martin assembled an impressive 95-14-1 record before returning to his alma mater in 1945 as an assistant. When legendary Dutch Meyer stepped down in 1953, Martin got the call to replace him. Under Martin's guidance (1953–66), the Frogs achieved a 74-64-7 record, including three conference titles and five bowl appearances.

November 30, 1935: Two Champs

The SWC produced two football national champions in one season. Southern Methodist University entered a game against TCU in Fort Worth with a SWC title and a trip to the Rose Bowl on the line. Adding further

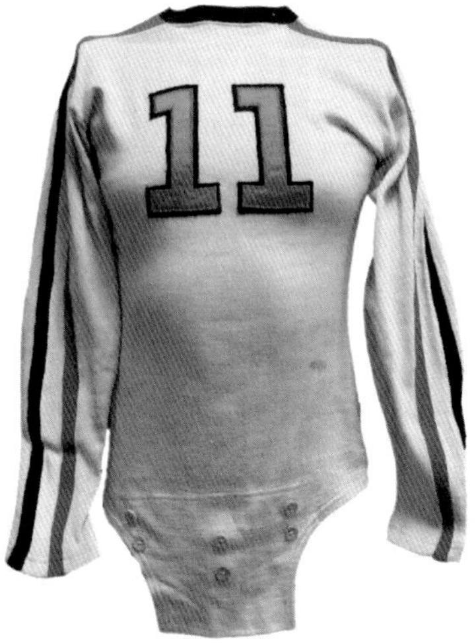

SMU football legend Bobby Wilson's 1936 college all-star jersey. *Courtesy of the Texas Sports Hall of Fame.*

meaning to the game was the financial burden that the Great Depression had left on the SMU athletic department. With the game tied 14–14 late in the fourth quarter, SMU lined up to punt. But instead of kicking, SMU faked the punt, resulting in a thirty-seven-yard touchdown by Bobby Wilson and a 20–14 SMU victory. The team's subsequent appearance in the Rose Bowl netted the athletic department $85,000 and put its finances in the positive for the year. SMU would lose in the Rose Bowl, and TCU would go on to defeat LSU in the Sugar Bowl, establishing its own claim to the national title.

DECEMBER

December 1, 1956: Krebs Leads the Mustangs

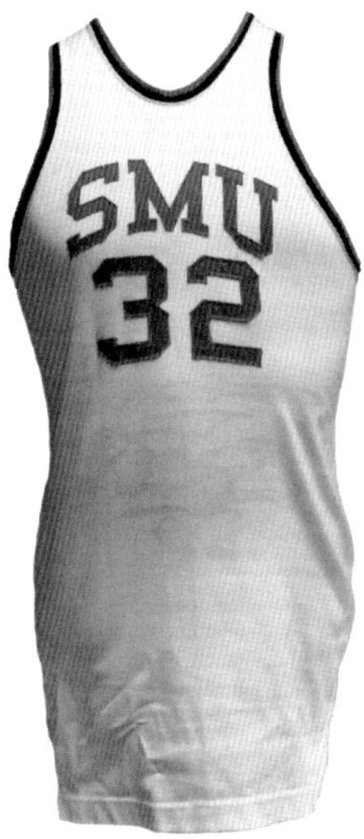

Led by Jim Krebs, the SMU basketball team began its season with an 82–67 victory over North Texas State. The Mustangs would go on to a SWC championship and a trip to the Final Four. The team's great season would lead future star Max Williams to commit to SMU. The team was coached by Doc Hayes, who led SMU basketball for twenty years, during which the team captured eight SWC titles and seven NCAA tournament berths.

Jim Krebs's SMU basketball jersey. *Courtesy of the Texas Sports Hall of Fame.*

December 2, 2002: Catch 1,000

In a *Monday Night Football* game featuring the Oakland Raiders and the New York Jets, Raiders receiver Tim Brown recorded his 1,000th career reception, just the third NFL player to reach that mark. Brown (class of 1984) had been a star since his days at Woodrow Wilson High School, going on to win the Heisman Trophy in college. When Brown won the trophy, Woodrow Wilson became the first high school to produce two Heisman Trophy winners—Davey O'Brien (class of 1935) was the other. Woodrow Wilson would induct the duo into its first "Hall of Fame" class in 1989, along with other Wilson students, including golfer Ralph Guldahl and auto-racing legend Carroll Shelby.

December 3, 1950: Layne to Box

Two Texans led the Detroit Lions, as Cloyce Box of Hamilton, Texas, caught twelve passes for 302 yards and four touchdowns from Bobby Layne, a native of Santa Anna, Texas. The Lions defeated the Baltimore Colts, 45–21.

December 4, 1997: Brown to Texas

Mack Brown was announced as the newest head coach of the University of Texas. Although Brown's tenure at Texas was rocky at times, he proved to be worth the hire when, in 2005, he led the 'Horns to their first national title since 1970. Brown recorded two Big 12 titles and six Big 12 South titles during his tenure at Texas (1998–2013). He finished with a record of 158-48.

December 5, 1998: Aggies Win the Big 12

In a stunning upset, No. 10 Texas A&M defeated No. 1 Kansas State, 36–33, in two overtimes to win the Big 12 title. Down by fifteen points entering the fourth quarter, the Aggies mounted the biggest comeback in the championship game's history before prevailing on a thirty-two-yard touchdown pass from Brandon Stewart to Sirr Parker in the second overtime. Dat Nguyen led the Aggies defensively, recording an interception and seventeen tackles.

December 6, 1969: Game of the Century

No. 1 Texas and No. 2 Arkansas faced off in a game with national title implications. The contest has been called the "Game of the Century." ABC convinced the two teams to move the game from October 18 to the end of the year, hoping to increase the meaning of the match. It paid off, as the two teams worked their ways to the top of the polls. The Longhorns would win, 15–14, in front of a crowd that included President Richard Nixon and Billy Graham.

December 7, 1952: Night Train

Dick "Night Train" Lane recorded his first pick-six as the Los Angeles Rams defeated the Green Bay Packers, 45–27. A twenty-four-year-old rookie, Lane hadn't played football in several years since leaving Scottsboro Junior College to join the military. He was signed as an undrafted free agent by the Rams because of his combination of size and speed, and the gamble paid off. Lane would set the NFL record for interceptions in a season as a rookie. The record still stands, despite the NFL season being four games longer today than it was in 1952. Lane would record another pick-six the following week against Pittsburgh, helping the Rams to a 9-3 finish despite the team starting the year 1-3. The Rams would lose to Bobby Layne, Doak Walker, Buddy Parker and the Detroit Lions in the 1953 championship game.

December 8, 1940: Turner Leads Chicago

The Washington Redskins, led by Sammy Baugh, met the Chicago Bears and Clyde "Bulldog" Turner at Griffith Stadium in Washington, D.C., for the NFL championship. After beating Chicago, 7–3, in the regular season, Redskins owner George Preston Marshall told reporters that the Bears were crybabies and quitters. George Halas, Chicago's head coach, routinely repeated and showed his players the comments in preparation for the showdown. On the opening drive, Chicago established control, running for a sixty-eight-yard touchdown on the second play. Baugh responded, driving Washington to the Chicago twenty-six-yard line, but

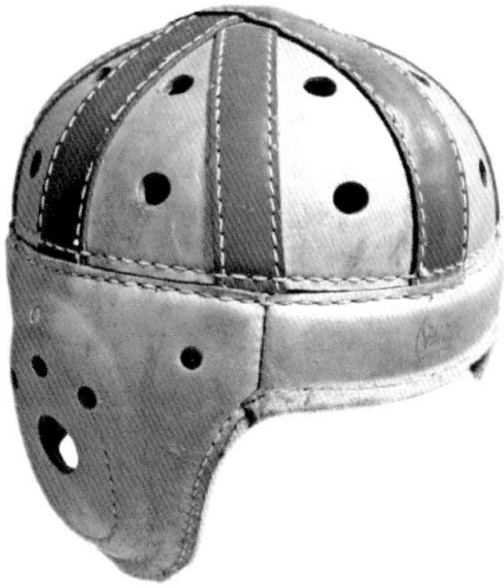

Clyde "Bulldog" Turner's college all-star helmet. The helmet is silver with red and blue stripes on top. *Courtesy of the Texas Sports Hall of Fame.*

receiver Charlie Malone dropped an easy touchdown pass in the end zone that would have tied the game. Things spiraled from there. Chicago went on to score eleven touchdowns, including a twenty-yard interception return for a touchdown by Hardin-Simmons University legend Turner. Turner also recovered a Redskin fumble that set up the NFL-record tenth touchdown. The final score, 73–0, remains an NFL record for margin of victory. It was the first time all season the Redskins had been shut out. Furthermore, the Redskin defense had only allowed opposing offenses to score 142 points all season (eleven games) before allowing half that total in one game. After the game, a reporter asked Baugh if things would have turned out differently had Malone caught the initial game-tying touchdown. "Sure," Baugh responded. "The final score would have been 73–7."

December 9, 1972: East Texas State Wins NAIA

Harvey Martin leads East Texas State to a 21–18 win over Carson-Newman to capture the National Association of Intercollegiate Athletics national title. Martin was a late bloomer at South Oak Cliff High School before joining the Lions. During his early collegiate seasons, Harvey made little impact, but by his senior season, he was ready to make waves. He became a force at defensive end, making All–Lone Star Conference and All-NAIA All-American. The season paid off, as Martin was selected in the third round of the NFL draft by his hometown team, the Dallas Cowboys. Martin was more than worth the selection, making four Pro Bowls and being named 1977 NFL Defensive Player of the Year and co-MVP of Super Bowl XII with defensive tackle Randy White. (It was the first and only time co-MVPs were named in a Super Bowl and the first time a defensive lineman was named MVP.) In that game, the Cowboys defeated the Denver Broncos, 27–10, for their second Super Bowl title.

December 10, 1938: Mighty Mites

Coach H.N. "Rusty" Russell led the Fort Worth Masonic Home into a Texas high school playoff game against vaunted Highland Park. Russell led the Masonic home—a school with about 160 kids—to a 127-30-12 record from 1927 to 1942. The school played in Texas high school football's highest classification. Over those sixteen seasons, Russell would take the team to the playoffs ten times. He left the Masonic home to coach Highland Park in 1942, leading a team that featured Bobby Layne and Doak Walker to the 1944 state championship. Russell was then hired by SMU, helping to bring Walker to the school.

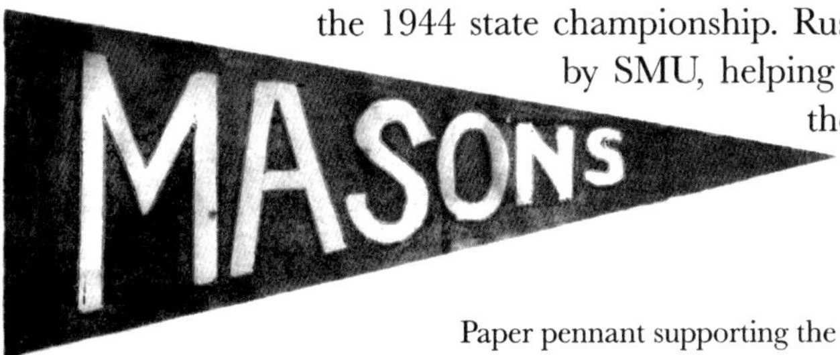

Paper pennant supporting the Masonic Home Mighty Mites. *Courtesy of the Texas Sports Hall of Fame.*

December 11, 1957: Crow Wins the Heisman

John David Crow of Texas A&M is presented the Heisman Memorial Trophy. The first Aggie to bring home the award, Crow also holds the distinction of being the only player under Bear Bryant to win a Heisman.

December 12, 1937: Joe Routt

After being named a two-time All-American at Texas A&M, Joe Routt was selected in the second round of the NFL draft by the Cleveland Browns. Routt never played a down of professional football, because, according to his wife, "He didn't want to go north." Upon graduation, Routt joined the U.S. Army Reserve, commissioned as a lieutenant. At the outbreak of World War II, Routt was called to active duty as an infantry officer. During his training, he was recruited by the army, along with a few other A&M football players, to play for the army football team in exhibition games against all-stars from professional teams. The aim of the games was to raise money for the armed forces and the USO, so, naturally, Routt and the other army

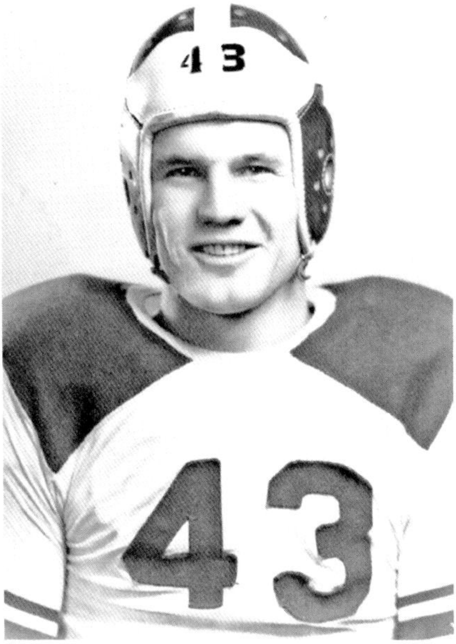

Portrait of Texas A&M's Joe Routt. *Courtesy of the Texas Sports Hall of Fame.*

players received no compensation for playing. After training, Routt was assigned to the 405th Regiment, 102nd Infantry Division, rising to the rank of captain. While stationed in France, the staunch Texan had an incident with a U.S. general. As one writer recalled: "Captain Routt, Commander of an infantry company, kept the Lone Star Flag of Texas flying from his tent on the Western Front and once had the audacity to ask an American general to salute it. The general wheeled about, snapped to attention and responded with a very snappy salute." Routt's unit was sent to the front lines for the Battle of the Bulge, engaging in constant enemy contact from November 28, 1944, to Routt's death on December 10. After Routt's commanding officer was killed, he valiantly reorganized his men to counterattack and avoided encirclement. Just as the troops were about to reach safety, Routt was gunned down by machine-gun fire from an enemy tank. For his actions, Routt received the Bronze Star and Purple Heart. When he heard of Routt's passing, E.J. Kyle (Kyle Field's namesake) said, "Joe was as modest and likeable a man as I ever have known. When I bought a copy of the midnight *Post* on Wednesday and read that Joe Routt had been killed in action, I went to my room and cried like a baby. The knowledge that so many other fine American young men were being killed, and will be killed, figured in my grief." On April 12, 1949—the day of Aggie Muster—Routt's body was returned home to his family in Brenham, where he received a full military honors burial. On November 29, 1950, the Texas A&M Board of Directors renamed a major avenue north of Kyle Field Joe Routt Boulevard. Routt entered the Texas Sports Hall of Fame in 1952 and the College Football Hall of Fame in 1962. His citation upon entering the College Football Hall of Fame summed up Routt perfectly: "In war as in football, Joe Routt was a true leader of men, ever prepared to make the ultimate sacrifice."

December 13, 1998: Murray Breaks Record

Once deemed the best rodeo cowboy by *Sports Illustrated*, Ty Murray won a record-breaking seventh All-Around title at the Professional Rodeo Cowboy Association.

December 14, 1958: Dillon Stars in Green Bay

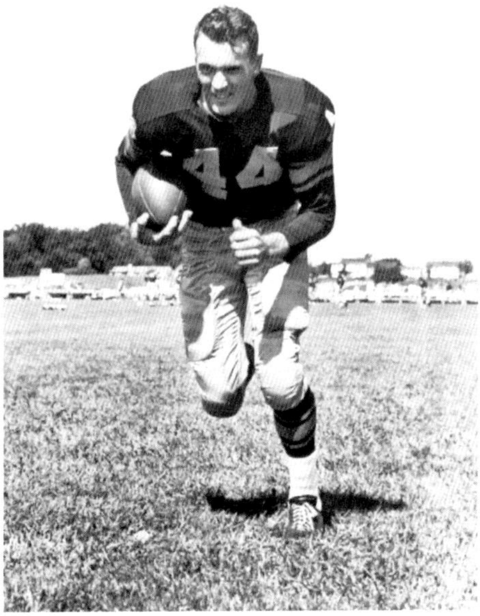

Bobby Dillon in his Green Bay Packers uniform. *Courtesy of the Texas Sports Hall of Fame.*

The Green Bay Packers' season ended with a disappointing 1-10-1 record. However, former UT standout Bobby Dillon was a bright spot on the roster. In 1958, Dillon became just the second NFL player to record more than fifty career interceptions. From 1953 to 1958, Dillon reeled in forty-seven interceptions for 934 yards and five touchdowns. An outstanding achievement for any player, it was even more impressive because Dillon had vision in only one eye, the result of a childhood injury. Dillon would play just one more year, 1959, when the Packers were 7-5 (Dillon's only winning season), which also happened to be Vince Lombardi's first as head coach. Later, Dillon would say he could tell things were about to turn around in Green Bay, but he couldn't pass up a job back in Temple, Texas. He had been working for Wilsonart in the offseason, and the company wanted him to start working full-time. It turned out to be the right choice, as Wilsonart would become an international leader with over $1 billion in sales. Dillon never regretted retiring at the age of twenty-nine, but he did regret not winning a championship, which Lombardi and the Packers achieved two years later. Dillon still holds the franchise record for career interceptions.

December 15, 1996: Goodbye, Houston

The Oilers played their final game in Houston, a 21–13 loss to the Cincinnati Bengals. Just three days before, Bruce Matthews was selected to his ninth consecutive Pro Bowl, matching Mike Munchak for the franchise record.

December 16, 1999: Williams Passes Away

Legendary golf coach Dave Williams passed away in Wharton, Texas, on this date. He had led the University of Houston to sixteen NCAA championships and coached future PGA players, including Fred Couples, Steve Elkington, John Mahaffey, Bill Rogers and Fuzzy Zoeller. Williams-led teams won fourteen conference titles and 340 tournaments over his thirty-six-year coaching career. Many consider Williams the father of college golf, as he helped transform college competitions from match-play format to stroke-play format in 1955.

December 17, 1988: Friday Night Lights

Permian High School fell to Dallas Carter in the state semifinals. Today, the game is immortalized in the movie *Friday Night Lights*. Not surprisingly, the movie took some artistic liberties with the story. While Permian lost the title game on a last-second play to Carter in the movie, in reality, the game was a state semifinal contest that Carter came back to win dramatically, 14–9, in the fourth quarter. The real game was played at UT's football stadium, not in the Astrodome, as depicted in the film. While the movie misinterprets or misrepresents other compelling pieces of the Permian team and the 1988 high school football season, one of the biggest is the fact that Carter had to forfeit its state title after beating Converse Judson in the final, 31–14. It would become public knowledge that Carter played an ineligible player, so the title was forfeited to Judson.

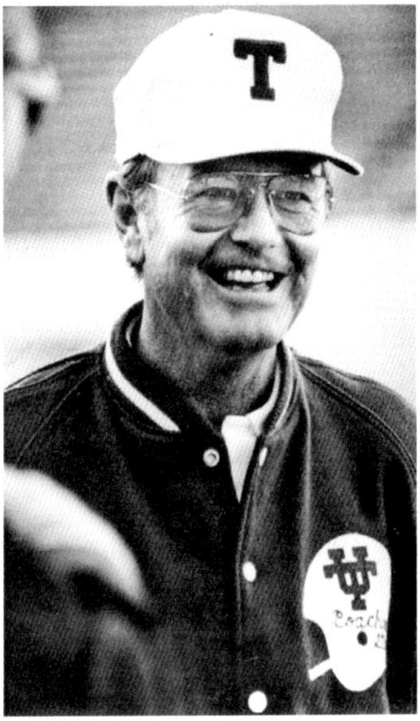

Coach Darrell K. Royal during his time at the University of Texas. *Courtesy of the Texas Sports Hall of Fame.*

December 18, 1956: Texas Gets Royal

Darrell Royal became the twenty-fourth head coach of the University of Texas football team. UT first offered the job to Bobby Dodd of Georgia Tech. The school was reportedly also interested in Duffy Daugherty. But after a four-hour interview with Royal, UT knew it had its man. Royal was immediately successful, posting a 39-13-2 record in his first five seasons.

December 19, 1959: Steinke Leads Texas A&I

Brenham, Texas native Gil Steinke coached Texas A&I to its first NAIA championship, defeating Lenoir-Rhyne, 20–7. The legendary coach would lead the Javelinas to five more titles over his career (1954–76). Known as an early leader of integration in southern football, Steinke would recruit and play kids who were white, African American or Hispanic, regardless of their social background.

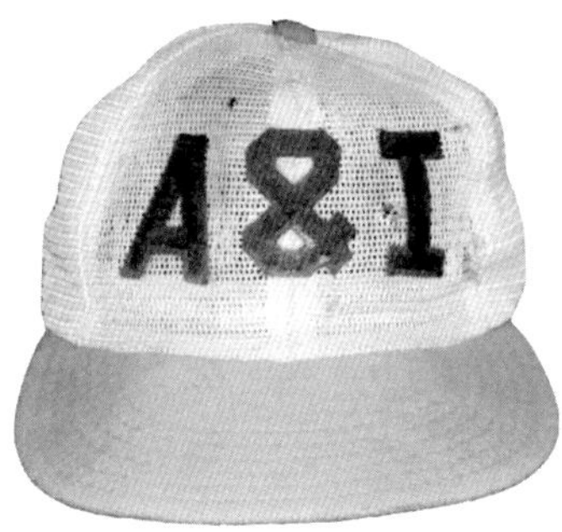

Gil Steinke's Texas A&I coaching hat. The bill is yellow, and the lettering is dark blue. *Courtesy of the Texas Sports Hall of Fame.*

December 20, 1970: Cowboys vs. Oilers

The Dallas Cowboys and Houston Oilers met for their first regular-season game, a result of the AFL-NFL merger. After Houston took a victory in the preseason, the Dallas Cowboys exacted revenge, pummeling Houston (2-10-1) by a score of 52–10. The 'Boys would finish the regular season 10-4 and advance to Super Bowl V.

December 21, 1963: Bears Win Bluebonnet

Baylor defeated LSU, 14–7, in the 1963 Bluebonnet Bowl. James Ingram caught eleven passes for 163 yards, including two touchdown passes from Don Trull in the fourth quarter. Trull threw for 255 yards in the game, while the Bears held the Tigers to 108 total yards.

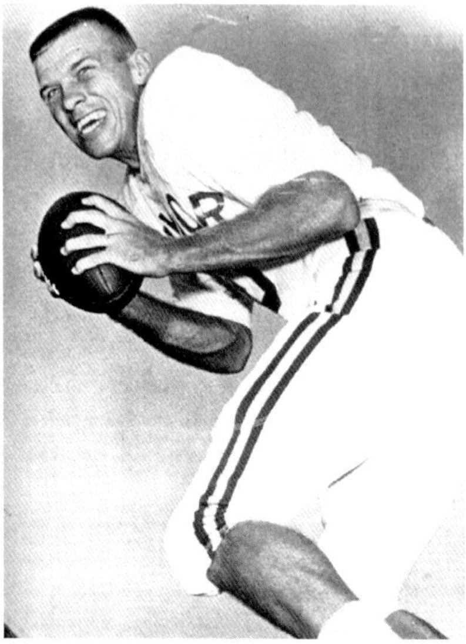

Portrait of Baylor's Don Trull. *Courtesy of the Texas Sports Hall of Fame.*

December 22, 1922: Tyson's First Title

Waco High defeated Abilene, 13–0, to claim coach Paul Tyson's first UIL-sanctioned state title. On the team were stars Ben Boynton and John Drew Johnson. Johnson scored all of Waco's points in the final four minutes of the game. Tyson would go on to lead Waco to one of the greatest high school football dynasties in history, taking the Tigers to six straight finals, winning four of those games. Tyson was sought out by people such as Knute Rockne and Pop Warner for his excellent football mind.

December 23, 1962: Texans Win AFL Title

Lamar Hunt's Dallas Texans won the AFL title over the Houston Oilers at Jeppesen Stadium on the campus of the University of Houston. The game ended in the fourth quarter as a 17–17 tie before the Texans prevailed in two overtimes (the Texans had blocked a field-goal attempt at the end of regulation to force the OT). It was the first professional football championship decided in overtime. With a final time of 77:54, it was the longest game played at the time. The wild finish captivated the nation, as 56 million people tuned in to watch the game on television.

December 24, 1961: Oilers' Second Title

The Houston Oilers won their second consecutive AFL title. The Oilers had won the first ever AFL title the year before and would make it to their third consecutive title game in 1962. Of course, the Texans would win the 1962 title game, giving the Lone Star State all three of the AFL's first three championships.

December 25, 1950: Rote's Birthday

The son of SMU All-American and NFL star Kyle Rote, Kyle Rote Jr. graduated from Highland Park High School in Dallas. He then enrolled at Oklahoma State University to focus on football, but after an injury, he transferred to the University of the South in Sewanee to play on its varsity soccer team. (The school had one of the few soccer programs in the country that offered a scholarship at the time.) First noticed by Lamar Hunt, Rote was drafted in the first round of the North American Soccer League by the Dallas Tornado in 1972. Given a year to develop, Rote became a full-time starter in 1973, leading the NASL in scoring—the first American to accomplish the feat. Rote also won the television competition *Superstars* three times in a four-year period.

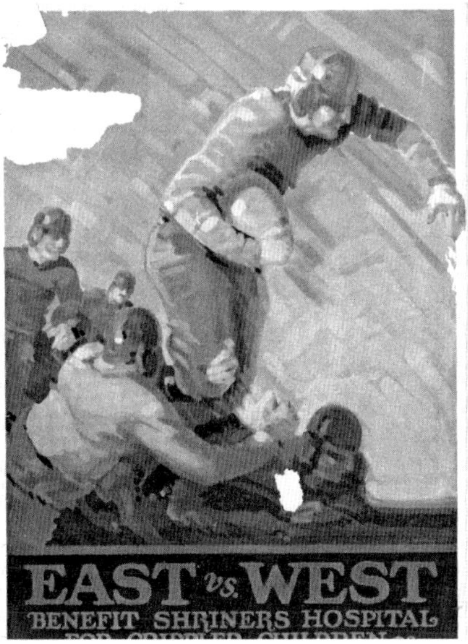

East-West Shriners program from 1927. *Courtesy of the Texas Sports Hall of Fame.*

December 26, 1927: East-West Shrine Game

In the third East-West Shrine Game, the West, led by Texans J.V. Sikes (TAMU), Joel Hunt (TAMU), Rags Matthews (TCU) and Gerald Mann (SMU), defeated the East, 16–6. It was the first East-West game to include players from the SWC. Matthews was named the game's MVP.

December 27, 1953: Lions Over Browns

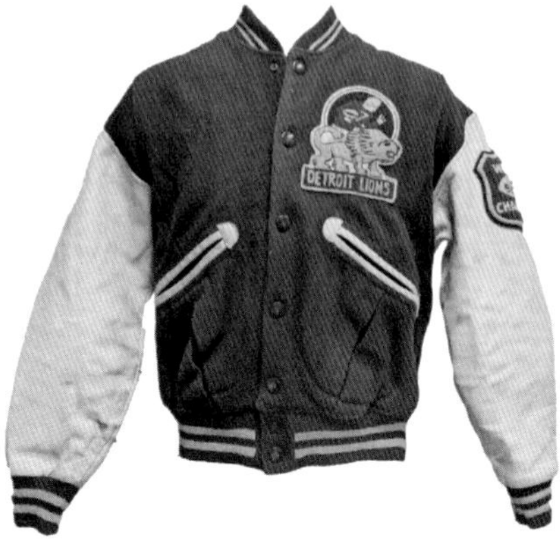

Bobby Layne's Detroit Lions jacket presented to him and other players for leading the Lions to back-to-back NFL championships in 1952 and 1953. *Courtesy of the Texas Sports Hall of Fame.*

Bobby Layne led the Detroit Lions 80 yards to score with three minutes left in the 1953 NFL championship game, as the Lions beat the Cleveland Browns, 17–16. The year before, Doak Walker and Bobby Layne each scored a touchdown while leading the Lions to the 1952 world championship, again beating the Browns, 17–7. Four years later, Tobin Rote of Rice led the Lions to a 59–14 rout of Cleveland for the title. Rote threw four touchdown passes, completed twelve of nineteen passes for 280 yards and ran for another touchdown.

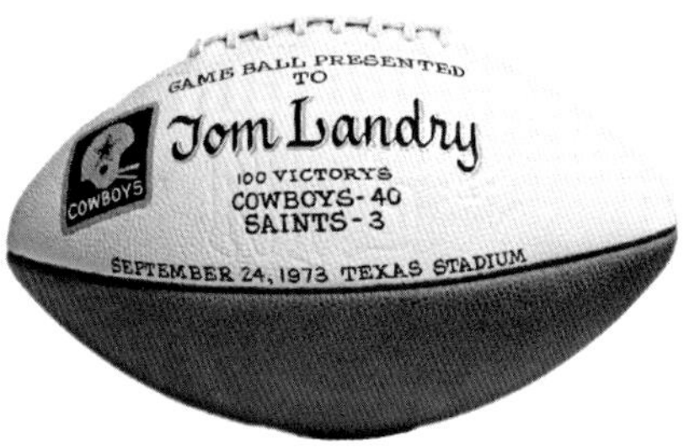

Tom Landry's 100th victory game ball. *Courtesy of the Texas Sports Hall of Fame.*

December 28, 1980: Landry Wins 200th

Tom Landry won his 200th game as the Dallas Cowboys defeated the Los Angeles Rams, 34–13.

December 29, 1990: Ags Take Down Detmer

The unranked Texas A&M Aggies traveled to San Diego to take on the No. 13 BYU Cougars, led by Heisman Trophy winner and Texas native Ty Detmer. The Aggies, coached by R.C. Slocum, jumped out to an early lead thanks to the effort of running back Darren Lewis, who would finish the game with two rushing touchdowns and one passing touchdown. Up 37–7 at halftime, the Aggies' "Wrecking Crew" defense pummeled Detmer and the Cougar offense. Detmer would be knocked out of the game in the third quarter, and Texas A&M quarterback Bucky Richardson would win the game's MVP award after throwing for 203 yards and one touchdown while rushing for two touchdowns and catching another score. This would be the last time a Heisman winner played in a bowl game before New Year's Day, until the 2011 Alamo Bowl, which featured Baylor's Robert Griffin III.

December 30, 2000: Army All-American Bowl

Featuring the top high school football talent in the country, the first Army All-American Bowl was played. The first game was at Highlander Stadium in Dallas, but it has since moved to the Alamodome in San Antonio, where the game has been played annually since 2003 (the game was in Alamo Stadium in 2001 and 2002). The game also features the presentation of the Ken Hall Trophy, awarded to the U.S. Army Player of the Year. Many consider this to be high school football's highest honor. The trophy is named after Ken "Sugarland Express" Hall, one of the greatest individual high school football players of all time.

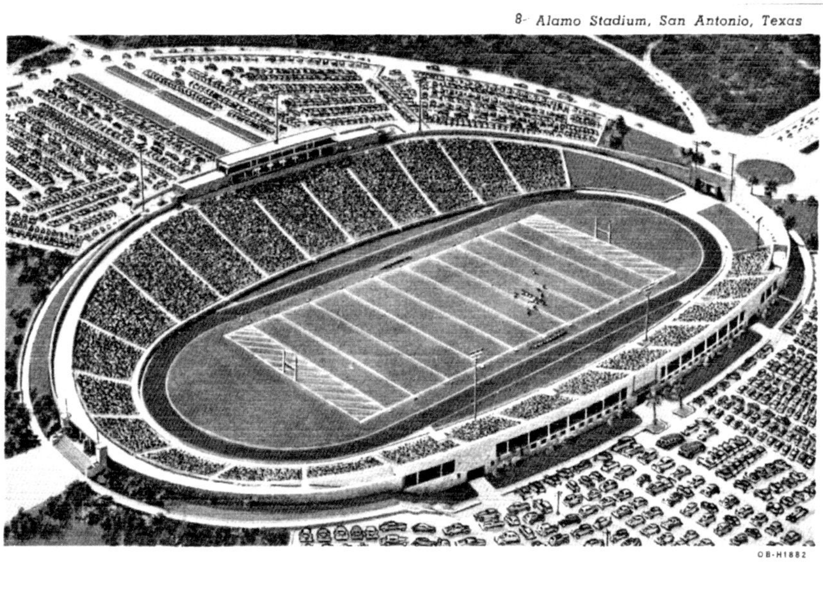

One of Texas's lesser-thought-of venues, San Antonio's Alamo Stadium, remains one of the state's great historic stadiums. *Courtesy of the Texas Sports Hall of Fame.*

December 31, 1967: The Ice Bowl

The Dallas Cowboys took on the Green Bay Packers for the NFL championship and a trip to Super Bowl II. Nicknamed the "Ice Bowl," the game was played in Wisconsin at Lambeau Field. To prepare for the anticipated cold conditions, Green Bay had installed an $80,000 turf-heating system designed by GM. However, the machine malfunctioned, leaving moisture on the field. When the tarp was removed, the moisture flash-froze in the -15 degree weather (an average of -48 degrees with wind chill). Dallas held a 17–14 lead with 4:50 left in the fourth quarter. Bart Starr then led Green Bay on a drive starting at their own thirty-one-yard line, eventually punching the ball into the end zone, giving Green Bay the win with a final score of 21–17.

ABOUT THE AUTHOR

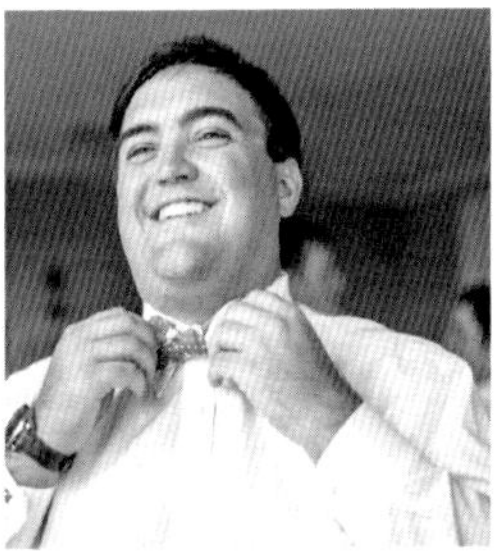

Ryan Sprayberry was born and raised in Texas before his passion for history took him to the Smithsonian in Washington, D.C., and the College Football Hall of Fame in Atlanta, Georgia. Today, he lives in the Texas Hill Country with his wife and son while working on a degree from Texas A&M to add to his undergraduate degree from Baylor University.